Finn Juhl. Life, Work, World

The book is published with the support
of the following foundations

Arne V. Schleschs Fond
Augustinus Fonden
Beckett-Fonden
dreyersfond
The Oticon Foundation
POLITIKEN-**FONDEN**

Finn Juhl

——

Life
Work
World

Christian Bundegaard

Translation: Max Minden Ribeiro
Picture editor: Birgit Lyngbye Pedersen

Contents

Foreword

It is a wonder that until now, no proper monograph on the architect and furniture designer Finn Juhl has been available.

Not just because he belongs to an inner circle of the most prominent Danish furniture designers of the so-called golden age in the decades after the Second World War, a group including Arne Jacobsen, Hans J. Wegner, Børge Mogensen and Poul Kjærholm, but also because in many ways Finn Juhl holds a special position within this circle.

Finn Juhl often went his own way, both in terms of the forms in his designs and likewise in his professional life. As such, above all others, Juhl became the leading figure when Danish furniture design and Danish applied art became world famous in the 1950s and 1960s under the branding of *Danish Modern*.

Finn Juhl – Life, Work, World tells this story and presents for the first time all of Finn Juhl's most significant designs in the aesthetic and idealogical context that they came about in.

The book could not have been written without the help of the business historian Per H. Hansen's thorough and inspiring research into the history of modern Danish furniture; the architect Esbjørn Hiort's brilliant book on Finn Juhl, which was republished in 2017; Professor Anders Brix's sharp sighted and considered professional critique and advise; the book's picture editor Birgit Lyngbye Pedersen's sense of the right angle for illustrations and Caroline Lemvigh-Müller's determined photo research; Niels Træsborg, Jan Leander, Michael Sheridan, House of Finn Juhl and Martin Feldt's expertise regarding Danish furniture on auctions and the vintage market; along with the publisher's editor Lil Vad-Schou's patient and congenial, octopus-like effort in holding the whole project together and on track.

The author offers them all a warm thank you.

Sóller, August 2018
Christian Bundegaard

Finn Juhl (1912–1989) was an avid traveller, often visiting traditional artist's destinations, such as Italy, France or, as here, Greece, specifically the ancient theatre in Epidaurus on the Peloponnese.

Introduction

If a single figure were to be credited with lifting Danish Design to world fame in the years following the Second World War, it would surely be the designer and architect Finn Juhl (1912–1989). It was in large part by dint of his breakthrough in the United States, his exhibition work at shows from Chicago to Zurich and as the interior designer behind both the Trusteeship Council Chamber at the United Nations Headquarters and Scandinavian Airlines' (SAS) ticket offices across the globe that the world first laid eyes on the Danish chair.

In reality, the picture is more nuanced. For one thing, Danish design was just one strand of a broader, Scandinavia-wide modernism that fed back into modernism internationally. For another, Finn Juhl was just one of a handful of talented young designers who together comprised a veritable golden age of Danish furniture design between the close of the 1930s and the beginning of the 1960s.

In those years Danish design was marked by a uniquely Scandinavian interpretation of modernism, a *Scandinavian Modern* that influenced the whole spectrum of design, from applied art to urban planning. While architects like the Dane Arne Jacobsen, the Finn Alvar Aalto, the Swede Gunnar Asplund and the Norwegian Sverre Fehn did not conceal the influence of Le Corbusier and Mies van der Rohe, they each in their own way gave modernism a more human face. They implemented an undogmatic, socially conscious functionalism, a meticulousness in planning and execution and an extensive use of warm, natural materials, such as brick and light Nordic woods. They emphasised organic compositions with curving forms that are sensitive to human scale.

While international modernism's long straight lines in concrete, steel and glass can seem impersonal, even embodying a cold monumentality that is neither completely removed from neoclassicist temples nor from the terrifying scale of fascist architecture, Scandinavian modernism is more down to earth – a continuation of local building traditions founded in the inherited knowledge of one's craft. Finn Juhl gained early insight into this attitude towards and interpretation of modernist concerns as an architecture student of Academy Professor Kay Fisker, one of the most influential Danish architects of the day. This was followed by ten years' employment under Vilhelm Lauritzen, one of the period's leading, most holistically minded and demonstratively modernist architects. Finn Juhl was assigned to Lauritzen's most acclaimed projects, including both *Radiohuset* (the Radio Building) and Copenhagen Airport. With Lauritzen's firm Juhl came to be responsible for interiors, and it was likely in light of this experience that he first chose to dedicate himself to furniture and interior design. During these years Juhl was also part of a rapidly growing environment, one among many young talents in the field of furniture design.

It was not only the designers that were gifted. There were also a number of critics, teachers and writers who helped to create a pronounced sense of identity, a strong work ethic and, in time, a fierce competitiveness that came to characterise the design community. The golden age in Danish furniture design was brought about by a couple of generations of architects and designers with links to a single school and an annual design fair, and in close partnerships with a few dedicated cabinetmakers. The school was the Furniture School in the Royal Danish Academy of Fine Arts, School of Architecture, where the architect and designer Kaare Klint had since the middle of the 1920s established a scientifically-minded approach to furniture design, based on careful study of the subject who would sit in the chair, eat at the table or fit their clothes into the wardrobe. The Klint School conceived of furniture design as its own discipline; a distillation of the different kinds of furniture to their fixed measurements and a thorough analysis of their functions. This functionalist idea was far removed from the pure aestheticising at play in certain aspects of modernism, but shared in its need to understand the fundamentals of an object in order to find its appropriate form. Finn Juhl would later term this task *the endeavour*.

In contrast to some of his colleagues, including Børge Mogensen, Ole Wanscher, Arne Karlsen and Poul Kjærholm, who in their own ways carried forward the traditions of the Klint School, Finn Juhl, like Hans J. Wegner and Arne Jacobsen, found an independent expression that at once extended the teachings that the school had established and explored a freer interpretation of the relation between form and function. None of the three had been students at the Furniture School. Wegner was trained as a cabinetmaker and educated at the School of Arts and Crafts, Jacobsen was educated as an architect and Juhl, who never graduated from the School of Architecture, was a self-taught furniture designer, his apprenticeship with Vilhelm Lauritzen notwithstanding.

The Klint School's approach had parallels in many contemporary functional studies. The work procedure of housewives for instance was just one area of research in the growing trend of applying scientific methods to everyday activities in order to optimise productivity. Generally, this effort was motivated in equal parts by an economic rationalism, a scientific curiosity and a growing social consciousness.

In architecture and design, this new interest in *the social* gave rise to what one might call a humanising of the designer's practice. People's aims and needs came to be considered more important than style or convention. For some architects, this new scientific attitude became a genuine ideology, driven by a fascination with machine aesthetics and the new technological possibilities of mass production. With this they anticipated increases in social goods, reason and progress overall. For others though, the core of this fresh approach lay in a new moral and aesthetic integrity, conceived as the disclosure of the materials and the methods by which artefacts are constructed. This had been demonstrated in machinery, but might equally be applied to design, which by contrast has its roots in craftsmanship and natural, traditional materials – wood for furniture, brick for buildings.

Carrying forward the lessons of their schooling and with the sense of participating in a breakthrough moment for design, a number of professional partnerships were forged between designers and cabinetmakers, in connection with *Snedkerlaugets Udstilling*, the annual furniture fair of the *Copenhagen Cabinetmakers' Guild Furniture Exhibition*. The fair was the year's major design event, where the public could view and even purchase the latest in Danish furniture. For the smaller cabinetmakers' workshops it was a vital platform in their increasing competition with a growing furniture industry. And for the designers, the exhibition provided exposure to the public – both customers and critics – expanding a minor field into a major cultural phenomenon, one that would eventually develop into the successful export of Danish furniture under the branding of Danish Modern and Danish Design.

That it was furniture and interior design that the architecturally trained Finn Juhl devoted himself to doubtless also had something to do with his interest in the fine arts, in particular ancient Greek and Egyptian sculpture, which he found to be reflected in the congenial compositions of modern sculptors such as Henry Moore, Barbara Hepworth, Jean Arp and his lifelong favourite, the Dane Erik Thommesen.

There is a tension between a freer art form, which is both functionally and expressively close to the plane of human experience, and the fixed, structural demands of a chair built to task. It drew Juhl and his longstanding collaborator, the cabinetmaker Niels Vodder, into a hard-fought battle with wood and its structural possibilities, often leading them to bold and original solutions.

Juhl's background in Scandinavian modernism and his interest in the visual arts converged in the consideration that all architectural tasks are interrelated, from the smallest scales of industrial design to the planning of buildings and cities. In a book in which Juhl describes his experiences as a teacher at the School of Interior Design in Copenhagen, he urges that town planning, the internal layout of apartments, and an apartment's furnishing should be considered a single interdisciplinary practice. Heavy and ill-fitting furniture, he argued, can be traced back to misguided urban planning. This was exemplified in the new builds shooting up everywhere at the time.

Finally, Juhl in both his personal and professional temperament was a typical architect, unable to entrust the critical details of a project to others, even less to chance. In his own house, which has been preserved as a museum, one can see for oneself an architect's characteristic need to delineate life or, in any case, its functions, spaces and utensils, from the forks in the drawers to the garden's landscaping. In each of his designs, this comprehensive approach and his art-historical background are locked in a running battle, played out from chair to chair, with the desire to resolve his objects' designs with an elegant flick of the wrist or a contrarian's cheeky, ironic remark.

Finn Juhl was perhaps not a great educator, but he was an engaging intermediary, gifted at getting things his way when a contractor or manufacturer doubted the wisdom of a project. Likewise, he was a formidable thinker and debater. He knew his art history and often had an excellent understanding of the theoretical implications of his projects. In any case, he had studied them as well as he was able. However, he often feigned to know little about anything and claimed to be essentially self-taught. And at the same time, as he put it himself, he liked to think that there was an artistic aspect to his practice, as there must be in all design tasks.

The present book tells the story of Finn Juhl and his work in five chapters. The story begins with his first, groundbreaking meeting with Scandinavian modernism at the *Stockholm Exhibition* in 1930 when he was just 18 years old, and it continues through to the present-day renaissance of his furniture, now classic pieces whose prices rocket at auction. This is in sharp contrast to the period between the 1960s and Juhl's death when he felt himself forgotten, his work fallen from favour. Yet this story cannot be told in isolation from the architectural and design history of the period, and indeed the history of ideas that shaped the social developments of the times. Juhl's career and his products then, are seen from a broader perspective, the long view, from which all artistic work can be contemplated.

The first chapter considers Juhl's studies at the Academy and his apprenticeship with Vilhelm Lauritzen. It also addresses the inception of modernism in Scandinavia and the figures of Kay Fisker and Kaare Klint. Both men developed a uniquely Scandinavian interpretation of modernism and both had a decisive influence on Juhl's work and self-understanding. The chapter is thus concerned with modernity as both an epoch and a concept. It considers the Danish architectural community as it transitioned from Neoclassicism to Functionalism and it questions what it means to design with both social responsibility and aesthetic quality.

The second chapter takes a closer look at Juhl's furniture, in particular his most significant chairs, those produced in the years following the war. It was then that Juhl established his own design studio, consolidating his method and so laying the foundations for his international reputation. Taking a broader perspective, the chapter considers the chair as a historical phenomenon and addresses the underlying rationale for design as such.

In continuation of this theme, the book's third chapter tells the story of Juhl's breakthrough in the United States. From his acquaintance with the influential contractor and intermediary Edgar Kaufmann Jr., to his work on the Trusteeship Council Chamber at the UN, his exhibition work and the various tasks that in the most literal sense kept Juhl flying throughout the 1950s. The chapter also offers a brief history of the American context; of consumer culture in relation to the craft traditions and natural materials that, not least in America, lent Nordic expression an exotic quality.

In the fourth chapter we come down to earth again, examining Juhl's heated debate with Børge Mogensen and Arne Karlsen concerning what one might call *furniture morality*. This is tied to Juhl's period of failing inspiration and declining demand, a period that ended with his slightly early retirement to his studio at the house he designed for himself in Ordrup. The chapter also traces Juhl's reflections on the relations between form and function, history and ideas, the fine arts and design.

The fifth and final chapter points in a new direction. It turns to how the legacy that Juhl inherited (from the art and ideas behind Scandinavian modernism), meets with the legacy that we inherit from him: his furniture and his house. The status of artefacts waxes and wanes as retro-waves or the pendulum of history casts out what is most valuable or instead, unexpectedly, grants the forgotten a renaissance. The latter is exactly what has happened with Juhl's furniture, which today holds cult status in Japan and in many cases has been put back into production.

Between the second and third chapters Finn Juhl's most important designs receive a thorough description and analysis.

Today, Finn Juhl's *Chieftain Chair* and *Poet Sofa* are considered modern classics, taking their place in the Elysium of chairs alongside Wegner's *Round Chair* and *Wishbone Chair*, Mogensen's *J39*, Jacobsen's *Ant* and *Egg Chairs*, the Eameses' *DAW Chair*, Thonet's *Vienna Chair*, Mies van der Rohe's *Cantilever* and *Barcelona Chairs*, and Kjærholm's *PK22*.

Not bad company. And Finn Juhl's legacy embodies those very qualities that lifted Danish design to world fame, simple but distinguishing properties like attentiveness, honesty and originality. What it means for a chair to possess these qualities is of course open to debate. It is a discussion that Juhl would undoubtedly have loved to take on one more time.

1912 —— 1939

The
Functional
Tradition

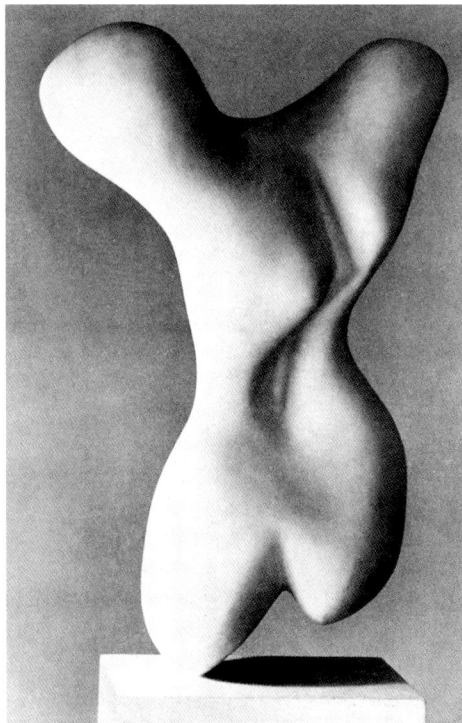

Abstract sculptures, such as Jean Arp's *Torso* from 1933, remained an important source of inspiration for Finn Juhl throughout his life, and his exhibition displays always included a sculpture.

The Functional Tradition

At first, Finn Juhl wanted to be an art historian. As a teenager he spent hours amid the collections of ancient Greek sculpture at the Glyptoteket Museum in Copenhagen and likewise at the National Gallery of Denmark when, once a week, it was open in the evenings. But his father, a textile dealer, did not trust he would be able to make a living as an art historian. Juhl's mother had died three days after his birth (January 1912) and Juhl's relationship with his father was far from close. Juhl described him as authoritarian, adding, "but I discovered early that if I heeded him, nothing would happen to me ..."[1]

Juhl's older brother Erik trained to be an engineer. For Finn, studying architecture was really a compromise with his practical, money-minded father. In his father's defence, the economic outlook in 1930, when Finn finished secondary school, was dire enough that it might influence a young person's choice of livelihood. In the United States, the Wall Street Crash of 1929 had led to a precipitous drop in growth, sky-high levels of unemployment and global shockwaves that were felt even in Denmark.

In this regard, Juhl shared the fate of another contemporary architect, Arne Jacobsen, who would also go on to represent Danish design on the world stage. Jacobsen was ten years Juhl's senior, and his father, who was also a merchant, was perhaps even less understanding than Juhl's of artistic aspiration. At school it was only in drawing classes that Jacobsen felt engaged, and he wanted to be a painter. Like Juhl's, Jacobsen's father pressed him towards architecture, believing it to be more financially secure. When Jacobsen was awarded a medal at the *International Exhibition* in Paris in 1925 and the programme described him as an *artiste*, his father commented, "This must be a mistake, my boy – you're no artist, and you're too fat to be a trapeze artist."[2] For both Jacobsen and Juhl, it became a lifelong ambition to unite the playful experimentation and formal suggestiveness of the fine arts with the traditions and functional utility of architecture and design.

Between Art and Function

Where the boundaries between disciplines are drawn has always determined the identity of craftsmen and their ability to make a living from their trade. From the Middle Ages, the guild system ensured, on the one hand, that products were of a certain quality and on the other, that conventions and practices were protected by a monopoly on both commissions and the education of the next generation. This holds true for the cabinetmaking tradition that Finn Juhl came to work closely with in his furniture production.

Whether he was designing furniture or houses, interiors or exhibitions, Juhl continued to draw on the fine arts[3]. In his interior designs he returned continually to the work of a select few favourites, including the painter Vilhelm Lundstrøm and the sculptor Erik Thommesen. He brought together colours, textures and lighting to complement one another, attempting to produce a total architectural space, with all of the careful detail a holistic, overall effect is composed of. In Juhl's furniture design, the abstract sculptures of Jean Arp, Barbara Hepworth, Henry Moore and Alexander Calder are clear sources of inspiration. And yet, perhaps more significant for Juhl was seeking to draw artistic expression into the heart of the design process, to make of design a space where aesthetic consideration and artistic expression are developed.

Finn Juhl used the two photographs shown here as inspirational models when he lectured and taught. Of Barbara Hepworth's *Two Forms* from 1935 he said, "Her abstract sculpture is an intense study of the relationship between two bodies, one reclining, the other in a never-released movement. It contains a portrayal of movement."

Finn Juhl's own aesthetic balances the playful experimentation and the technical analysis that had been established in his youth. It was functionalism but with a human face and demanded the same care for its cultural aspect as it did for its technical engineering. Without this balance, design would be arbitrary and superficial; we would lose sight of the intentions behind the product. Juhl held that "… there is so tight and intimate a relation between a thing's form and its function that the very language of form must be treated as part of the object's function, that is, in an equally intimate relationship with contemporary life in every other regard."[4] With his reference to contemporary life Juhl is suggesting that the question of balancing the technical with the human is not limited to aesthetics or the practice of art and design. When Finn Juhl was accepted into the School of Architecture at the Academy of Fine Arts in 1930, architecture too was profoundly influenced by the tension between tradition and an innovation that characterises modernity in general as a condition of life, the social structure and the mindset of Western civilisation, and that found its artistic expression in modernism.

The Price of Progress

Modernism can be seen as an attempt to live up to the pre-eminent demand of modern society: to be contemporary. While earlier movements had based themselves on established historical foundations, modernism attempts to reflect and interpret the shape of life in the modern world. It was a life in constant flux and without the providential safety net that since the Enlightenment, Western civilisation had gradually rejected as a fantasy. In place of faith grew a belief in humanity and its ability to achieve progress in freedom and guided by reason.

Freedom, reason and progress. But freedom and progress came at a price. A perceived loss of meaning, context and reliable signposts to guide one through the fragmentation, abstraction, anonymity and isolation that characterised life in the modern city, where people were reduced to cogs in the machine. This experience stood in stark contrast to that of previous generations, who had passed down their knowledge and values from one generation to the next, protected by the close ties of village communities and the rhythms of the natural world that they lived from. In modernity, by contrast, ceaseless change, industrial and scientific division of labour, technological and bureaucratic alienation and the individualisation of the conditions and values of life meant that the capacity for adaptation and renewal were critical if one was to navigate the markets that, with ever-increasing commodification, were coming to dominate all areas of modern life.

One of Finn Juhl's early watercolours (1934) from his time as a student at the Royal Danish Academy of Fine Arts. The inspiration of Le Corbusier is obvious.

As with music and painting, modernism first came to exert a real influence over architecture during the first decade of the 20th century. But while in the arts modernism was *formal*, namely the abstraction of and distancing from realist depiction, in architecture modernism developed into a new interest in architectural *content* – in the function of buildings. This might seem obvious, in as much as architecture should be concerned with the concrete use of buildings – they have to *house* people and not just look interesting. Nevertheless, this proved fiercely controversial.

The buildings at 2A and 2B Vodroffsvej (1929) by Kay Fisker and C. F. Møller. Danish modernism with windows in long horizontal bands, underscored by bands of brickwork in two colours.

Modernism – the international style or functionalism, as it was often called – was driven in no small part by an excitement with the architectural possibilities of modern engineering, in particular its use of wrought iron (in railway bridges, long glass-covered passages and the Eiffel Tower) and, later, iron-reinforced concrete. The new construction method, using iron and cast concrete floors supported by concrete columns instead of brick walls, allowed not only for expansive self-supporting spaces, but for components that were pre-fabricated and then assembled at the construction site. This meant that construction could be faster and cheaper and grow taller, but also that the buildings were lighter and airier, as large glazed sections brought the outside world to view. The long lines of these concrete facades were often even rounded, resembling the vast ocean-going steamers that were the period's great symbol of progress, and whitewashed to appear as clean as a modern laboratory.

The Architecture Machine

It was then paradoxically *form* that came to distinguish functionalist architecture, a form characterised by both a construction technique and an outward appearance that were immediately recognisable. Meanwhile, content, *function*, how it was that these modernist buildings realised their purpose, was not so outwardly apparent and so became a matter of ideological dispute. In a way, this made sense. Modernism reflected a modern world that came into being through industrialisation. This industrialisation depended in turn upon technological advances that themselves were bound up with a certain rational worldview, which since the Enlightenment had progressively permeated society and individual life. In the field of architecture, this rationality manifested in those construction techniques that came to distinguish functionalist buildings. Inspired by scientific progress, the matter-of-fact approach of engineers and the contemporary call for truth and transparency, architects began to display the *substance* of the building's construction honestly and unadorned.

At the same time, young, socially engaged architects came to see that architecture would have no right to call itself modern until it addressed the urban population, those who worked the machines that drove modernity, and whose living conditions were just as wretched as their working conditions. A suitable functionalist architecture must engage with the real needs for housing in modern society. With this, the formerly peaceable and retiring art form of architecture became an explosive political arena. In truth, the white, cold, clean structures of concrete, steel and glass did not help the young architects to convince the wider public of modernism's potential social benefits. The resistance was – and is – likely ethical, political and aesthetic at once. Many were simply not interested in having the inner structures that determine our everyday world revealed. First, Marx had laid bare the blueprint of the capitalist system. Then Darwin had revealed the building blocks of human evolution. Finally, Freud had gazed into our psyche and found dry rot and decay beneath all our thoughts and deeds. And now the engineers and the architects wanted to reveal the entire building as it was, a machine for living in; cold, transparent, stripped bare. No thanks.

Tradition and Innovation

The charge that modern architecture was cold and elitist was aimed at both the international white functionalist structures built for the few and the industrial prefab apartment blocks built for the masses. It still is today. The classical 'white' modernists like Le Corbusier, Mies van der Rohe and, in Denmark, Arne Jacobsen were headstrong avant-gardists and single-minded artists with little thought for the social aspects of their work or for its broader socio-economic, political or cultural impact on the world in which they built. But then neither the Bauhaus School nor the New Objectivity movement in Germany, with its shiny machine aesthetic and its confidence in the social potential of industrial mass production, was ultimately able to forge a compelling link between form and function, tradition and innovation.

On the one hand, authentic, high-quality craftsman-ship was fetishised as the core of all manufacturing. On the other hand, there was a boundless fascination with the equally authentic, unchecked, raw technology. With Titanic as the shining example, machines promised speed, freedom and new opportunities waiting beyond the horizon. This was the age of mass emigration. As mentioned, all the great functionalist buildings drew on motifs from the vast ocean steamer.

Ultimately, there was at best something a little risible about functionalism. At worst, it was a major disappoint-ment. At least, *tradition* had decided which of the heritage styles certain buildings should be built in: parliaments and courthouses should be classical, town halls gothic, churches romantic or gothic, palaces and stately homes baroque or in the National Romantic style, and farm-steads should look like farms. *Innovation* had not provided the key to the new house nor resolved the relationship between form and function. Modernism had promised to let function dictate form, but instead it seemed that the old styles had simply been replaced with a new one. Allowing that "form follows function", as the American architect Louis Sullivan had put it, turned out to be easier said than done.

The Nordic Ideal of Beauty

In Denmark too, modernist architecture struggled to find its breakthrough, although from around 1930, some of the country's leading architects began increasingly to lean in that direction. In fact, the most successful modernist expressions were more a continuation of established approaches to architecture than something radically new. Quite aptly and rather paradoxically, Kay Fisker, Juhl's teacher at the School of Architecture, described function-alism as the "functional tradition". Innovation as tradition, no less!

According to the architectural historian Nils-Ole Lund, "the demands of construction change, and architectural form is renewed, but values are the glue that holds it all together."[5] Values that in Denmark are based on the need to unite beauty and utility, form and function, by defining beauty as order. So when modernist rationality reached Denmark it was understood to be a rationality of beauty, a dream of order and harmony; a kind of decree or first principle by which something that functions well will also be beautiful. Combined with a Protestant-Calvinist work ethic and a social consciousness inspired by N. F. S. Grundtvig's writings, this translates into the typically Danish outlook: that with sufficient effort and care, things will come right.

The architect Kay Fisker (1893–1965), Finn Juhl's professor at the Academy. Fisker's Danish edition of international modernism, which emphasised the use of brick, Denmark's unofficial 'national building material', became trend-setting in Denmark.

Kaare Klint (1888–1954), the influential head of the Furniture School at the Royal Danish Academy of Fine Arts, School of Architecture during the years when modern Danish furniture design was making a name for itself. Klint's studies of proportions and functions introduced a modern, scientifically inspired approach based on rationally defined needs in furniture design, and coincided with a similar developments in building architecture.

The French-Swiss architect Le Corbusier at the entrance to his housing complex Unité d'Habitation in Marseille. A bas-relief shows *Modulor Man* – a sculptural edition of his *Le Modulor* system of proportions. Based on the proportions of the human body, the system can be used to dimension all the components of a building.

The founder of modern Danish furniture design and long-time head of the Furniture School at the Academy of Fine Arts, Kaare Klint, can be seen as the personification of this outlook. Klint's studies of utility and function aimed to determine the dimensions of all utensils and furniture according to a scale conceived on the basis of the proportions of the human body. Klint was both aristo-cratic and fiercely dedicated to his work. He was well-suited to his guru status. The Klint School has had an enormous influence on attitudes within Danish furniture design, an influence that has remained largely intact to this day. His systematic analyses of proportions and function were pioneering in a Danish context, albeit not unique internationally. Le Corbusier, for instance, was deeply immersed in parallel studies, and across a range of other disciplines at the beginning of the 20th century, inspired by the great new reach of scientific knowledge, many sought to quantify things that were not inherently quantifiable.

Sketch by Kaare Klint. Human proportions as the basic reference. The width of a folded shirt determines the width of the wardrobe drawer, and so forth.

Finn Juhl and Modernism

Was Finn Juhl a modernist? One can hardly doubt it. He sought a language of form that lay behind modernism, but repeatedly stressed the need for functionality and the objective and rational aspects of his craft. A typical architect, he thought in terms of order, unity, harmony, context and the aesthetic accordance between separate elements. So, for example, someone like Juhl who adored modernist art should also have a modernist and contemporary home, rather than a home representing some arbitrary historical period. Asked in an interview whether others ought to live as he did, Juhl responded, "I don't think people ought to do anything. But I don't understand how someone who reads progressive literature and listens to Stravinsky or other modern composers can do so in Renaissance furniture. In other areas we are in step with the style of the times … One cannot … expect that I, as a modern designer, recommend to contemporary people anything other than contemporary furniture."[6] But Juhl's modernism had its roots in the Danish tradition of *putting things in order* by means of inherited fine craftsmanship and guided by a human point of departure and a human end goal. Juhl's experiments and free play served to open design towards possible, as yet unknown, relations to function.

Finn Juhl was one of the first Danish furniture designers to consistently employ the key modernist technique of laying bare the relations between the component elements of a piece. Just as with modernist architecture's disclosed horizontal and vertical elements, an avant-garde of early modernism had experimented with designing constructivist furniture. The most famous is the Dutch designer Gerrit Rietveld's *Red and Blue Chair* from 1917 that, paralleling his compatriot Piet Mondrian's abstraction of coloured squares and rectangles, conceives furniture as a clean, geometric expression of flat rectangles. Likewise, the Bauhaus School had continued to investigate the possibilities of constructing furniture out of its geometrical components, although most furniture that reached production concealed its own construction, as had always been the tradition in the finer crafts. This uncovering of that which an object is comprised of approaches the core of the modernist view, that the true, the good and the beautiful are united, as had been dreamt ever since Antiquity.

Juhl with the family dog, Bonnie, in the garden at Kratvænget 15 in Ordrup. The plot was largely flat, but soil excavated from the foundation work was used for landscaping, creating a slight bowl shape that provided more privacy for both the house and the garden.

ORDRUPGAARDS PARK

DYREHAVEN

PROJ. TILBYGNING

EGET HUS, KRATVÆNGET 15. 1:100
BYGGET 1941-1942

KRATVÆNGET 15 ·
CHARLOTTENLUND
DENMARK
FINN JUHL
ARCHITECT M.A.A.
ORDRUP 7721
ORDRUP 6009

AUGUST 1970

N

Juhl's own house (1942) at
Kratvænget 15 in Ordrup shown in
a watercolour by Juhl from 1968.
At the time he had plans of adding
a second building to be used as
a studio, but the idea was never
realised, perhaps because his firm
was not exactly inundated with
work.

Juhl's own house Kratvænget 15
in Ordrup consists of two off-set
parallel buildings connected by a
lower building. The light, simple,
clear-cut forms with white plaster
cladding appear clearly defined, yet
calm, against the dark woodland
background. The structure
combines jazz rhythms with
a temple-like stature.

A Modern Home must have a Table Bench

It is perhaps a little scholarly to hold that a prosaic, concrete object like a chair has a rational, an ethical and an aesthetic dimension. But when Juhl in his armchairs and his light easy chairs separates the load-bearing wooden frame from the borne elements of the seat and back, this is precisely an expression of the modernist aspiration to honestly (the ethical) foreground the chair's construction (the rational) and so exhibit its formal beauty (the aesthetic). This also demonstrates an awareness of the relationship between form and function and thus of the specific structural roles of the different elements and materials. In functionalist modernism, the work ethic of the craftsman, the designer and the architect is transformed into an ethics *of the objects themselves*. By honestly revealing the elements it is composed of, the chair itself becomes an honest chair.

Finn Juhl's *Table Bench* of 1953 illustrates the striking results of a modernist functional analysis that aimed to find completely new kinds of furniture, answering to new, modern ways of living. Formally, however, the *Table Bench* also continues modernist architecture's rediscovered archetype of beam and column in clean, minimalist expression: a thin horizontal board supported by equally slender legs. At the same time, the *Table Bench* stands somewhere between traditional wood and innovative steel; between the cabinetmaker's craft and industrial production. Had Juhl opted for the stronger material of steel, he could have avoided using braces to support the *Table Bench* along its length, achieving an even more minimalist expression. Instead, he made a virtue of necessity, placing the legs – the columns – as far towards the ends of the board as possible, achieving the refined proportions and the floating impression that is so archetypally modernist.

When Charles and Ray Eames' revolutionary chairs in moulded, laminated wood appeared just after the Second World War, Juhl and many of his colleagues saw the possibilities they heralded. In part, this was the possibility of working with forms that could open modernist expression towards the soft curves of the human and natural worlds. In part, it was the possibility of producing on an industrial scale for a wider public who could not afford expensive, handcrafted furniture. Still, neither the markets nor the production had the global scope they have today. New developments could occur in one place without necessarily reaching people elsewhere. It took time before products reached beyond their original locality, and when they did finally show up, they often took some getting used to.

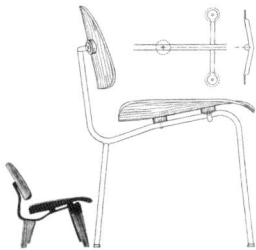

Finn Juhl often pointed to the American designer Charles Eames' furniture in moulded laminated wood as examples of industrial products that met contemporary demands for modern furniture.

Table Bench (1953). This advertisement demonstrates the dual function. A (surprisingly) rare example of multi-purpose furniture.

A Midsummer Night's Dream in Stockholm

During Juhl's formative years it was vital to be able to straddle both cabinetmaking and industrial production, local Neoclassicism and international functionalism, tradition and innovation. It shows in Juhl's work that he was a student of *both* Kay Fisker *and* Vilhelm Lauritzen; inspired by *both* Arne Jacobsen *and* Kaare Klint. It also shows that he himself recognised these debts and respected his mentors, even as he sought his own artistic expression from an early age and later, when to his mind they had ceased to cultivate the functionalist seed of modernism, distanced himself from them. That this seed found especially favourable conditions in the Danish soil, is underscored by the international perception of Danish architecture as "sane, sound and simple" according to a British architecture journal of 1948[7]. The Danish style incorporated a pragmatic restraint that in architecture, applied art and design manifested as an undogmatic search for harmony and authenticity as the very basis of the craft. This, in combination with a matter-of-fact sense of beauty, dictated that things should be simple, methodical and balanced.

Not least in light of this locally anchored, moderate approach, the more fanatical international architectural modernism had been, as suggested above, a quite limited and avant-garde phenomenon in Denmark. In 1930, however, it made its breakthrough in the Nordic countries, the same year Juhl enrolled at the Royal Danish Academy of Arts, School of Architecture. Juhl, his future teachers and all the significant Danish architects of the time flocked to Stockholm that summer for an architecture exhibition that has since become notorious as functionalism's great attempt to break into the mainstream – *The Stockholm Exhibition.*

The 18-year-old Juhl (centre) in May 1930, during his visit to the *Stockholm Exhibition.* It instilled Juhl and many other Danish designers and architects with modernism's ideals.

The exhibition was like a Midsummer Night's Dream, a modernist vision of things to come. Light, bright buildings floated like white sails and summer dresses in the breeze along Djurgårdsbrunnsviken's glinting waters. There were clean lines, visible constructions and housing designs based on careful studies of need and function, furnished with simple tubular-steel furniture in the style of Marcel Breuer. All the industry's latest and most innovative work was on show and the exhibition's centrepiece, an 80-metre-high mast with neon advertisements, stood lit throughout the summer nights like a great promise of infinite human progress. It was as though the structure wanted to lift from the ground and rise to the heavens, and as if this was not enough, the exhibition's striking restaurant was called *Paradiset* ('The Paradise').

Notwithstanding his usual sceptical reserve, even the stern writer and architect Poul Henningsen (known affectionately as PH) was positive about the exhibition. Indeed he was convinced it would prove influential for his profession moving forward. In a review he praised the exhibition for promoting "a new view of objects" and he hoped that "the inevitable effect that will be the result of the exhibition would lead away from direct, worthless imitation and towards an equally precise resolution of everyday tasks in terms of their own individual basis, as here this Sunshine Celebration has achieved".[8]

Modernising the Sense of Beauty

The *Stockholm Exhibition* was planned and organised by the Swedish architect Gunnar Asplund. This was his international breakthrough and he became one of the heroes of what many viewed as a distinctively human and moderate expression of modernism, one which the world came to call *Nordic Functionalism* or *Nordic Modernism*. Asplund was, moreover, both a congenial and close acquaintance of his contemporary Kay Fisker.

The most radical and socially conscious wing of the Danish Functionalist movement congregated at the journal *Kritisk Revy* (Critical Review) with PH and Ivar Bentsen leading the charge. This said, the journal also engaged with the formalism that lay behind both the international white modernism and the Danish, locally anchored, Nordic Neoclassicism. Uniting beauty and function was for the leading functionalists simply a continuation of architecture's foremost aim. Yet just as modernity, with its scientific reach and its industrial production, looked set to provide the technical basis for functionalist unity and wholeness (exactly when progress, in other words, looked ready to take off) it was the prevailing notion of beauty that stood in the way.

The *Stockholm Exhibition* in 1930 was one of the first coherent manifestations of modernist architecture, design and crafts and was pivotal in establishing the strong international reputation of Scandinavia as a place where modernism and the new welfare state seemed to form an ideal union.

Even Poul Henningsen (1894–1967), the sharpest cultural critic of the time, who was no fan of stylistic trends, such as the "ice cold tubular-steel furniture" of the Bauhaus style, had to admit that "the atmosphere" at the *Stockholm Exhibition* was unique.

Eight of Denmark's most prominent furniture designers photographed at the design and crafts sales exhibition Den Permanente and reprinted in *House and Gardens* magazine in 1963. From left: Ejnar Larsen, Arne Jacobsen, Aksel Bender Madsen, Orla Mølgaard Nielsen, Peter Hvidt, Ib Kofod Larsen, Hans J. Wegner and Finn Juhl in his *FJ45 Chair*. In front, the *Judas Table*.

"To bring the sense of beauty into accordance with the present social situation has always been the task of art," wrote PH in his review of the *Stockholm Exhibition*, "and thereby the individual who has overcome his initial doubts about 'the new' will come upon a happier and more harmonious beauty than before. And later such a modernisation of beauty will lead to possibilities for socio-economic and socially salubrious progress. We cannot at present build a normal house without sacrificing a large sum on that honest ambition's altar, sums that otherwise could better the room's spaciousness and decor. Progress with respect to new building materials and methods is, among other things and to a great extent, both dependent on and curbed by the prevailing sense of beauty."[9]

The atmosphere and aspiration of the exhibition accentuated a tension between tradition and innovation, form and function – and for the upcoming furniture designers, between craftsmanship and industry production. The experience became a watershed for all the influential architects and designers of the time, including Kay Fisker and another of Juhl's mentors from the School of Architecture, Vilhelm Lauritzen. Each of them in their own way introduced 'the modern' into Danish architecture, shifting the beauty ideals towards a more contemporary, more democratic functionalist ideal. Regardless, it took the broader public a long time to develop an enthusiasm for *funkis*, as the new style was then called.

The Stone Axe and Neoclassicism

As in art academies across Europe, the Danish art academy had undergone a youth rebellion. The old styles and sweeping redundancies eventually had to give way to a more impartial and contemporary approach. It was undoubtedly a much needed revolution. To give one example, up until 1918, submissions for the Academy's final exam had to be in one of three styles: antiquity, middle ages or renaissance. On excursions out into the world, this younger generation now began to take the measure of frank, simple houses whose details were lifted out of anonymity and into current architecture. This pursuit of authenticity lead them back towards antiquity, but also into a more local historical engagement: to the form of the stone axe and the content of the farmhouse, as Fisker put it. And when Fisker began to describe the characteristically Danish combination of Neoclassicism and Functionalism as "the functional tradition", the neoclassical elements were never really so classical. On the other hand, the end result was certainly modern, just in a less conspicuous way than international functionalism.

Thus, the younger generation wanted to *construct* a tradition, just as 'the new' and 'the innovative' too must be constructed to live up to the demands of the times. In buildings which signalled this new direction, like Carl Petersen's Faaborg Museum, and Fisker and Aage Rafn's stations along the Gudhjem train line, there is an admiration for C. F. Hansen's unpretentious neoclassical *Church of Our Lady* in Copenhagen, only seen and interpreted through the traditional Danish farmhouse, whose functions, forms and materials have been decided by tradition. Kaare Klint's chair for the Faaborg Museum is a simplified, modern interpretation of the ancient Greek klismos chair, much like the Austrian Thonet brothers' *No. 14 chair*.

This search for authenticity in both the Nordic building tradition and the solid beauty of earlier classical architecture has been termed a *doricism* in Nordic architecture. So when the young Finn Juhl was drawn to ancient Greek art he was perhaps already on the trail of an interest in the free but as yet unknown forms that lay behind established styles. This interest would come to define his own works.

Finn Juhl at the Academy

After two preparatory years at the Academy of Fine Arts, students chose one class and one teacher to follow during their first year at the Academy proper. Finn Juhl – like Arne Jacobsen before him, who had graduated in 1927 – chose Kay Fisker. In 1924 Fisker had taken over the so-called 'Danish Class'. The class had been established by Hack Kampmann and the young rebel generation of 1913 as a means of shifting the Academy's emphasis from the detached study of styles towards the real challenges facing Danish towns and cities: schools, stations, dairy plants, doctor's residences etc.

With a nose for the demands of the time, Fisker transformed the class into a study of housing. Perhaps he was not the most socially engaged, but Fisker saw that the combination of an acute lack of housing, state funding and municipally purchased low-cost construction sites would ensure work for those architects who knew how to build housing. He had experienced this himself during the 1920s with a string of large apartment blocks such as Hornbækhus in Copenhagen. Fisker had built many quality houses, published books, edited *Arkitekten*, met with all of the times' most prominent personalities and was a popular lecturer. Fisker's training of future residential architects likely contributed to the replication of Denmark's housing standards in many places across the world.

Later in his career when Juhl grappled with the relations between house, interior design and furniture, he no doubt drew on his experiences under Kay Fisker. Juhl's conviction that housing associations, urban planners, architects and furniture designers should work together to conceive and design housing and likewise guide the public in furnishing their apartments might have first arisen during his time in Fisker's class. Fisker thus set his students the task of researching the different kinds of residential architecture in Copenhagen, and the systematic overview, complete with floor plans, was published as a proper typology in *Arkitekten*[10].

Fisker also designed furniture, applied art and interiors. He was the architect behind the Danish pavilion at the *Paris Exhibition* of 1925, furnishing it with his own designs, among them a wing-back chair that looks to have inspired Finn Juhl. Fisker made a large number of sketches for furniture and furnishing proposals, writing desks, work chairs, dining tables, cupboards and even a bedroom for a Director Schou, complete with an arcing, carriage-shaped double bed in Italian walnut that puts one in mind of a boat trip down the Nile. Fisker also produced a series of functional silver objects during the 1920s. Later he collaborated with the B&W and Helsingør shipyards, designing ship's cabins for many Danish ferries, including those that chartered passage to England and Bornholm.

Making One's Own Way in Functionalist Formalism

Finn Juhl always maintained that as a furniture designer he was self-taught and that he had originally begun to design furniture because his brother lacked a work table. After designing a table for his brother, he later designed one for himself when he established his own studio, just as cabinetmakers in the past had always set out by designing their own toolbox. In fact, he was self-taught in so far as he did not attend the Furniture School at the Academy. Juhl was certainly observant of the developments around him. This is clear in his first attempts at upholstered furniture, which were very similar to those exhibited by Arne Jacobsen and other contemporaries at the annual furniture fair of the Copenhagen Cabinetmakers' Guild (Snedkerlauget), where Juhl would later be a frequent participant[11].

Finn Juhl came of age in a tradition that was largely functionalist in the sense demarcated by those contemporary architects and designers whose practice spanned Neoclassicism and Modernism: "we can detect a change in people's lifestyles, and as ever, this is followed by a corresponding change in the configuration of the home. Naturally, we try at first to incorporate these changes into the existing pattern, but simultaneously an avant-garde of modernists will fight to elucidate the most radical consequences of the changed relations … Philip Johnson's house is just such an avant-garde attempt and will of course never be considered as the standard."[12] Juhl refers here to the American architect Philip Johnson's famous *Glass House*.

Under Fisker, Juhl developed his own eye for home design in all its aspects. And when he reached his fourth year at the Academy, Juhl came under the tutelage of perhaps an even more decisive influence, the teacher Vilhelm Lauritzen, who hand-picked Juhl for a summer internship at his design studio. What was supposed to be a single summer came to last 11 years.

Juhl's efforts to assert his independence from his own father were transferred into efforts with his professional 'father', Kay Fisker, and the father of Danish furniture design, Kaare Klint. Though he was not named, the architect behind Hornbækhus may well have felt himself the target when Juhl remarked that "the efforts to make apartment blocks more human" was a stand against "the insipid, never-ending rows of terraced houses or tower blocks that monotonously repeat the same balcony detail."[13] Likewise Klint, in his play with balance and mathematics, had abandoned the duty towards function – the functional rationality. Of Klint's famous *Spherical Bed* for instance, Juhl rebuked "My things are created for humans and the human body – and I think it seldom that a sphere goes to sleep."[14]

According to Juhl, this lost rationality lead to a formalism that, in turn, let down the lesser talents of the industry by departing from the typically high standard of Danish craftsmanship along with the intuitive understanding of form and function's interrelation. In the spirit of PH, Juhl railed, "Nearly everybody works for museums; very few for development and for life."[15] For Juhl, almost paradoxically, the designer's imagination was inhibited and their products were tedious precisely to the extent that they weren't controlled by a functionalist rationality.

Juhl actively promoted modern interior design. Commenting on Philip Johnson's *Glass House* from 1949 in the book *Hjemmets Indretning* (Furnishing the Home) from 1954, he wrote that although the house was extreme, it represented a clear and unequivocal vision of things to come.

In contrast, he examined a set of Kay Bojesen's cutlery that he saw as "infinitely forthright. All is addressed: function, material, production method, weight, cleaning, and the cutlery feels immediately pleasant."[16] However, one should not think that the design of the cutlery had demanded less thought or study than products which obviously resulted from thoroughgoing calculation or fastidious studies of style. You can sketch with loose lines just as long as you are sketching on top of something solid. It is a common artistic experience that a lack of restrictions can be the greatest restriction of all. The point is of course, that this is an experience from the fine arts. Architects and designers always work within the limitations of their field. In truth, Juhl was not attacking Fisker or Klint, so much as offering a constructive critique of the functional tradition and the conditions of functional analyses.

Finn Juhl, who sought to think and sketch his way out of the bonds of presuppositions and a language of form that was impersonal or timid, wanted simply to help revive the functional tradition.

In his teaching and in articles, lectures and debate events, Juhl advocated the new aesthetic. Furniture manufacturers still preferred to deliver what the general public wanted, and many used 'architect-designed' as a term of offence. Like several of his colleagues, Juhl felt that education was needed if quality furniture – modern, practical and simple – was to succeed.

1. Kay Bojesens sølvbestik.

2. A. Michelsen: Sølvbestik tegnet af Ole Hagen.

3. Vilh. Hammershøj: »Støvfnuggenes dans i solstrålerne«.

FORTID nutid fremtid

Foredrag holdt af arkitekt Finn Juhl i Landsforeningen d. 14. januar 1949

Dansk kunsthåndværk har idag et fællespræg over sig. Man taler om tradition og mener håndværksmæssig tradition, soliditet og en vis nøgtern udtryksform, der karakteriseres som typisk dansk.

Enhver tale om de danske præstationer på dette område må nødvendigvis begynde med en anerkendelse af det fine gennemsnit.

Når der alligevel inden for visse faggrene begynder at opstå tvivl om tilstrækkeligheden af de opnåede resultater, har dette vel både ydre og indre anledning.

Edgar Kaufmann jr., direktør for den kunstindustrielle afdeling på MUSEUM OF MODERN ART i New York, aflagde et besøg her i sommer som landsforeningens gæst. Den høfligt udtrykte mangel på enthusiasme, som vore præstationer aflokkede ham, kom måske som et chock for mange, der havde drømt om en vældig eksport til guldlandet U. S. A.

Den gryende kritik i den ellers så venlige presse efter sidste snedkerlaugsudstilling er en anden ydre anledning. I fagpressen er Svend Erik Møller gået i rette med snedkerne for udstillingens mangel på initiativ og dens direkte kedsommelighed. Udstillingen var kedelig, og måske den kedeligste i en række af efterhånden mere og mere kedelige fremvisninger. Snedkerne var måske bange for, at de gyldne tider var forbi, og tiden var forpasset, hvor man kunne tillade sig at eksperimentere.

Skal snedkerne have skylden? Efter min opfattelse har arkitekterne i de tidligere rosværdige år været så glade for at omtale deres andel i det samarbejde, der var disse udstillingers fineste værdi, til at det er anstændigt nu at lade snedkerne bære byrden, mens vi andre lusker ud ad bagdøren.

Det var arkitekternes og møbeltegnernes område og part i arbejdet, der i virkeligheden blev kritiseret. Snedkerne er lige dygtige til arbejdsudførelsen. Kan man med rette sige, at fremragende ideer fra konkurrencen før udstillingen ikke blev antaget til udførelse? Det kunstneriske initiativ ligger ikke hos snedkeren, det ligger hos arkitekten, og svigter det, et fejlen hans.

Denne erkendelse af, at soberheden måske snarere er manglende fantasi eller ialfald hæmmet og kvalt fantasi, er vel i sig selv anledning til, at man fra landsforeningens side har ønsket at diskutere nutid og fremtid inden for møbelfaget.

Jeg vil gerne føre Dem på en rundrejse i den lilleverden, som betinger min måde at arbejde på, i håb om, at den på mange måder må komme ind på Deres område og derved afstedkomme kontakt og diskussion.

For at begynde på et helt andet område end møblerne vil jeg vise Dem 2 sølvbestik, det ene tegnet og udført af Kay Bojesen, det andet tegnet af arkitekt Ole Hagen for A. Michelsen.

Kay Bojesens ting er uendeligt ligefremme. Alt er husket: funktion, materiale, fremstillingsmetode, vægt, renliggørelse, og de udløser et umiddelbart behag. Ole Hagens bestik er mere elegant. Tingene ser omtrent ligeså enkle ud, men der er en mærkbar forskel. Man ser tydeligt glæden ved materialet, især i slidpræget (det meget tynde gods), og man mærker en dybtgående og streng bearbejdelse af formgivningen med støtte i ældre generationers stilprægede arbejder.

Hagens et decideret formet og tænkt af en æstetiker og udløser et medvidende og respektfuldt behag. Bojesens er fornemmet og formet af en humørfyldt kunstner. Det ligefremme i hans bestik har ikke krævet mindre tanke eller studium end Hagens.

1940 —— 1949

The Origins
of the Chair

Juhl debuted as a furniture designer at the Cabinetmakers' Guild Exhibition in 1937 with an overstuffed easy chair and sofa, a folding table with a dining chair and a wall-mounted bookcase.

Overstuffed furniture such as Flemming Lassen's *Trætte mand* (Tired Man) from 1935 – now one of the most expensive Danish furniture designs ever sold at auction – was widely popular, also among young designers and architects.

At Vilhelm Lauritzen's studio, Juhl was probably responsible for much of the furnishing at *Radiohuset* (1945), taking the lead on lamps, furniture and so forth. The early (1934) facade drawing of the project seen from the street Julius Thomsens Gade shows the building's consistent functionalism: horizontal lines, smooth surfaces, asymmetrical composition.

An Overstuffed Expression

Apart from a drawing table for his own use – a fitting place to begin – the first pieces of furniture Finn Juhl designed were overstuffed chairs. They are in the soft and comforting, ursine style that many Danish architects, Arne Jacobsen and Flemming Lassen included, were attempting in the 1930s. Flemming Lassen thought that his own voluminous, furry armchair, the *Tired Man* of 1935, brought to mind a polar bear mother's warm embrace on the ice caps[17]. Arne Karlsen, a historian of Danish furniture design, argues that these pieces had no direct precursors in the history of furniture construction, and that designers had to place their trust in the cabinet-makers and upholsterers' ability to devise a stable structure[18].

The cabinetmakers and trained furniture designers had difficulties seeing the constructive challenges in upholstered furniture. Their expertise was rather in static refinement and delicate joints. But the public took to the soft armchairs, and this cheerful, almost goofy play with forms was no doubt an enticement for Finn Juhl. He debuted as a furniture designer at the annual furniture fair of the Copenhagen Cabinetmakers' Guild in 1937, exhibiting among other pieces an overstuffed sofa and armchair. Their armrests – like real arms or th e flippers of a seal – reach diagonally upward, as though the chair literally wants to catch the man or woman who, coming home from a long day's work, would like nothing more than to sink into its protective embrace.

In all of these overstuffed models, evidence of con-struction is hidden away in a manner uncharacteristic of modernism. Their plump, cheery designs resulted from a free play with form that sought to create something full-bodied and alive. They are not especially convenient, though, and gradually, as it was discovered that comfort depends more on the flow of lines and the surface gradient than on the thickness of the padding, designers could work at refining the contours and surfaces to create lighter models that flaunt their own construction.

The influential architect and writer Steen Eiler Rasmussen, who would go on to become something of a sage of Danish architecture, wrote in a review for the newspaper *Politiken* that Juhl's furniture resembled deflated rubber balls. Naturally, the young architect was put out: "… and I thought my fate was sealed, and I was finished. Then I met an old classmate on the high street *Strøget* who shouted 'Congratulations! I saw that you were in the papers.' He hadn't read it at all. That taught me that the opinions of the press are quickly forgotten, whether they are good or bad. The most important thing is just to be written about …"[19]

From *Radiohuset's* Door Handles to Furniture Provocateur

In 1937 Finn Juhl was 25 years old and newly married to the dentist Inge-Marie Skaarup, and since his summer internship away from the Architecture School in 1934, he had been employed by Vilhelm Lauritzen's design studio. Here he quickly became one of the leading designers on *Radiohuset* (the Radio Building), the headquarters of DR (Danish Broadcasting Corporation). It would be a distinc-tive and revered cornerstone of Vilhelm Lauritzen's architecture. *Radiohuset* was perhaps the first large-scale thoroughly functionalist construction in Denmark. It is so holistic a work that all the furnishings, from furniture and light fittings to door handles and coat hooks, were designed anew and tailored for the building. Though Finn Juhl's signature appears on many of the drawings of the furnishings, he always insisted that Vilhelm Lauritzen designed the furniture for *Radiohuset*.

If this is so, Juhl may have learned from Lauritzen in his increasing separation of the supporting wooden frames from the supported padded seat and back elements, for this feature characterises the armchairs designed for *Radiohuset* in 1938. Likewise the wing-back sofas in the studio foyer, where performers in the concert hall could relax between sessions, have certain similari-ties with Finn Juhl's own sofa from the same year.[20]

Juhl, aged 27, was photographed for a newspaper when he took part in one of the Guild's first furniture fairs in 1939. He exhibited a sofa, a 'tilt radio' and a drinks cabinet, the latter demonstrated with practised ease by the designer himself. Modern and stylish.

Nutidshjem med Diskotek og Vippe-Radio

Bernild

That year, Juhl exhibited the first chair in a sequence of furniture that would be regarded as controversial, unusual and sometimes downright provocative. The zoological theme is more than just an allusion here. The frame's supporting triangles, which form the front and back legs, clearly mimic the anatomy of "grasshoppers poised to spring" as a reviewer described the two exhibition pieces.[21] 'Chair legs' are a dead metaphor, but Juhl's playful approach reinterprets the figure of speech, breathing new life into it. The motif has been around almost as long as there have been chairs. We see it, for instance, in the ancient Egyptian chairs from ca. 1500 BC engraved with lion's feet. And if one recalls Juhl's interest in ancient history, in particular ancient Egypt, it becomes clear that the *Grasshopper Chair* (1938), as it came to be known, is a free variation on this theme.

The joint connecting the front legs to the armrests and the top rail is irrationally acute and the question is whether it is a case of originality and provocation, or whether it represents the architect's incomplete understanding of viable furniture joints? This structural challenge likely excited the interest of Juhl and his collaborator over the next 20 years, the cabinetmaker Niels Vodder.

Likewise, the use of both wooden poles and beams renders the expression of the *Grasshopper Chair* a little unclear. It was produced in ash with an upholstered seat and back. The model was only produced in two copies, and it would probably take additional product development or experiments with new materials to bring it into production again. This in spite of the characteristic organic form, which both embraces and supports.

An early photograph (left) of the house at Kratvænget in Ordrup, where one of Juhl's two *Grasshopper Chairs* are seen on the left next to the organically shaped coffee table. The *Grasshopper Chairs* were designed for the Cabinetmakers' Guild Exhibition in 1938 (below), and both chairs remained in the house, until Juhl's first wife took them with her when the couple divorced.

A Wild Experiment with Wood

Finn Juhl met Niels Vodder through Mogens Voltelen, something of a live wire and *enfant terrible* who had been a secretary for PH and a staffer at *Kritisk Revy*, among other activities, and who agitated energetically for his furniture ideas. Voltelen's *Copenhagen Chair* (which Vodder had produced) was reportedly purchased by Bertolt Brecht. Arne Karlsen described it as "the closest Danish furniture came to a sociopolitical manifesto".[22] It was probably not the political so much as the reckless-ness and the free play with form that attracted Juhl to Vodder. And it was with Vodder at his side that Juhl himself set out to explore the structural limits of wood. Since Juhl did not have the schooling or experience in static mechanics, construction or the properties of wood of some of his Furniture School-educated colleagues, Vodder became an invaluable partner. It was probably in large part the collaboration with Vodder that allowed Juhl to cut loose and experiment with bold expressions and constructions, as Vodder was always able to build the joint or effect the state of balance that brought the wild forms good.

Although this was hardly experiment for experiment's sake, in looking back years later Juhl would recall the free inventiveness that ran through the overstuffed furniture period as a cheerful counterweight to the monkish restraint that at times can overtake the Danish cabinet-making tradition.

The close dialogue that unfolded over 22 years between Juhl and his working partner, cabinetmaker Niels Vodder, was unique and played a key role in shaping Danish Modern.

The Pelican and Free Flight

Juhl's true ambition was something different, however, and this becomes especially clear with the *Pelican Chair* of 1940 and the *Poet Sofa* of 1941. The *Pelican Chair* again alludes to the animal kingdom, although visually it does not resemble the waterbird so much as "tired walruses", as one critic dubbed it, a term not exactly intended as praise.[23]

When Juhl's furniture initially received a cool reception it was likely not because they were not considered functionalist enough. At the time there was still only a small avant-garde promoting international modernism and its aesthetic. Besides, Juhl's furniture really was quite functionalist. True, the overstuffed chair and sofa were heavy and unwieldy, but for the most part these kinds of furniture had always been so. They were also really quite comfy, and this too was beginning to be talked about. Juhl always worked from matter-of-fact analyses of the functional aspects of his furniture, although their free, artistic expression has perhaps encouraged a myth to the contrary. For instance, Juhl often sought the perfect arm, lumbar and shoulder supports, experimenting with solutions that allowed people to sit facing each other in his sofas or lounge sideways in his armchairs, legs slung over the armrests.

No, what was provocative was that pieces like the *Pelican Chair* are not simply inspired by modern sculp-ture, they are well on their way to becoming sculptures themselves. Not in a functional sense, since they are not without utility, as all fine art at least reserves the right to be. Rather, they are sculptural in an aesthetic sense. The chair carves out a space around itself, and in inter-acting with that space it effects an irritation, even a resistance, giving rise to meanings, associations and a sense of something different, something unusual. This is what art can do – stir an awareness that things are not always as we are accustomed to their being. Sculpture poses a bodily challenge to furniture. Its organic forms remind us that the purpose of all design is its use: handling, touching, enclosing. Fundamentally human, bodily acts.

The *Pelican Chair* is perhaps not one of Juhl's most accomplished works, but neither is it content to be 'nice' or 'non-descript'. It is its own presence within a space, and like most of Juhl's chairs, it is difficult to coordinate with other furniture. It is exactly because he felt an obligation toward the functional tradition and at the same time understood fine art to pose a serious bodily challenge to traditional forms of the chair, that Juhl also felt compelled to stress that "furniture is furniture – that is, applied art – not sculpture".[24]

A modern vision of interior design
from the early 1940s. The *Pelican*,
the *Poet*, a tilt radio, a practical Juhl
coffee table with sliding leaves,
Arne Jacobsen's *Bellevue* lamp and
a Lundstrøm painting on the wall.

During the early years, Juhl's furniture seemed provocative, and reviews were mixed. The same applied to the launch of the *Pelican* at the Cabinetmakers' Guild Exhibition in 1940.

Juhl was still working on overstuffed chairs when he and Vodder exhibited at the Cabinetmakers' Guild Exhibition in 1941. As usual, the display featured a sculpture. Here, a plaster relief by Sigurjón Ólafsson.

Snedkerlauget's Furniture Fair

At least as important as the arts for Finn Juhl's development and career was the professional milieu he operated in. In fact it was the fracture lines within this milieu that gave rise to challenges and assignments, imposed constraints and sparked curiosity. For almost all of the years that Juhl was active as a furniture designer, the annual furniture fair of the Copenhagen Cabinetmakers' Guild functioned as just such a decisive, professional setting, as, in another period, the exhibitions that Juhl designed would. All of Juhl's colleagues exhibited at the fair and it was also here that two other great names of the period made their debut, Hans J. Wegner in 1938 and Børge Mogensen in 1939.

The Danish cabinetmakers had begun the fair as an enterprise in 1927 in response to competition from both the growing furniture industry and the increase in furniture imports from overseas. With it they aimed to secure a place for the cabinetmaking trade and its traditions in modern society. In connection with the fair, the organisers ran an annual design competition, which attracted all of the best young talents. During the first years, it was Kaare Klint (who in 1924 had founded the Academy of Fine Arts' Furniture School) who defined the competition brief. In 1930, the year that Juhl began his studies in architecture and the *Stockholm Exhibition* paved the way for the breakthrough of Nordic functionalism, 13 cabinetmakers were each paired with a designer with a view to exhibiting together. These collaborations laid the seeds for what is now considered Danish furniture design's golden age.

During this golden age, not only was a vast amount of internationally considered high quality furniture produced, Danish furniture was an export success, not least on the lucrative US market. Many of these pieces are today considered classics, a handful of the most outstanding designers are world-renowned and even the typically more anonymous cabinetmakers and manufacturers are well known among connoisseurs. The golden age lasted almost exactly as long as cabinetmakers and designers continued to exhibit in the annual furniture fairs, that is to say, until 1966. That year the Copenhagen Cabinetmakers' Guild discontinued the fair, and Danish handcrafted furniture fell out of style, "a lost cause" as one of the cabinetmakers put it.[25] And despite later attempts to resurrect the furniture fair, it was never the same. Still, the Danish furniture industry today commands decent market shares and as modern antiques – classics, as they are called – furniture from the golden age is perhaps even better known and more coveted than in its own time.

Two of Juhl's most prominent colleagues during the Golden Age of Danish furniture design: Hans J. Wegner (far left) and Børge Mogensen (second from the left), while they were still students at the School of Arts and Crafts in the late 1930s.

Cabinetmakers, Designers and the Klint School

In his great work on the rise and fall of modern Danish furniture design, the business historian Per H. Hansen outlines the precise position that the Cabinetmakers' Guild Exhibition occupied when Finn Juhl made his debut: "By the close of the 1930s the furniture fair was stronger than ever. An artisanal functionalism had been established that rejected both old period furniture and the more drastic funkis-inspired experiments."[26]

The driving force behind the collaboration between cabinetmakers and designers was an agreement to fuse fine craftsmanship with functional design. In this, both Klint's technical approach and his aesthetic played a significant role. Klint's teaching at the Academy involved thorough studies of the human measurements that chair, table and bed should meet and the dimensions of the items to be placed in cabinets, cupboards and drawers. It aimed to find the minimum requirements and the basic, functional prerequisites of each design task. In this way one could pass on the knowledge carried in the tradition whilst also providing guidance in solving new problems. This practice was well known in architecture, but in the tradition of the Art Academy it had come to play a lesser role than the study of period styles.

In the natural sciences there had been recent successes identifying the fundamental components of different phenomena and materials and formulating them mathematically. This inspired Klint to use geometry to formulate a set of rules for the composition of different kinds of furniture. So it is that Klint's famous sideboard, designed to hold a 12-piece dining service, attempts to resolve a perennial storage problem: that even when things are put away they invariably leave a lot of unused (and so wasted) space within the storage unit. This is not such a problem if one lives in a mansion, but in an average home large, bulky furniture encroaches on the limited floor space available.

Two of Børge Mogensen's best-known furniture designs: the *Shaker Table C18* and *J39*, nicknamed *The People's Chair*. Both designed for FDB Furniture in 1947 (below).

There is a big gap between Arne Jacobsen's *Egg Chair* from 1958 and his early chair from the late 1920s, and not just in years (below right).

In *Danish Furniture Design* Arne Karlsen describes this work process: Klint and his students measured "a large number of Danish and foreign models of each piece in a dinner service: plates, cups, pitchers, knives, spoons, forks, etc. By comparing the length, width, and diameter of the pieces, they discovered the variations in the measurements were surprisingly small, and that it was possible to establish a simple series of dimensions according to which they were able to determine the measurements of shelves, trays, and drawers *without* limiting their use for predetermined purposes. They furthermore discovered that the same simple numerical ratio could easily be used for the different heights. By coordinating the norms they found for the *inner* dimensions of storage furniture with the *outer* dimensions determined by human measuremen ts, it was finally possible to create a valid, scientifically based *common* foundation for planning a large number of storage pieces: side boards, service cabinets, etc". At the same time Karlsen points laconically to an inherent problem for both the Klint School and their furniture: "Factory owners found their artistic expression too meagre – a typical reflection of the times and of the norms in taste that Kaare Klint was up against."[27]

Functional Analysis and a Personal Style

Perhaps Klint was not especially interested in uniting form and function. He prioritised function: analysing the requirements of different kinds of furniture in terms of their dimensions and usages. By contrast, he set little store by "aesthetic refinements. On the basis of these dry [functionalist] facts one can learn to construct a piece of furniture that anyone can endow with their own artistic expression to suit their tastes and the times."[28] In terms of their expression, Klint's best pieces simplify older furniture styles by stripping away all ornamentation in the pursuit of the furniture's basic form. Klint's *Safari Chair* of 1933 has its precursor in British officers' field chairs from the colonial era, and his *Church Chair* of 1936 recalls Mediterranean spindle-back chairs with rush seats.[29] In some cases, the basic form's geometry took over completely and led into formalism. In other cases he drew so close to the English *Chippendale* furniture he so greatly admired that one may well wonder how a modern functional analysis could result in so uncomfortable a sofa in a quite outdated style.

At the same time, Klint's conservative aesthetic was merely a reflection of the fact that Danish designers did not immediately embrace the functionalist idiom. Looking at the first furniture of a young Arne Jacobsen for instance, one can barely believe that it was designed by the international ultramodernist behind the *Ant* and *Egg* chairs.[30]

Kaare Klint's most prodigious student, Børge Mogensen, conceived his own distinctive functionalism. It was inspired by the Shakers' simple furniture and anonymous traditional furniture styles. Without compromising on quality, Mogensen designed modern furniture that could be industrially produced. Consequently his pieces were manufactured at a much lower cost than handcrafted furniture and so could reach a far broader public.

Like all of his contemporaries, Finn Juhl was inspired by Kaare Klint. Juhl thought that there was a need for "old, tried and tested, well-functioning models to be taken up again and used as the basis for designing modern furniture." This is precisely what the Klint School practiced and preached.[31] Juhl praised Klint's furniture for its "strength and stringency" and Klint's working method along with it. He wrote of the "almost fanatical obsession" which made Klint a natural role model for his students. Yet, it may have been because Juhl's own first attempts at furniture did not take place in the School of Furniture, but instead as he designed the interiors for *Radiohuset* with Vilhelm Lauritzen's design studio, that Juhl developed a freer personal expression than that contained in the Klint School's teachings or in their view of the relationship between form and function.

The Egyptian Chair and the Mystique of Simplification

Finn Juhl's *Egyptian Chair* was designed for the Cabinetmakers' Guild Exhibition in 1949. It was produced by Niels Vodder and shares the structure of a chair found in Tutankhamun's tomb. Seen in profile, the vertical back legs extend upwards to meet its slanting back, comprising an acutely angled triangular frame. This rests on a horizontal supporting rail which runs between the front and back legs. The backrest and seat are rounded, and Juhl confessed to borrowing both this motif and the triangle from the ancient Egyptian chair, which he had studied at the Louvre. In the spirit of Klint, Juhl simplified and modernised his model, stripping away its ornamentation and its lion's feet.

When modernist furniture designers felt this need to simplify, it was bound up with a more general experience of a loss of quality in modern society – the quality of products but also the quality of life. Although, naturally, designers and architects were not harder hit by this than others, they perhaps felt a special obligation to do something about it. They shared this analysis of the social situation with the period's social reformers, some of whom were Marxists, although the majority were likely some variety of utopian socialists or straightforward idealists. The downside of progress – even of civilisation itself – was that the down-to-earth, tactile practices in craft production were being alienated and disappearing as a result of the new divisions of labour and industrialisation. Rousseau had already seen human beings suppress their nature in the name of the enlightenment. Technologies created by others were replacing the artisans' own tools. Quality itself was becoming homeless.

In the countries that had first been industrialised, counter movements had sprung up. The English Arts and Crafts movement, for instance, quickly found support across Europe and North America. It aimed to promote both social reform and the handing down of fine craft traditions across different practices. There were also movements such as the *Deutscher Werkbund* (German Association of Craftsmen), a coalition of artists, architects, designers and industrialists who, rather than risk isolating the craft traditions by opposing the manufacturing industry, forged partnerships between artists and manufacturers to secure the quality of their products.

The Danish cabinetmakers of the Copenhagen Cabinetmakers' Guild made an effort to stress that good craftsmanship united the useful and the beautiful and was also the more ethical choice. Authenticity was marketable in part *because* it made for the simplest and most beautiful designs.

Juhl's *Egyptian Chair* was inspired by an Egyptian chair from ca. 1400–1300 BC, which is at the Louvre in Paris. It is seen here in a mural from Chancellor Sennefer's tomb at Thebes (Luxor) from ca. 1430 BC. Finn Juhl loved the chair's simple geometry and borrowed its construction principles with the triangular gables and the rounded seat and back.

Decline and Originality

One of the problems with this narrative of resisting industrialisation is that it is a tale of decline roughly modelled on the Fall of Man. Once upon a time, long ago, everything was better. Something original was lost, and ever since, we have tried to recover it. Little wonder, then, that many since the Romantic period had a burning interest in the history and origins of things big and small. Digging into the earth, seeking out the sources and taking up again the styles of past eras, searching for something sturdy enough to resist the storms of progress that had blown us backwards out of Paradise.

Following the path back from Danish handcrafted furniture and the modernist love of simplicity, one comes across a handful of recurrent models. One is the English *Windsor chair* from the 17th century. It has a steam-bent top rail (or bow) held fast by characteristically thin, round, vertical spindles above the mid-rail. The seat is solid wood, and the turned chair legs thrust right up into its base. This was always a frank, simple model and it received further simplification in the Thonet brothers' *Bentwood Chair.* Kaare Klint returned again and again to his English *Chippendale* chairs from the 18th century. Hans J. Wegner studied and imitated the thousand-year old Chinese chairs with their broad back splats and fine, curving armrests. And as mentioned above, Børge Mogensen found an exemplar in the unpretentious, finely mortised furniture that the Shakers had begun to produce in North America at the close of the 18th century.

When one traces the origins of the chair itself, one discovers, strange as it seems, that in broad strokes things haven't changed much since the first examples we know. Sitting on something presumably has practical origins in the need simply to lift oneself off the cold, damp earth, but for a long time it was the bench and the stool, modelled on the overturned tree trunk and the tree stump respectively, that fulfilled that function.

The individual chair has a long history even so, although it is in large part passed down to us through images. Few chairs from the ancient world survive, among them the chair of Tutankhamun's tomb, which was excavated in 1924. From ancient Greece we know the *Klismos* chair with its broad, in-curving top rail and its out-curving legs. It has been reinterpreted repeatedly in more recent times by the Danish 18th-century painter Nicolai Abildgaard, Kaare Klint and IKEA among others. It seems that among the ancient Greeks the chair was quite common. Images from Greek antiquity shows musicians sitting with their instruments on chairs. In ancient Egypt, by contrast, the chair was reserved for the most distinguished figures and symbolised grandeur. This is reflected in the hieroglyph for 'a person of rank' which depicts a man seated on a chair. Something similar is true of the Middle Ages and up into the 18th century, when many farmhouses only had a single chair, placed just inside the door, on the off-chance of a distinguished guest.

But despite the chair's varying status there is little difference in the basic constructions of the oldest known chair, depicted in a sculpture from the Cyclades from 5000 years ago, the 500-year old chair depicted in Bruegel's painting from the 16th century and a modern chair. And perhaps this speaks to fact that the chair's original beauty was easy to determine and preserve, provided one knew the craft tradition that stood behind it.

For Finn Juhl, it was the originality in the suppleness and vitality of ancient Egyptian furniture that made it a paragon. Just as in the archetypal shapes and organic power of primitive tools, he found in Egyptian furniture a latent strength that fascinated him. This experience of vitality in something as static as a chair is probably more characteristic of his own sculptural approach than the more restrained procedure of the Klint School. Juhl once named the sculptor Alexander Calder's mobiles as an underlying inspiration, and it is true that the seat, back and arm supports of his *Chieftain Chair* are very close to the amorphous, floating bodies in Calder's work.

Juhl's Own Projects in the Shadow of the War

Finishing all the details in the designs for *Radiohuset* took a long time. The outbreak of the Second World War in 1939 delayed construction further, leading to import restrictions and so shortages of materials. This was compounded by a particularly hard winter. And when the building was finally nearing completion, the tempo was slowed down and its opening postponed by almost two years, so that the new headquarters of Denmark's national broadcaster would not become a Nazi propaganda machine in German hands. So Juhl had steady work and perhaps was not too busy to sketch a little on his own projects. He said himself that in the course of his days at Vilhelm Lauritzen's design studio he might think up a chair and on clocking off, would jump onto his bike and race home to draw it that evening:

"Of course I made loose sketches of how I thought the model should look, and when I felt that there was something to one of them, that was when I really started to draw. It was an intense physical and mental strain to hold onto the little bit of hope or the thought that I had … It could very well be that I would skip the little sketch I had started with, because I was working alone and so could just say 'stop' and move on to a new idea. As a result, I may have designed some chairs which you won't see anymore, because they were a little too 'complete'. It was not that they weren't thought through, but rather that they were overthought, as I kept having new ideas throughout the process, so the design ended up being unclear or too complicated."[32]

It might seem a turbulent time to be sketching furniture with the Second World War raging and Denmark under Nazi occupation. It is certainly true that not all of Juhl's colleagues came through these years so lightly. Arne Jacobsen was Jewish and so had to escape to Sweden in 1943. As did PH, who had been a little too open in his criticism of the occupying power, among other things with the publication of the ballad '*You bind us by mouth and hand*'. But for the Germans, the agricultural country of Denmark was foremost a wartime pantry from which provisions could be sent to the soldiers on the front. For this reason, the occupying forces had an interest in the country continuing to operate as usual. Luckily, this also applied to the Cabinetmakers' Guild Exhibition, and Finn Juhl seized the opportunity to make a name for himself. His products were clear expressions of his own self-willed talent. They had something to say, and while they may at time have missed the mark, they always had an artistic daring that caused a stir.

Radiohuset on Rosenørns Allé in Copenhagen with typical modernist motifs, including the curved hangar roof with the portholes and the serial bands of windows. The combination of yellow brickwork and white details in the form of window sills and frames was and is a recurring feature in the Danish strand of modernism. Today, the building houses the Royal Danish Academy of Music.

Finn Juhl's Best Chair?

While there is still a youthful irony to the *Grasshopper Chair* and the wing-back sofa from 1939, there is already a greater resolution to the chairs Juhl exhibited at the Cabinetmakers' Guild Exhibition in 1943. The critics wrote that he and Niels Vodder seemed to have found one another. The following year, Juhl's offering was even more sincere. He exhibited a mature and consummately original adaptation of his primitive and archaic fore-runners: the armchair *FJ44*, produced by the cabinet-maker Niels Vodder in Brazilian rosewood and Cuban mahogany. It has a leather seat and was exhibited as part of a dining room set. Initially, only 12 were produced, not least because of how ambitious its construction turned out to be. Juhl and Vodder would spur one another on, experimenting with how far wood could be bent, stretched and burdened. Thus, the entire back section of *FJ44* is cut from a single length that lends the chair its bone-like expression; the "animalistic, pleasurable character"[33] that Juhl had first observed in ancient Egyptian furniture.

FJ44 was Juhl's favourite among his own furniture designs, perhaps because it is both uncompromising in the demands the construction makes on the structural properties of the wood, and because conceptually it finds a cultivated way to introduce the animalistic and primitive into decorous living spaces.

Even more sophisticated is the easy chair that Juhl exhibited the following year: *FJ45*. It has been said that this chair occupies a position in Juhl's oeuvre that mirrors that of Hans J. Wegner's *Round Chair* (1949). Perhaps *FJ45* is Juhl's best chair. It has an organic suppleness that relates it to the *Grasshopper Chair*, but both technically and aesthetically it is a far more integrated whole.

It is the first of his chairs in which Juhl worked earnestly at the distinction between the supporting and the supported. The thinly padded, continuous seat-and-back element floats effortlessly between the armrests' strong sweeping lines and the back legs, which slant outward, as though ready to take off. Individually, these motifs were not unknown. They are found in the works of many other of Juhl's contemporaries, for instance in the tubular steel furniture of the Bauhaus School, in Charles and Ray Eames, Mies van der Rohe and Alvar Aalto. And among Juhl's Danish colleagues, in Tove and Edvard Kindt-Larsen's prizewinning project from the 1940 instal-ment of the Copenhagen Cabinetmakers' Guild's annual furniture fair. However, in opposition to many of the pioneering chairs in tubular steel or laminated wood, Finn Juhl's chair, though it is incredibly slender, is made of solid wood. It is the static boldness in the slim lengths of wood, the sweeping form and the refined joints that make *FJ45* so unique. This is high-quality design and eminent craftsmanship from long before computer-controlled saws and milling machines.

Juhl and Vodder's stand at the Cabinetmakers' Guild Exhibition in 1944 was a breakthrough for Juhl. The ensemble consisted of the *FJ44 Chair*, a wall-mounted cabinet with painted panels, a hot table and a dining table where the leaves, borne by hinged frame elements fit flush with the table when they are not in use.

Juhl incorporated his new furniture
designs in his own home. In the
living room, the *FJ45 Chairs* are the
original display models from the
Cabinetmakers' Guild Exhibition,
the bookcase was part of the
interior from the beginning, and
the sofa was added later.

Considering the sculptural quality of his furniture generally and *FJ45*'s armrests in particular, Juhl confessed years later that he had had to balance his desire to draw free forms with a need to compensate for his lacking an education in furniture modelling and static mechanics, hence "measuring virtually everything I came across to gauge how high armrests ought to be, how high the seat should be and how deep – I had no idea, because I hadn't learnt to design furniture."[34]

FJ45 was an authentic experiment that would likely have been unthinkable without the close collaboration between designer and cabinetmaker. As Arne Karlsen makes clear, the delicate diagonal bracing beneath the seat had never been attempted, and the "stress on the very boldly curved back part of the armrests made demands of wood quality and craftsmanship that no one had ever dared make before."[35]

This audacity made the chair into a classic – not just in Denmark but in international furniture design. In 1959 it appeared in an industrially produced variant, *BO59* or the *Fireplace Chair* that enabled it to reach a much larger public. The *45 Chair* has also been produced as a two-person sofa. In 1945 Juhl designed a worktable in panels of warm, light Brazilian rosewood, which can be seen today in Juhl's study in his house on Kratvænget. *FJ45* was awarded a gold medal in 1951 at the *Triennale Design Exhibition* in Milan and was acquired by the Museum for Modern Art in New York for their furniture collection.

A Fine Year

With *FJ45* the reviews finally came good. And 1945 was a fine year in other regards too. The war ended, *Radiohuset* finally opened, and Juhl had the confidence to leave Vilhelm Lauritzen's design studio and cast out on his own. He established his own studio in a high-ceilinged, ground-floor apartment at Nyhavn 33 in Copenhagen. That same year he was employed as a teacher at The School of Interior Design, a private institution in Copenhagen.

Even so, Juhl continued to participate in the annual Cabinetmakers' Guild Exhibition and competition, as ever in partnership with Niels Vodder. In 1946 they exhibited *FJ46*, an armchair with a thinly padded seat and back. It has a wide frame which, characteristically for Juhl, broadens where the burden is greatest. Correspondingly, the back sweeps inwards as it descends, providing support for the sitter's lower back and lending the chair its distinctive expression. It has very thin side rungs that are invisible from certain angles and grant the chair's frame a light expression, complementing the floating seat, whose support is visible only where the frame is broadest.

Just like *FJ45*, *FJ46* was awarded a gold medal at the *Milan Triennale Design Exhibition* of 1951. And like *FJ45*, it is included in the furniture collection at New York's Museum of Modern Art.

As a teacher at the School of Interior Design Juhl taught the modern principles of a unity of needs-based functionality and aesthetic, which applied to all items, from furniture to utilitarian objects, textiles, colour schemes and works of art.

Finn Juhl balancing a mobile in the style of Calder in front of the shelving system he designed for Bovirke in 1955. On the shelf, one can see, among other things, architectural models, his watercolor of the Georg Jensen store facades in Toronto and a book about the British modernist artist Ben Nicholson. The rugs on the floor are by Anna Thommesen.

Finn Juhl's studio in Nyhavn, Copenhagen in the 1940s. To apply colour washes to his drawings he recruited employees among his students at the School of Interior Design. Note that the table lamp, which also appears in the photograph above, is by another architect, namely Arne Jacobsen – it is his *Bellevue* lamp from 1929.

Seats and their Sitters

"Finn Juhl has designed an easy chair, armchair, or whatever you want to call it, so alive that it quivers with vitality. It is expensive and it is delicate, but then a derby winner will always be so..."[36] wrote a journalist from *Politiken*, reviewing the 1949 instalment of the Cabinet-makers' Guild Exhibition. In spite of its being a large chair, the easy chair *FJ49A*, also known as the *Chieftain Chair*, retains its suppleness and as with Juhl's earlier animal designs, it feels almost like a body in motion caught mid-moment.

The padding in the chair's armrests consists of metal plates built up by a blacksmith and covered with felt and leather, for Niels Vodder had little experience with laminated wood. Juhl's description of the development of the *Chieftain Chair* confirms the impression of both a grand gesture and a stroke of good luck. "I was home alone, and I began around 10 a.m. with a sketch, only 5 cm high, just four vertical lines connected with 'something'. And around 2 or 3 a.m. I had painted it, and off it went." He added, though, "It may be that it had existed in my thoughts for some time, as a vague idea that I would like to make a large chair, for instance."[37]

It is said that that the *Chieftain Chair* received its name because Juhl felt the chair was a little pompous in its design, and when setting up the exhibition, he joked that it was a gift for the then king of Denmark, Frederik IX. It was customary for the royal couple to open the Copenhagen Cabinetmakers' Guild's annual fair. By the time of the opening, however, Juhl had cold feet. It would not do to embarrass His Majesty. Juhl maintained instead "that it was for some negro chieftain."[38] And the *Chieftain Chair* was exhibited before background pictures of stone dolmens and spear-wielding African hunters.

Still, it did not exactly hurt sales that the King, the Minister for Foreign Affairs and the Minister for Trade were all photographed sitting in the chair. The effect of this kind of exposure can be enormous and permanently shapes a chair's image. In addition to King Frederik in the *Chieftain Chair*, his diametric opposite Bertolt Brecht sat in Mogens Voltelen's *Copenhagen Chair*. Then think of Kennedy and Nixon, who both sat in Wegner's *The Chair* during the final televised debate of the United States presidential election of 1960. Today *The Chair*, also known as the *Round Chair*, is a permanent fixture of DR's (Danish Broadcasting Corporation) *Deadline* debate programme, precisely because it signals political debate at the highest level.

Once King Frederik IX had been photographed in the *Chieftain Chair* at the Cabinetmakers' Guild Exhibition in 1949, both Minister of Foreign Affairs Gustav Rasmussen and, here, Minister of Commerce Jens Otto Krag seized the obvious photo opportunity. Note the typical Juhlian selection of archaic artefacts on the wall.

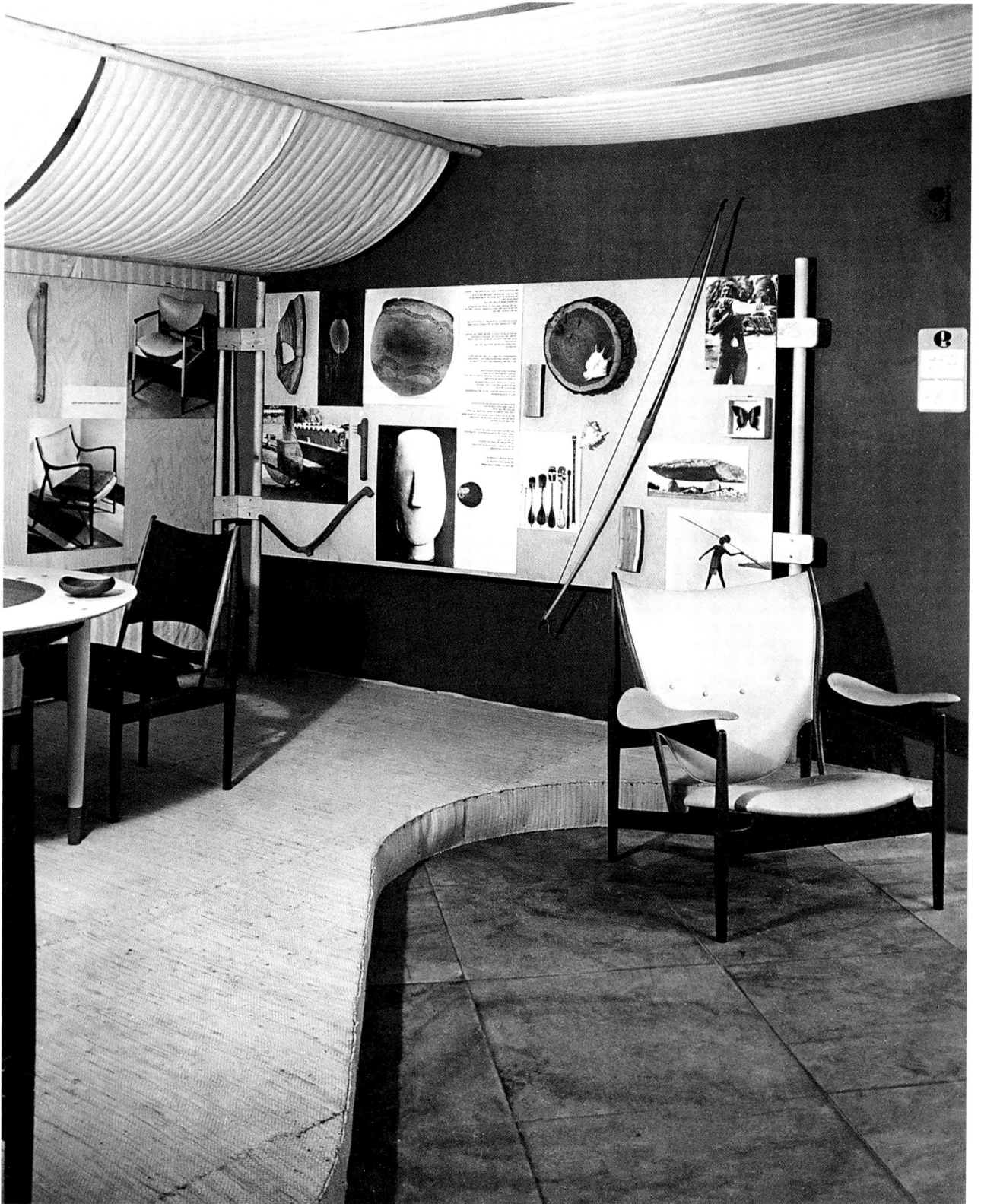

Waving baldachins as an evocative
fifth wall at Juhl and Vodder's
stand at the Cabinetmakers' Guild
Exhibition in 1949.

The *Chieftain Chair* on the cover
of cabinetmaker Niels Vodder's
furniture catalogue.

FINN JUHL

M Ø B L E R
F U R N I T U R E
M Ö B E L

NIELS VODDER

S N E D K E R M E S T E R
BILLE BRAHESVEJ 2
K Ø B E N H A V N V
TELEFON NORA 7551

The Myth of Misunderstood Genius

Later, the myth began to take hold that Finn Juhl was a misunderstood genius in his native country, and that it was only after succeeding abroad that he began to be recognised in Denmark. But that is only a myth. Juhl garnered recognition, deservedly, for his best chairs of the 1940s. And they led to a long sequence of commissions across the architecture and design spectrum, from everyday utensils and furniture to interiors, exhibition work and houses. In fact, Juhl reached new heights, designing the interiors of aeroplanes for Scandinavian Airlines (SAS). Some felt that success came too easily to Juhl, or that his style was gratuitous and opportunistic. This was likely jealousy. True, Juhl might occasionally give the impression that his successes were simply jest and luck and chance. But he was not being coy when he later said that there had been some tough years before his work was recognised.[39]

Throughout the 1950s Juhl continued to design many fine chairs, some of which were variations on his best designs from the 1940s. Others, however, were bolder and more mature, and perhaps his interiors disclosed his true talent – a sense of coherence, wholeness, balance and the subtle use of detail. Exactly as in his most successful chairs.

It is easy to see parallels in Hans J. Wegner's production. Already in Wegner's debut chair from 1938 one can discern some of the same motivations and the same search for resolution that, in a different expression, characterises Juhl's work. Perhaps out of the corner of their eyes they noted that the other was engaged in the very same endeavour. Including Børge Mogensen in the comparison further highlights the temperament, expression and philosophy that distinguished Danish design during this period. Juhl had grown up in Frederiksberg, a municipal enclave in Copenhagen, Wegner was from the town of Tønder and Mogensen from Aalborg. Through his employment with FDB Furniture, Mogensen quickly developed a clearer and more singular direction for his products, based on the demands of industrial production.

Wegner and Mogensen were trained cabinetmakers, unlike Juhl. Wegner and Juhl worked more or less independently all of their lives, whereas Mogensen had an employer for a long period. Wegner and Juhl became world-famous. Mogensen's *Spoke-Back* sofas were at least world-famous in Denmark. All three aimed for the heart and the origins of the design process, finding inspiration in their Chinese, ancient Egyptian and Shaker forebears. Juhl and Mogensen philosophised and debated their own and others' furniture. They ended up furiously and publicly at odds. By contrast, Wegner kept a lower profile, getting on with the job at hand. Juhl spoke openly about the problematic aspects of the Klint School, whereas Mogensen extended and developed it loyally, although he brought his own personality to bear on it. Wegner felt the full force of the schoolmaster's disapproval when Klint suggested that his unorthodox *Flag Halyard Chair* resembled a gynaecologist's examination table.

On the basis of his handful of masterpieces from the 1940s, Finn Juhl spent another 10 years at the top. Those chairs were sprung from a bold experiment with the limitations and possibilities of wood. While they were inspired by the ancient, the archetypal and the primitive, they also took as their basis modern functional analyses. What is more, they were driven by a powerful compulsion towards original and personal expression. And the 1940s chairs achieved something else crucial for Juhl. They constituted a point of departure so supple and so vital that in the years that followed the 1940s Juhl was able to hold on to the artistic freedom usually reserved for the fine arts and the serious playfulness that is essential to all creative work.

Selected
Presentations

Grasshopper Chair

Year	1938
Manufacturer	Niels Vodder
Measurements	W 87 cm, H 91 cm, D 103 cm
See pages	35, 48

The *Grasshopper Chair* is an experiment from the young designer's furniture laboratory, an attempt to take organic forms literally and translate them into man-made artefacts and applied artworks. Finn Juhl was perhaps the first, but he was far from the only one to pursue this idea, and the *Grasshopper Chair* was followed by several Danish chairs named after animals, including the *Ant*, the *Pelican* and the *Swan*. The chair marks the transition from overstuffed furniture to visible frames in Juhl's work. It also marks his first attempt at conceiving the supporting frame as an independent element – one that expresses its static necessity as form. The sharply angled legs are so reminiscent of a grasshopper's that one has to assume the insect was indeed an inspiration. These legs have none of the fluid joinery so recognisable in his later works. The joint connecting the front legs to the armrests and the top rail is acute; too acute in fact, to be rationally motivated, and is rather an attempt to experiment with what is and is not possible in a viable furniture joint. The confluence where the vertical slats supporting the chair's back sweep into the supporting triangle of legs and armrests is visible, as had become usual under the influence of Klintian honesty. In this case, though, there is a discordance that is not especially fortunate. The combination of poles and beams also render the chair's expression a little unclear. Finn Juhl had the *Grasshopper Chair* produced in maple. The free-standing seat-and-back element with its wing-back motif lend it significant weight, direction and presumably – for few people have ever actually sat in a *Grasshopper Chair* – a degree of comfort that would be characteristic of his future exploration of organic furniture with its enveloping and supportive forms. The *Grasshopper Chair* may have been a fleeting idea, realised in collaboration with the cabinetmaker Niels Vodder, who was always, and congenially, ready to experiment. It was never put into production, and the two chairs that were exhibited at the Cabinetmakers' Guild Exhibition in 1938, are the only two in existence. For some years they were located at Finn Juhl's home at Kratvænget in Ordrup. Eventually however, they were sold to collectors, who acquired some of the rarest of Finn Juhl works.

Pelican Chair

Year	1940
Manufacturer	Niels Vodder
Measurements	W 85 cm, H 68 cm, D 76 cm
	seat height: 37 cm
See pages	36

The *Pelican* easy chair is the best example of Finn Juhl's playful engagement with overstuffed seating, a type of furniture that for generations was, and probably still is, most popular with the general public. To most people, the notion of 'the good chair' does not conjure images of the uncompromising beauty of a Poul Kjærholm model or the iconic form of Arne Jacobsen's *Egg Chair*, so much as a high-backed, generously padded easy chair, such as the protective wing-back chairs dating from a time when the fireplace was the only source of heat. At that time a chair was required that closed in around the sitter, offering protection from draughts on all sides except that which faced the fire. Like the *Poet Sofa*, the design of the *Pelican Chair* clearly represents the marriage with modern sculpture that Juhl continued to develop and refine. Like a figurative-abstract sculpture by Henry Moore or Jean Arp, Finn Juhl's furniture echo the forms of the human body, and this resonance takes on a functional purpose: supports, statically bold load-bearing constructions with a light and delicate appearance and forms that embrace the sitter or allow for a number of sitting positions. The design forms its own space within a space, a refuge for rest and recreation.

The *Pelican Chair's* slightly caricatural expression reflects the enjoyment of a designer playing with possibilities – the organic form seems on the verge of leaping straight into the animal kingdom. However, Finn Juhl is no postmodernist, and he stops short of making a joke of the expression. Nevertheless, it is provocative to design furniture that looks as though it could have been taken from a child's drawing, and when the *Pelican Chair* was exhibited at the Cabinetmakers' Guild Exhibition in 1940, the critics were not laughing, referring to the bird as a half-dead walrus.

Today, the model has been put back into production and is even said to be Finn Juhl's best-selling chair. It is easy to see why. The *Pelican Chair* seems an affable sort, a chair with a good sense of humour. In the ongoing tug-of-war between, on the one hand, 'good taste', as dictated by fashion and the elites through lifestyle magazine articles about beautiful homes and, on the other hand, people's more intuitive sense of cosy living, subtle provocations, like the *Pelican Chair*, will always find an audience.

VODDER. 5 STAND PAA SNEDKERNES UDSTILLING I KUNSTINDUSTRIMUSEET 1940. STOL I MAAL 1:5. OPSTALT AF VÆG I MAAL 1:10.

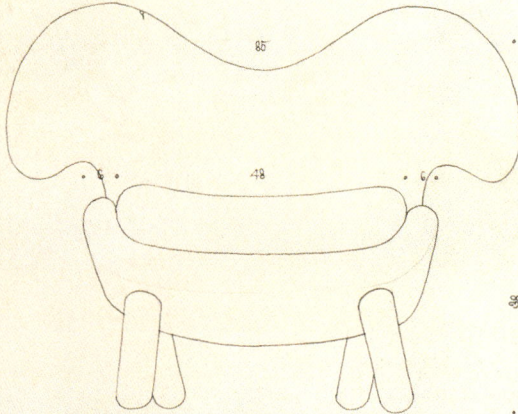

SETT FORFRA
STOLEN HAR LYSTGRAAT BETRÆK, HYNDEN "LARKSPUR"-BLAA AHORNBEN

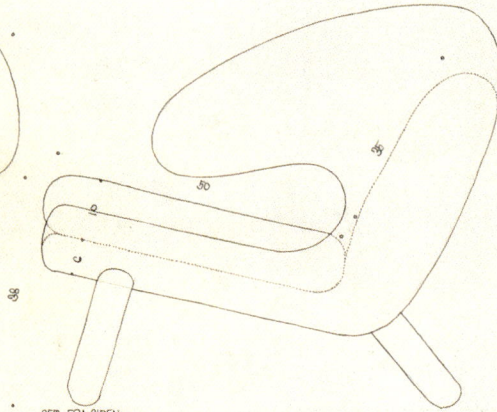

SETT FRA SIDEN
SETT OVENFRA

ALLE PLANCHER FRA "LA CERAMIQUE ANCIENNE DU PÉROU". OVENSTAAENDE PL.26

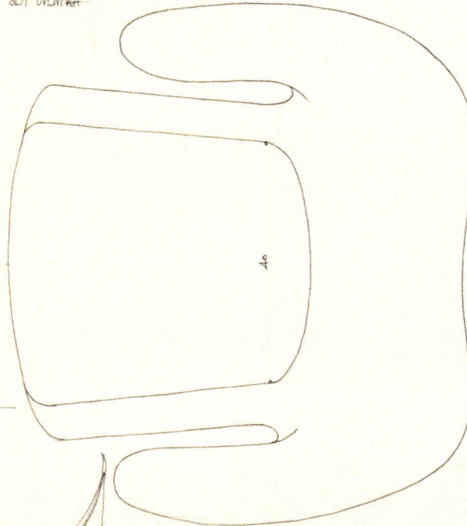

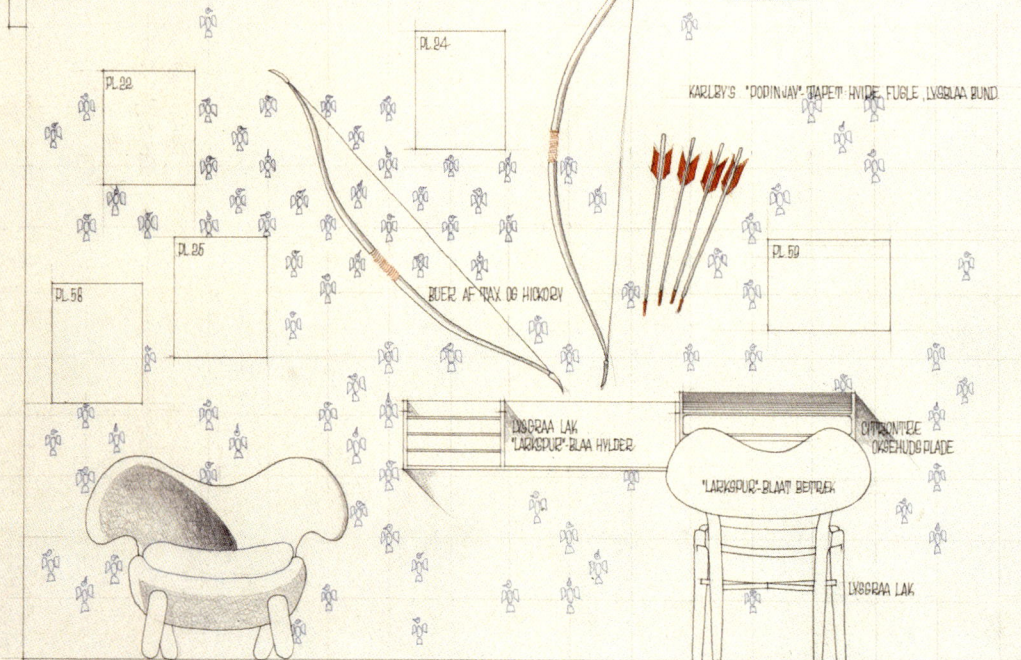

KARLBY'S "PODINJAY"-TAPET. HVIDE FUGLE, LYSEBLAA BUND.

PL.22   PL.24   PL.59

PL.25

PL.58

BUER AF TRÆX OG HICKORY

LYSGRAA LAK
"LARKSPUR"-BLAA HYLDER

OPMONTERE
OKSEHUDS PLADE

"LARKSPUR"-BLAAT BETRÆK

LYSGRAA LAK

Finn Juhl
26 AUG 1940.

Poet Sofa | FJ41

Year	1941
Manufacturer	Niels Vodder
Measurements	W 136 cm, H 87 cm, D 80 cm, seat height: 38 cm
See pages	36

The sofa *FJ41* received its name, the *Poet Sofa,* because it resembles in large part another Finn Juhl sofa, which was only produced in a single edition and which featured in the Danish comic series *The Poet and the Little Mother*, which was adapted into a popular film. The sofa is without doubt one of the best-known of Juhl's works. Not just in light of this stroke of luck in its marketing, but because it possesses all of the most important characteristics of a Finn Juhl piece. It is – to adopt the usual cliché – sculptural. The photograph on page 40-41 from the Copenhagen Cabinetmakers' Guild Exhibition in 1941 shows two *Poet Sofas* in the company of an abstract wall sculpture in plaster by the Faroese artist Sigurjón Òlafsson. Juhl was heavily influenced by contemporary modernistic sculptors and he always exhibited his furniture in interplay with abstract art. On the other hand, the free form also leaves room for functionality. Finn Juhl understood people and conceived form, expression and comfort as a whole. The characteristic armrests are a typical Finn Juhl solution. They are a humorous touch, which at the same time renews our notion of the armrest with their distinctive and interesting finish. They are also a good hand support and offer help when lifting oneself up from seated. It is also typical of Juhl that the backrest embraces two sitters in conversation. The sofa positions them naturally, angled slightly towards one another, so that they need not twist in their seats to make eye contact. This design is a proposed solution to a problem: two people in conversation. Intimate conversation perhaps, but without their being seated uncomfortably close, nor drifting away from each other, nor sitting too formally with straight backs. Rather, back and lumbar supports, a rest for one arm and the possibility of many different postures have been thought into and ensured by the design. This lends the little *Poet* an air of sophistication that is almost akin to the Empire Style, so that although it belongs to the class of overstuffed furniture, the sofa immediately strikes one as *petite*. The sofa is a little, romantic sculpture for two. One might say it is the lady to the *Chieftain Chair's* gentleman, and in this way it describes an aspect of the creator's persona, which spanned both the coquettish and the coarse. The *Poet Sofa* is as slim in the waist as the *Chieftain Chair* is broad in the breastplate.

FJ44

Year	1944
Manufacturer	Niels Vodder
Measurements	W 52 cm, H 74 cm, D 60 cm, seat height: 46 cm
See pages	48, 158

FJ44 pursues the idea of extending the sitter's skeleton into the chair that bears it. It also makes allusions to ancient domestic tools made of bone and animal animal hide. As such it was nicknamed the 'bone chair' and is said to have been Juhl's personal favourite. Like the *Grasshopper Chair,* it is an attempt to realise an idea, boldly and consistently, with scant regard for tradition or the technical limitations of wood. However, *FJ44* is a far more mature and successful experiment, and as Juhl's first chair with armrests, it also catalysed his period of productivity during the mid-1940s, when *FJ45*, *FJ46* and the *Chieftain Chair* were designed. Both the construction and joints are ambitious, to put it mildly. For example, the torsioned back is carved from a single length of wood. This necessitated the use of hardwood, and for *FJ44*, Juhl and his trusted partner cabinetmaker Niels Vodder used Cuban mahogany or Brazilian rosewood. Vodder's acrobatic mastery of the material is impressive. Nevertheless, the boomerang-shaped strut, which lends rigidity to the chair and absorbs some of the stress by converting the pressure on the seat to traction, does not prevent a fragility at the joint between the back section and the back legs when weight is applied to the armrests. Indeed, photographs of models reveal that as a rule, *FJ44* required repair work after sustained daily use. *FJ44* was exhibited as part of a dining room set at the Cabinetmakers' Guild Exhibition in 1944. The interior is said to have been commissioned by a dentist named Ravn. In addition to *FJ44* it included a dining table, a hot table and a mounted cabinet featuring sliding doors with painted sections. Finn Juhl was one of the first modern Danish furniture designers to employ colour in the form of painted sections and panels. The use of colour supported his ambition of planning and managing an interior design through the use of directional features. Types of wood, textile qualities and colours should be selected to ensure a coherent and flexible design. For instance, it should be possible to use a chair from one room as an extra chair in another without breaking with the overall expression. That may seem obvious today, after 75 years of interior-design magazines, but at the time it was a novel concept that sprang from the modernist ambition of getting rid of period furniture and interiors that reflect historical traditions instead of contemporary needs. Only 12 *FJ44* chairs were ever produced and rumour has it that Juhl bought back some of those that had been sold. One of them can be viewed in his house today.

FORFRA

FRA SIDEN

ARMSTOL AF CUBA MAHOGNI MED SÆDE, BETRUKKET MED OKSEHUD

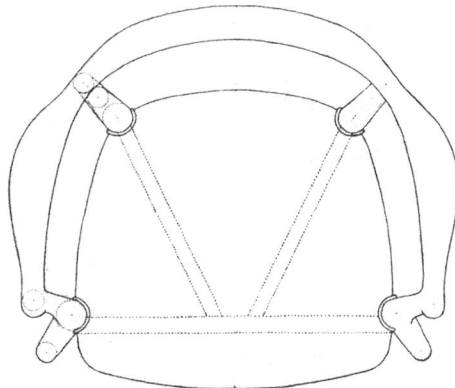

OVENFRA

1944

Work Desk

Year	1945
Manufacturer	Niels Vodder
Measurements	W 94 cm, H 72 cm, L 202 cm

Finn Juhl is best known for his chairs and sofas, but he has also designed many tables – including coffee tables, dining tables, and desks. His tables have never received the same attention as his seating however, perhaps because the table is less suited to spectacular and experimental expressions. Juhl designed the *Work Desk* in 1945 and it was produced by Niels Vodder for the Cabinetmakers' Guild Exhibition in 1945. It was later manufactured by Baker Furniture in the USA. Juhl gave the desk a central position in his contemporary interior at the National Museum of Decorative Arts and Design in Trondheim, Norway. But initially, the *Work Desk* was designed for Juhl's own home, just as it is reported that Juhl first began to design furniture when, at a young age, his brother did not have a desk. The dark walnut tabletop is distinguished from the lighter oak frame and the stretcher beam has a rounded, brass trim so that one can rest one's feet with shoes on without wearing down the wood. The Danish furniture manufacturer House of Finn Juhl has brought the table into production again under the name of the *Kaufmann Table,* a nod to Edgar Kaufmann Jr., the curator from the Museum of Modern Art in New York, who was decisive for Finn Juhl's international breakthrough and became a close friend.

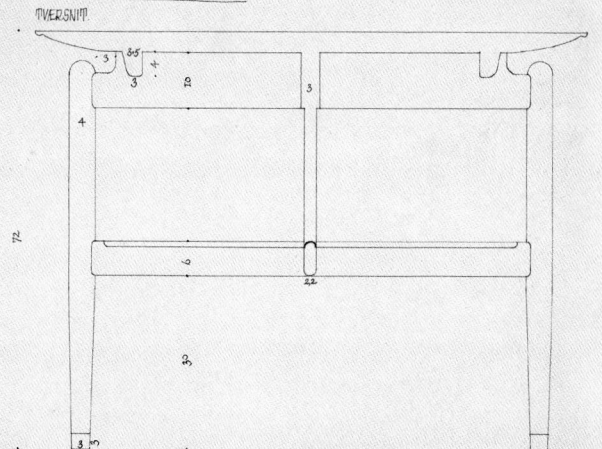

LANGSIDE, MAAL 1:5.

ENKELTHED AF SNIT I BORDPLADE, MAAL 1:1.

KORTSIDE

TVERSNIT

FOR ET ~~BORDPLADE~~ ER BORDPLADENS FLADE DET AFGØRENDE. DER ER DERFOR GJORT ALLE ANSTRENGELSER FOR AT FAA DEN TIL AT DOMINERE. DEN UDFØRES I LYS ASK, MENS RESTEN UDFØRES I GREENHEART. DEN VALGTE KONSTRUKTION MED TILBAGETRUKKET STEL TILLADER ANVENDELSE AF SPRODSER UDEN DERFOR AT FORHINDRE BORDET BRUG VED KONFERENCER, LIGESOM DEN GIVER MINIMALE SARGE VED LANGSIDERNE. SPRODSERNE BEKLÆDES PAA OVERSIDEN MED MESSING, SAA AT DE UDEN BESKADIGELSE KAN STØTTE FØDDERNE, NAAR MAN LENER SIG TILBAGE I STOLEN FOR AT MEDITERE OG LÆSE AVIS. BENENE HAR MESSINGKRAVER AF HENSYN TIL RENGØRING.

.PLAN

Nyhavn Desk | BO69

Year	1945
Manufacturer	Bovirke
Measurements	W 94 cm, H 72 cm, L 202 cm

In 1945, when Finn Juhl established his first design studio at Nyhavn 33 in Copenhagen, he designed a work desk for the cosy rooms with a view to the canal. It was a single table with a wooden worktop, an oxidised steel frame and wooden feet. The desk from Nyhavn was produced by Bovirke under the name *BO69*. In 1956, when his design studio was commissioned to design the interiors of Scandinavian Airlines (SAS) ticket offices across the globe, Juhl relocated the studio from the 40-m^2 space in Nyhavn to larger premises at Sølvgade 38 with room for an expanded workforce. This turned out to be wise, as the commission grew into an extensive project lasting for five years. SAS understood early that a modern, international company could use design to brand itself, and Finn Juhl was internationally recognised and could deliver hallmarked *Danish Design*. By the time the table moved with the design studio to Sølvgade it had been produced in various editions, among them a *Nyhavn Dining Table* with two drop-leaf sections which was launched in 1953. In connection with the relocation, Juhl designed a drawer unit for the original desk featuring three drawers with coloured fronts. The table was relaunched in 2009 by House of Finn Juhl.

FJ45

Year	1945
Manufacturer	Niels Vodder
Measurements	W 67 cm, H 88 cm, D 73 cm, seat height: 42 cm
See pages	48, 153

FJ45 was Finn Juhl's first successful attempt at the elegant separation of the chair's bearing construction from the borne elements, which along with their organic forms is the most distinctive characteristic of his chairs. The thinly padded one-piece seat-and-back element appears to float, suspended between the dramatic curvature of the armrest and the obliquely angled back legs, which lend the chair an air of being ready to pounce. In traditional chairs, such as the *Windsor Chair*, the backrest is fastened with tenons hidden inside the seat. The appearance of floating and the visible construction were some of modernism's favourite tricks, programmatically demonstrated in Gerrit Rietveld's *Red and Blue Chair* from 1917. It is also evident in tubular-steel furniture from the Bauhaus School and in Charles and Ray Eames', Mies van der Rohe's and Alvar Aalto's work. Finn Juhl's chair however, is made of wood, and it is the challenges of this living material that rightly place *FJ45* at the pinnacle of his work. It is a highly ambitious design and sublime craftsmanship, at a time long before computer-controlled processes made their way into the woodworking factories. In its elitist refinement of dimensions, forms and joints, it stands out in comparison to most of the industrially made furniture from the shortage-ridden post-war years. Designed in four hours in a burst of inspiration, *FJ45* marks Finn Juhl's most successful attempt at dismantling the distinction between individual works and a series, fine art and design, and indeed it was awarded a gold medal at the 1951 Design Triennial in Milan as well as being purchased for the permanent collection at the Museum of Modern Art in New York. What is more, it exists in a two-person bench. In 1945 Finn Juhl also designed a desk with a warm light Brazilian rosewood table top, which features in the study of Juhl's house at Kratvænget in Ordrup. The *FJ45 Chair* was produced by Niels Vodder untill 1959. In the years 1978-1984 Søren Horn manufactured the model, from 1989-2001 Niels Roth Andersen produced it, and it was relaunched in 2004 by House of Finn Juhl.

70

42

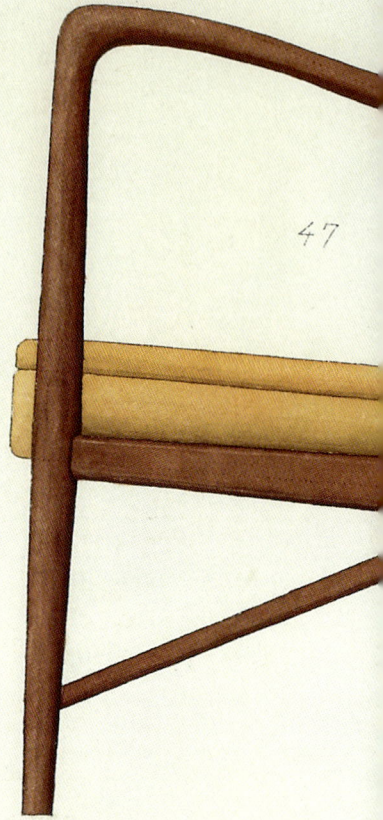

47

69
50

ARMSTOL 1945

48

78

KRATVÆNGET 15
CHARLOTTENLUND
DENMARK

FINN JUHL
ARCHITECT M.A.A.
ORDRUP 7721
ORDRUP 6009

FJ46

Year	1946
Manufacturer	Niels Vodder
Measurements	W 52 cm, H 82 cm, D 53 cm, seat height: 44 cm
See pages	50, 158

Finn Juhl's interest in archaic artefacts and, for example, the primitive domestic utensils of traditional cultures, naturally involved a curiosity for 'the original chair'. Accordingly, his furniture often incorporate forms and motifs from the earliest Egyptian chairs. Needless to say, this is especially evident in the *Egyptian Chair* (1949), but *FJ46*, with its U-shaped back, pointed back struts and upright posture, draws on Egyptian inspiration. Its complex expression is also a good illustration of the sheer pleasure Juhl took in creating an armrest that follows the angle of the human arm, allowing the person to adopt a relaxed, natural posture and use the full and generous width of the chair. The slender supporting struts under the seat are almost akin to Mikado sticks, and playfully engage with the space they are suspended in. They seem to connect with their anchor point on the sturdier rear strut almost by accident. This may seem anything but functionalist, but the static tension is probably perfect. *FJ46* is fairly rare, perhaps in part because the armrests make it a less popular choice for private homes than dining chairs or armchairs, while as a conference chair it was likely too exclusive. That undoubtedly played a role in Finn Juhl's decision in 1953 to simplify the design, making it better suited for industrial production at the Bovirke factory – as BO72. The Museum of Art & Design (now Designmuseum Danmark) in Copenhagen was remarkably slow to purchase furniture by Finn Juhl and so intentionally lagged behind design museums across the world. In the catalogue for the museum's retrospective Finn Juhl exhibition in 1982, museum director Erik Lassen admitted that at a private party he had once loudly 'proclaimed that the Danish Museum of Art & Design was pleased to note that it was the only museum in the world that did not own any of Finn Juhl's furniture.' Since 2008, House of Finn Juhl has produced the Bovirke model of the chair.

FJ48

Year	1948
Manufacturer	Niels Vodder
Measurements	W 69 cm, H 80 cm, D 63 cm, seat height: 44 cm
See pages	158

Finn Juhl and the cabinetmaker Niels Vodder's contribution to the Cabinet-makers' Guild Exhibition in 1948 was titled *An Art Collector's Study*. In fact, it included two rooms: a living room with an open fireplace and a study. The living room was furnished with the *Fireplace Chair* and a 'footstool table'; the study with a desk, a chair with armrests, a sofa bench and a coffee table. The chair was *FJ48*, whose broad, powerful volume antici-pates the large *Chieftain Chair* that Juhl designed the following year. *FJ48's* frame is comprised of large, semi-regular rectangles with straight struts and armrests. It bears two curved shells that constitute the seat and back. As such, the lines of *FJ48* are less organic and 'bodily' than in Juhl's earlier chairs. The Danish furniture manufacturer House of Finn Juhl has put the model back into production. In particular, the oak version with teak 'toes' and armrests highlights the lines and stature of the chair, making clear that Juhl was both inspired by and closer in his formal intentions to his colleague Hans J. Wegner and the Klint School than is generally recognised. The furniture for *An Art Collector's Study* seems to have been designed to accommodate a man-about-town – perhaps Finn Juhl himself – rather than the general public. The *Fireplace Chairs*, which were never put into production, were constructed from maple and Cuban mahogany with wool upholstery and an ox-hide neck cushion. When pushed together, they almost made up a small sofa. In a tongue-in-cheek detail typical of Juhl and his hedonist inclinations, the armrests feature carved-out recesses with a brass tray designed to hold a whisky tumbler. *FJ48* was one of the designs that Baker Furniture put into production in connection with Finn Juhl's American breakthrough in the early 1950s.

OPHOLDSSTUE FOR EN KUNSTSAMLER. ØVERST: VINDUESVÆG, NEDERST: REOLVÆG MED BLOMSTERVINDUE.

SOFABÆNK I CUBA MAHOGNI OG AHORN.   I:5
LÆDERBETRÆK. KONSTRUKTION SOM ARMSTOL.
SOFABORD I CUBA MAHOGNI OG AHORN   I:5
UNDER KLAPPERNE ER EN LØS BAKKE MED GLASPLA-
DE. UDTRÆKSRIGLE, HELE BORDKASSEN OG 'FØDDERNE'
AF MAHOGNI, RESTEN AF AHORN. BEHANDLING: KLAR
LAK.

Chieftain Chair

Year	1949
Manufacturer	Niels Vodder
Measurements	W 100 cm, H 93 cm, D 88 cm, seat height: 35 cm
See pages	52, 178, 323

The *Chieftain Chair* is probably the most well known and most striking of all Juhl's furniture designs. Although it is a large chair, it meets the modernist call for lightness and transparency, allowing our gaze to run through the spaces that emerge between the bare frame and the padded elements. It is a sculpture and a spatial component one can walk around and, as such, it is an example of the ultimate departure from the Empire-style tradition of placing furniture up against the wall. The many inter-secting elements of the frame include a variation on the triangle motif from the *Egyptian Chair* and also reference the spears and tools of indige-nous peoples. Juhl underscored this point by exhibiting the chair alongside indigenous utensils and artworks, such as a stone axe and bow and arrow, as well as photographs of stone dolmens and spear-wielding African hunters. The seat, back and armrests appear to be suspended freely upon and between those parts of the frame which support them. "Like four botched omelettes hung up on a rack," wrote one of the reviewers, the architect Odd Brochmann. Juhl happily conceded that, "considered as an omelette, it really was no good." Incidentally, the interior frame within the padded elements was not made of wood. This led to a complaint from one of the more fundamentalist cabinetmakers when the Danish Museum of Art & Design first considered purchasing the chair for their collection. Instead it was comprised of metal sheets built up by a blacksmith and covered with felt and leather. The *Chieftain Chair* incorporates many forms and potential references, so that the whole structure clamours with meanings – it is not a chair that is content with being a wallflower. Like Juhl's earlier 'animal' chairs it feels like a gesture frozen in time; a body in motion caught mid-moment. Each year, when the Finn Juhl Prize is awarded to one or more young furniture designers, the recipient takes home a scale model of the *Chieftain Chair* in addition to the prize money. The chair was relaunched in 2002 by House of Finn Juhl.

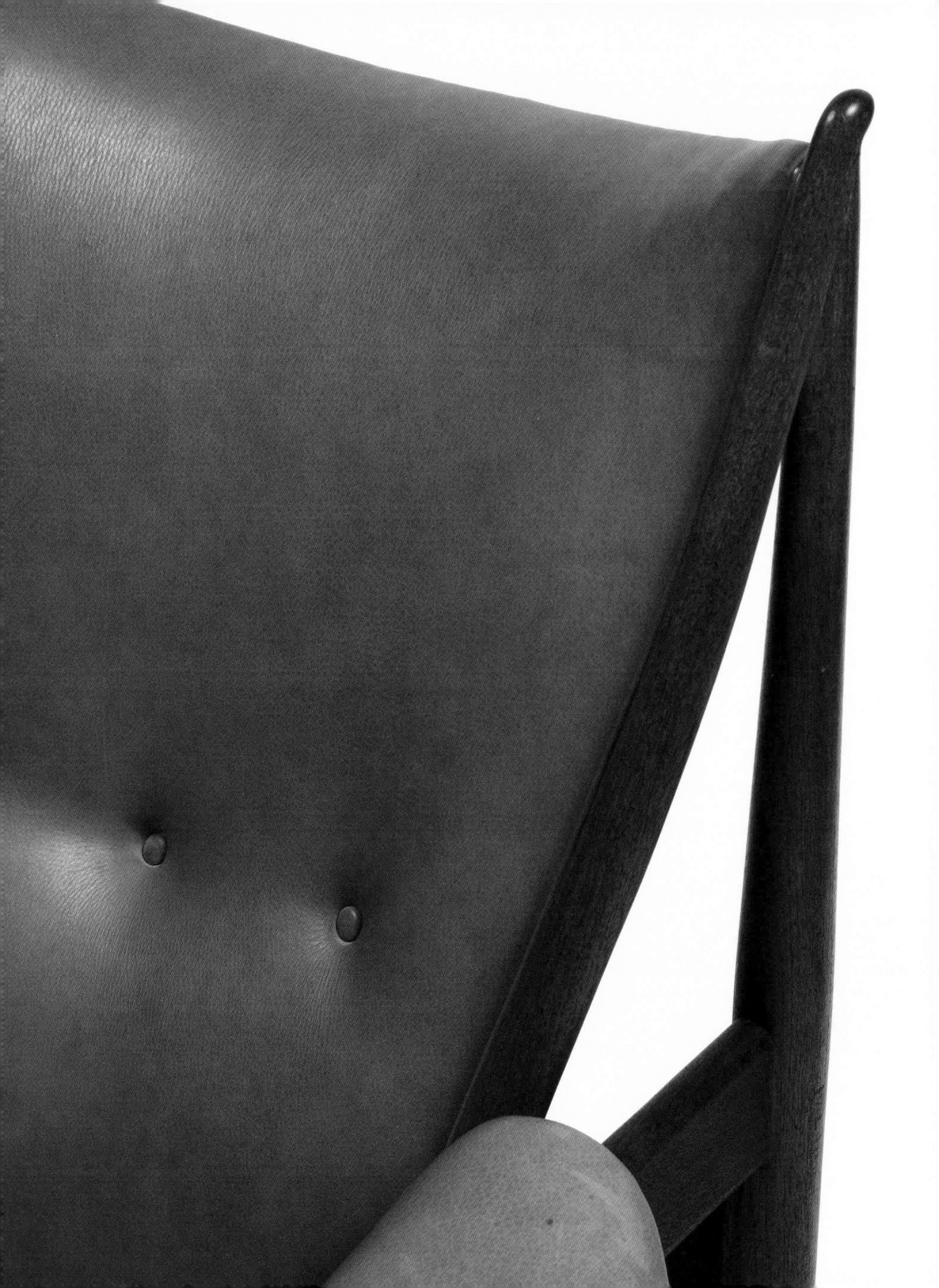

Egyptian Chair and Judas Table

Year	1948 and 1949
Manufacturer	Niels Vodder
Measurements	The Egyptian Chair: W 56 cm, H 90 cm, D 54 cm, seat height: 44.5 cm
	The Judas Table: W 120 cm, H 72 cm, L 180/290 cm
See pages	44

The *Egyptian Chair* and the *Judas Table* were not designed as a set. Nonetheless, Finn Juhl placed them together in the dining room of his own house in Ordrup. The *Egyptian Chair* is inspired by a chair from ancient Egypt (from approximately 1400–1300 BC) that features in the Louvre Museum's collection in Paris, where Juhl saw it and, like so many other furniture designers, was immediately enthused by its elegant combination of geometric elements. The steep back legs, the seat's side rungs and the straight slanting back form two triangles, lending the chair its distinctive, intuitively appealing profile. Finn Juhl borrows both from its static and strong design principle and aesthetically pleasing geometry. In his own version, Juhl cuts an open arch into the lower section of the back to make the chair more comfortable. That also lifts the seat free of the side rungs, so that the seat instead rests on the front and back rungs and seems to float when viewed in profile. A reinforced slat between the back legs is arched, mirroring the curvature of the sitter's back. Juhl also borrowed the small 'hooks' at the top of the back legs, but left out the lion's feet at their base. The result is a modern abstraction of an ancient design, where the figurative is eliminated while the principle is retained and supplemented by a personal interpretation. Not unlike – of course – modern sculpture. The *Egyptian Chair* has been returned to production in oak, teak and walnut, with textile or leather upholstery.

The *Judas Table* is an extendable table that Niels Vodder originally produced in Brazilian rosewood, although later versions exist in smoked oak and with a dark-wood table top and a frame in lighter teak. The table received its name after a classic Finn Juhl gimmick: the tabletop has thirty silver inlays the size and shape of coins – like Judas' blood money – that indicate the placement of the dinner service for four, six, eight and ten place settings. At once practical and playfully eccentric. The table was relaunched in 2014 by House of Finn Juhl.

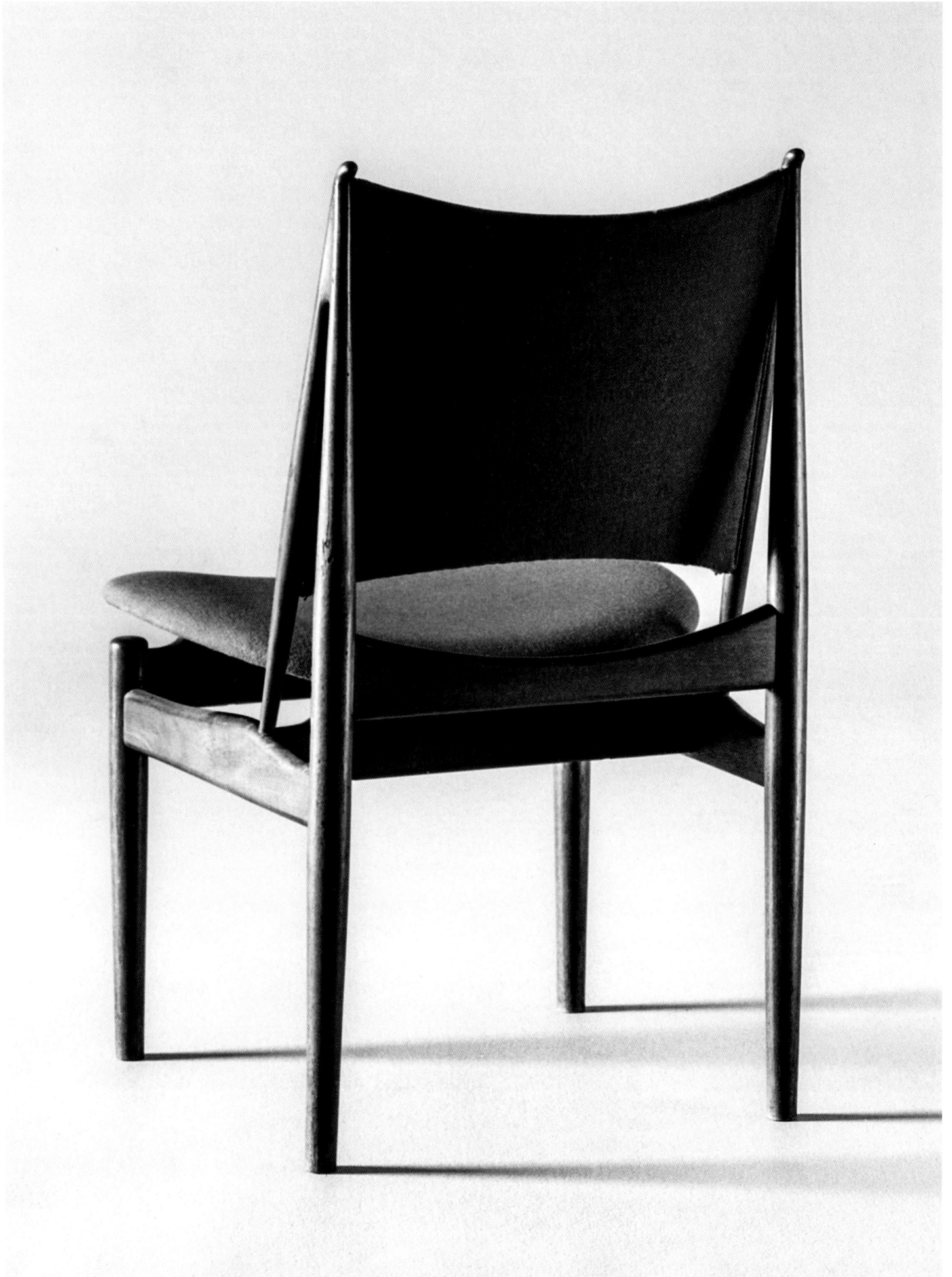

STOL, 1:5, I MEGET MØRK, TÆT TRÆSORT. SÆDE OG RYG I 8 MM KRYDSFINÉR MED FLAD STOPNING. HELULDENT, JAVAVÆVET BETRÆK

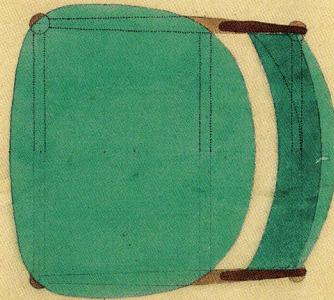

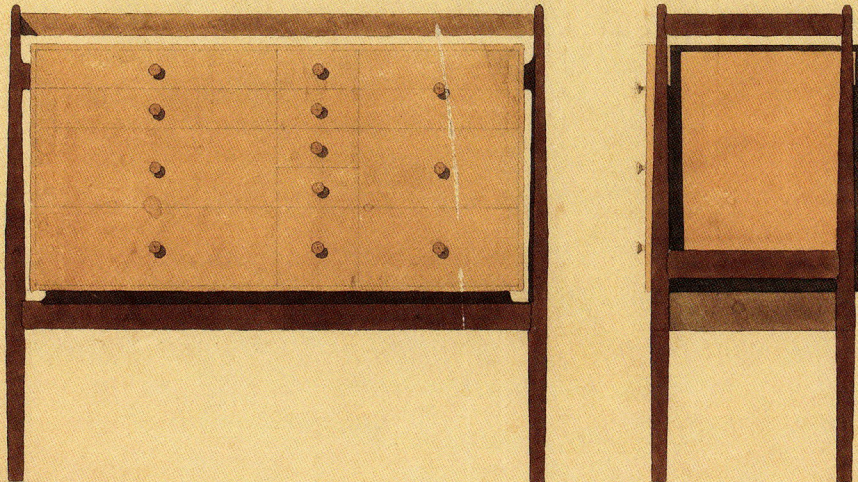

SØLVTØJ-SKÆNK, 1:5, I TEAK OG OREGON PINE. OVERFELSEDE SKUFFER MED SKJULT SKURT. SKUFFER INDVENDIGT AF AHORN.

3·1949·

SPISEBORD 1:5, 1:10, 1:1

ELLIPSE M. LILLECIRKEL 140 CM DIAM. OG FOKUS I LILLECIRKLENS SKÆRING MED STORAKSEN. HØJDE: 72 CM. PLADE: 22 MM MØBELPLADE M. 2 MM TEAK-FINER OG TEAKKANT. BØGESTEL M. TEAKFØDDER. NEDFELDEDE SØLVPLADER TIL MARKERING AF KUVERTER FOR 4, 6, 8, 10, 12 OG 14 PERSONER.

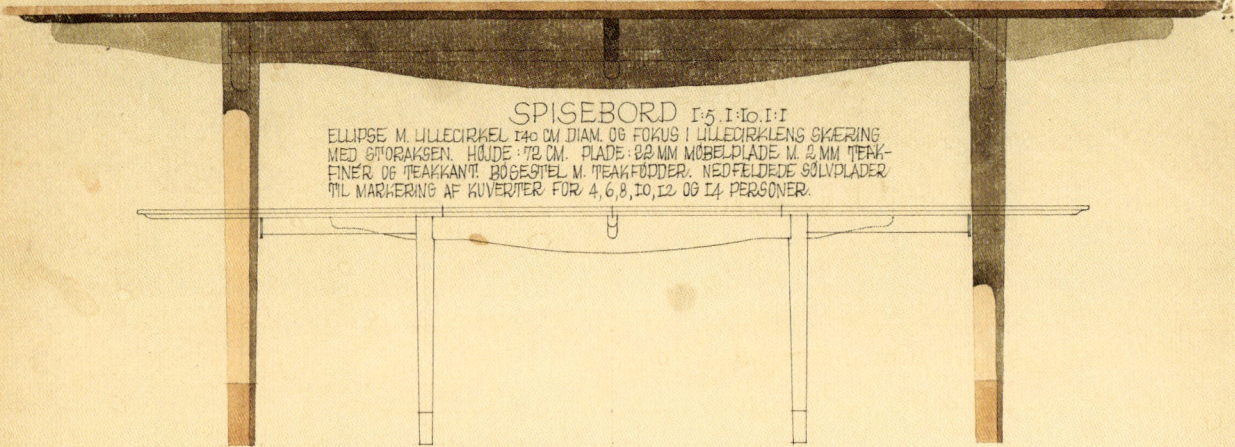

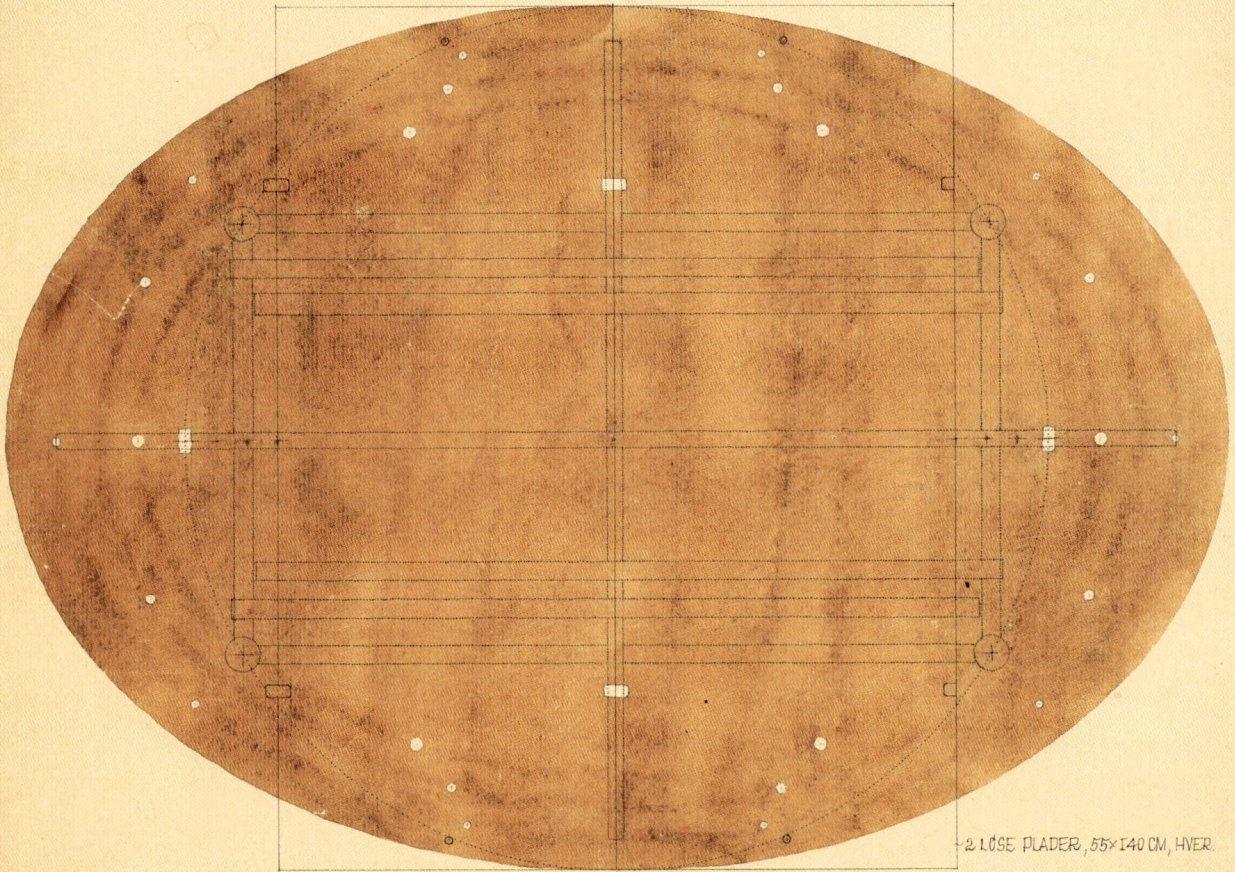

2 LØSE PLADER, 55×140 CM, HVER.

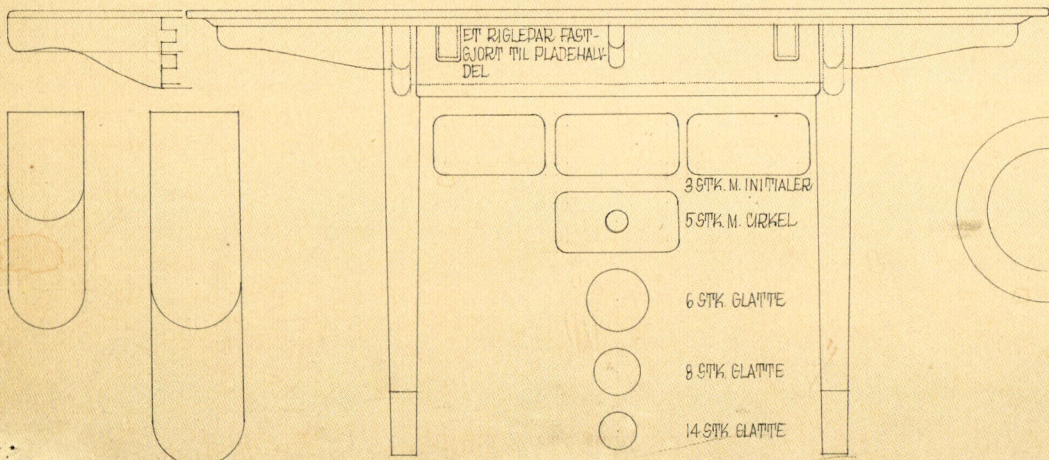

ET RIGLEPAR FAST-GJORT TIL PLADEHALV-DEL

3 STK. M. INITIALER

5 STK. M. CIRKEL

6 STK. GLATTE

8 STK. GLATTE

14 STK. GLATTE

1950

Wall Sofa

Year	1950
Manufacturer	Niels Vodder
Measurements	W 192 cm, H 102 cm, D 80 cm, seat height: 37 cm
See pages	206

Finn Juhl designed the *Wall Sofa* for his furnishing of *Interior-52* at the National Museum of Decorative Arts and Design in Trondheim, Norway, where his commission was to create a modern interior that was typical of its post-war time. At one end of the room Juhl placed a panelled wall, and opposite it he decided to have the wall painted a dark green that complemented a sofa suite, consisting of an *FJ45* chair and the *Wall Sofa*, with a turquoise and ultramarine seat and a grey back. In an extended model, the sofa also features in the interior of one of the few houses that Finn Juhl designed, Villa Aubertin (1952) by Nakskov Fjord in Denmark. The *Wall Sofa* is close to pure sculpture and so indicates why Juhl in an interview took the opportunity to insist that it was indeed furniture that he designed, and that there was a difference between the fine and applied arts. Visually, the overstuffed sofa's asymmetric and organically shaped back is liberated from the almost invisible frame. The seat and back are upholstered with fabric in separate colours to amplify the impression of them as two independent parts. It is one of Finn Juhl's most expressive pieces of furniture – a cousin of the *Pelican Chair*, *FJ44* and the *Chieftain Chair*. The sofa was relaunched in 2007 by House of Finn Juhl.

The Delegates' Chair | FJ51

Year	1951
Manufacturer	Niels Vodder
Measurements	W 74 cm, H 84 cm, D 67 cm, seat height: 44 cm
See pages	173

In 1950 the internationally unknown designer Finn Juhl was appointed to design the interior of the Trusteeship Council Chamber at the new United Nations building in New York. In furnishing the chamber, Juhl displayed his formidable ability to create unity in complex spaces, and the chamber became his principal architectural work. Among the many furnishings, Juhl designed a chair for the delegates, which was produced by Niels Vodder. The *Delegates' Chair* was exhibited at the Copenhagen Cabinetmakers' Guild Furniture Exhibition in 1950 and again in 1951 in a revised version, as Juhl was not satisfied with his original design. In its revision, the chair's back and top rail were reconfigured and the back was lowered. In the years 1951-1959 the chair was manufactured by Baker Furniture.

Baker Sofa

Year	1951
Manufacturer	Baker Furniture
Measurements	L 195 cm, H 98 cm, D 80 cm, seat height: 44 cm
See pages	207

In 1948 Edgar Kaufmann Jr. wrote an article about Finn Juhl in the reputable interior design magazine *Interiors*. It was read by Hollis S. Baker, the CEO of Baker Furniture, based in the 'Furniture City' of Grand Rapids, Michigan. In 1950 Baker travelled to Denmark and visited Finn Juhl at his design studio in Nyhavn to persuade him into a collaboration. Baker envisaged Juhl's modern furniture supplementing the American manufacturer's line of period furniture. The following year, an initially sceptical Finn Juhl entered into a contract with Baker Furniture, albeit only after visiting Grand Rapids and being convinced that the factory's industrial production methods could live up to the high quality standards that he was accustomed to in Denmark, a tradition shaped by skilled and meticulous Danish cabinetmakers. Under a series named Baker Modern, Baker Furniture came to produce twenty-four pieces of furniture designed by Finn Juhl. One of the first was a sofa, which has since become known as the *Baker Sofa*. It was first exhibited at the Copenhagen Cabinetmakers' Guild Furniture Exhibition in 1951. The *Baker Sofa* is an extension of Juhl's earlier overstuffed furniture such as the *Poet Sofa* and the *Pelican Chair*, though here as a development of the classic, high-backed coupé sofa. Juhl however, divides the back into two to make the sofa more flexible and to lighten the design expression. Thus, one can rests one's arm between the upper and lower sections of the sofa's back, while the protective wing-back motif is preserved. The light, visible wooden frame appears almost to be the pedestal for a sculpture in the style of Henry Moore, formed by the upholstered element. The collaboration between Finn Juhl and Baker Furniture showed that Danish handcrafted furniture could be produced outside of Denmark and by others than the Danish cabinetmakers. In this way, Baker Furniture's production contributed to establishing Finn Juhl's furniture on the American market as well as paving the way for other Danish furniture designers in the United States. After 50 years, Baker Furniture discontinued production of the sofa in 2001. In 2009 the model was relaunched in Denmark.

THIS SOFA TRIES TO SOLVE DIFFERENT PROBLEMS :
GOOD SUPPORT FOR "THE SMALL OF YOUR BACK" IN NORMAL POSITION,
RELAXED POSITION WITH YOUR FEET UP – IN BOTH CORNERS.
AND EVEN THEN REST FOR YOUR ELBOWS , AS WELL AS FOR YOUR HEAD –
THIS EFFECTUATED BY THE DIVIDING UP OF THE BACK IN TWO PARTS –
GOOD REST !

BAKER FURNITURE, INCORPORATED
Grand Rapids 2, Michigan

SOFA

FINN JUHL, architect m. a. a.
Nyhavn 33, Copenhagen K. Danmark
Telephones: Palæ 6618 - Ordrup 8000

date: 26 MARCH 5? rev.

no. 22

Japan Chair

Year	1953
Manufacturer	France & Søn
Measurements	W 61 cm, H 78 cm, D 70 cm, seat height: 35 cm
See pages	213

At the beginning of the 1950s Finn Juhl was a well-established name in furniture design, and an increasing number of furniture manufacturers approached him with a view to collaborating. After Bovirke and Søren Willadsen came France & Daverkosen, which later changed its name to France & Søn. The company was based in Ørholm, by the Mølleåen river, north of Copenhagen, and had originally been a mattress factory. C.W.F. France, the CEO, wanted to expand the company into seating cushions and commissioned Juhl to design furniture suitable for such cushions. The company had a reputation for high-quality products and quickly saw opportunities on the international market. After Fritz Hansen it was the best-known furniture manufacturer during the 1950s and 1960s. Finn Juhl designed the *Japan Chair* for France & Søn in 1953 and a matching sofa followed in 1957. Juhl used to say that "deviation is in the details" and the *Japan Series*, consisting of a chair, two sofas and a footstool, is a good illustration of his point. The series' expression was the simplest that had been seen from Juhl at that point. The *Japan Chair* is an open easy chair without armrests, which combines Japanese simplicity with functionalist geometry in both the distinctive top rail that supports the seat's back and the broad seat, whose convex shape offsets the concave back. Some of the elements could have been borrowed from traditional Japanese building traditions, such as the transverse rungs between the lightly tapering legs, which bring to mind the entrance to a Japanese temple. The rungs end in concave mouldings that lend it a striking visual refinement – a strategy typical of Juhl. Likewise is his accentuation of the distinction between the supporting and supported by showing the back to be separated from the frame by brass spacers. The *Japan Series'* minimalist idiom distances it from Juhl's earlier furniture and demonstrates his openness to new impulses, whether towards a 3000-year old Egyptian chair or the interest in Japanese design that crashed like a tsunami through Western architecture and design during those years. These pieces were manufactured in teak with wool upholstery on the seat and back cushions, just as France & Søn had requested. While other furniture manufacturers through the 1960s attempted to use new materials such as plastic or light alloy metals in their production, France & Søn stuck to wood, in particular the so called 'precious timbers'. They became the teakwood furniture manufacturer *par excellence*. In 2007 House of Finn Juhl relaunched the chair.

Table Bench | BO101

Year	1953
Manufacturer	Bovirke
Measurements	L 112 cm, H 39 cm, D 45 cm
See pages	23, 161, 215

Finn Juhl's *Table Bench* from 1952 is a clear result of the functional analyses that modern architects had begun to employ. Their aim was to design objects that satisfied contemporary needs instead of merely revisiting the designs and types of historical styles. The *Table Bench*, which was available in different lengths, was an answer to the need for a more open, light and airy decor, where fewer pieces of furniture could carry out several functions at once. Daily life, social conventions and consumer spending were changing rapidly and, literally speaking, furniture should not stand in the way of a freer expression in the home, where it was quite acceptable to jump around in pyjamas, lie across the table – sorry, the bench – and turn up the latest jazz records on the gramophone. Hence, free-standing pieces of furniture were designed that could be placed more freely, and which took up less space than heavier furnishings in symmetrical arrangements. Finn Juhl began relatively early to design furniture for industrial production alongside his continued collaboration with Niels Vodder. The *Table Bench* is one of a series of furniture designed for industrial production by Bovirke. It is exceptional in Juhl's production in that the combined tabletop and seat is wooden but has an underframe of oxidised iron. The tabletop is teak or Brazilian rosewood, and the toes on the metal legs are produced in the same material. The design has been renewed with a wool-covered cushion in a single colour that can be folded in half. Brass trim prevents the cushion from sliding. The *Table Bench* was one of Finn Juhl's most successful models in the United States after it featured in the touring exhibition *Design In Scandinavia* (1954–1957), an exhibition that Juhl had designed himself. Today, the *Table Bench* is a classic that commands high prices at auction. Juhl's intentions regarding the *Table Bench* are revealed in his book *Hjemmets Indretning* (Furnishing the Home), which was published in 1954. The book was intended as a help to those who "wanted an appropriate way to live, and in accordance with what the times prescribe", as it says on the back cover. The *Table Bench* was just such a concrete helping hand from a modern furniture designer to those who were following fashion. The table was relaunched by House of Finn Juhl in 2012.

Reading Chair | BO62

Year	1953
Manufacturer	Bovirke
Measurements	W 52 cm, H 74 cm, D 58 cm, seat height: 45 cm
See pages	213

The *Reading Chair* from 1953 was one of the first of Juhl's chairs that was initially designed for industrial production using the technology of the time. Up until the close of the 1940s Finn Juhl designed all of his furniture for handcrafting by the cabinetmaker Niels Vodder. Just as in many of the corresponding partnerships between Juhl's colleagues and specific cabinetmakers, Juhl's close collaboration with this congenial and skilled craftsman allowed him to experiment with the possibilities and constructive solutions that his materials afforded, while remaining on the firm ground of high-quality craftsmanship. With the advances in machinery, the years after the Second World War allowed designers to adapt their designs to industrial production. The cabinetmakers also industrialised, and Vodder was in fact one of the first to adapt to the new times. It was, however, in collaboration with the furniture retailer Poul Lund's company Bovirke in Frederiksberg, a municipal enclave within Copenhagen, that Finn Juhl began to design furniture suitable for industrial production that was cheaper to manufacture. His *Reading Chair* for Bovirke finds a simple solution to a common need. The horizontal top rail, which sits upon an extension of the back legs that itself reaches above the backrest, can be used as an armrest when one is sitting backwards or sideways in the chair. The slanting, buttressing stretchers between the legs indicate that this little chair is not content to resemble any old piece of classroom furniture. Bovirke's export of the chair was by no means small, and the *Reading Chair* eventually became a trademark for the company. Furthermore, it was one of the chairs that Baker Furniture in the United States brought into production. The *Reading Chair* is made in oak with a backrest and top rail in teak or walnut. In another version, the frame is painted black. The seat has a face veneer of teak or Brazilian rosewood and textile or leather upholstery. Since 2018 House of Finn Juhl has manufactured the chair.

NOWADAYS A DINING CHAIR IS USED FOR MANY OTHER
PURPOSES, THAN SEATING PEOPLE AT MEAL-TIMES
THIS CHAIR HAS A RATHER LOW BACK, CORRESPON-
DING IN HEIGHT TO THE DINING TABLE-TOP, AND IT
ALSO HAS A HORIZONTAL ARMREST, WHICH CAN BE
USED, WHEN A PERSON IS SEATED INFORMALLY.
TWO VERSIONS ARE SUGGESTED:
ALL IN WALNUT WITH UPHOLSTERED SEAT,
                 - A SYCOMORE VENEERED PLY-
WOOD SEAT.
SEAT RESTING ON RUBBER ON TOP OF FRONT RAIL, AND
ON METAL-HARDWARE WITH RUBBER 'CUSHIONS' BACK.

ARMREST IN SOLID WALNUT

CHROMIUM FINISH
BLACK RUBBER

3 LAYERS OF SOLID WALNUT

BAKER FURNITURE, INCORPORATED
Grand Rapids 2, Michigan

DINING CHAIR II

FINN JUHL, Denmark m.a.a.
Nyhavn 33, Copenhagen K, Denmark
Telephones: Palæ 0010 - Pa. 2 2000

date: 14. NOV. 1952 rev.

scale: 1:1 - 1:4

75

Bowls for Kay Bojesen

Year	1951 and 1954
Manufacturer	Magne Monsen
Measurements	H 6 cm, D 15 cm,
	H 7.5 cm, D 23 cm,
	H 13.5 cm, D 28 cm,
	H 15 cm, D 37 cm
See pages	178

Finn Juhl stated that his life's ambition was to fill his own house with furniture, carpets, curtains, light fittings, glassware, and silverware that he had designed himself. He did not quite achieve that goal, but he was well on the way. With persistent curiosity and tenacity, he took on all the types of applied art that such a task would involve. Thus in the early 1950s he designed a silver cutlery set for Georg Jensen and a steel dining service for Bing & Grøndahl. Neither of these came into production at the time. However, a set of teak bowls from around the same period was produced. The bowls were designed for the silversmith and designer Kay Bojesen and produced by the turner Magne Monsen. One can see from both the original sketches and the bowls themselves that the designer handled wood in his usual intrepid way, treating them almost like wet clay, out of which is formed an asymmetric, amorphous and bold bowl, which is related to the traditional olive-wood utensils of Mediterranean countries. Just as with the earlier, 'bodily' chairs from the mid-1940s, Finn Juhl's bowls induce the wood into doing something it could really only do when alive, trunks and branches twisting naturally outward. And it was nature itself that limited the production, for there is no longer wood available for the largest of the bowls. The teak trees that were used at the time had grown very slowly and had stood untouched for many years. Today, teak is only available from plantations and these trees grow too quickly for this purpose. As with Kay Bojesen's own woodwork, Finn Juhl's bowls are highly coveted and command high prices at auction. Achitectmade has produced the smallest size since 2003.

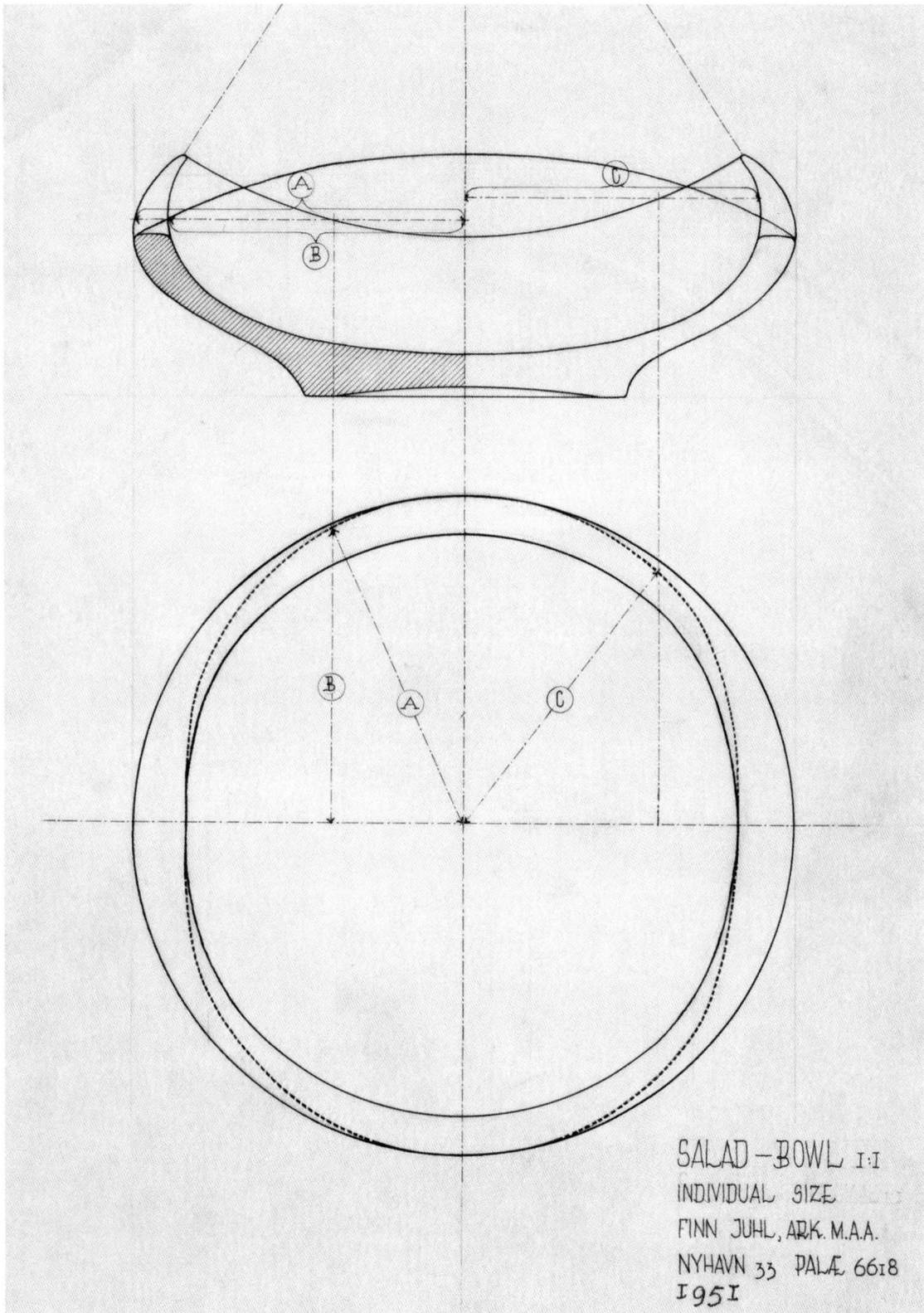

SALAD—BOWL 1:1
INDIVIDUAL SIZE
FINN JUHL, ARK. M.A.A.
NYHAVN 33 PALÆ 6618
1951

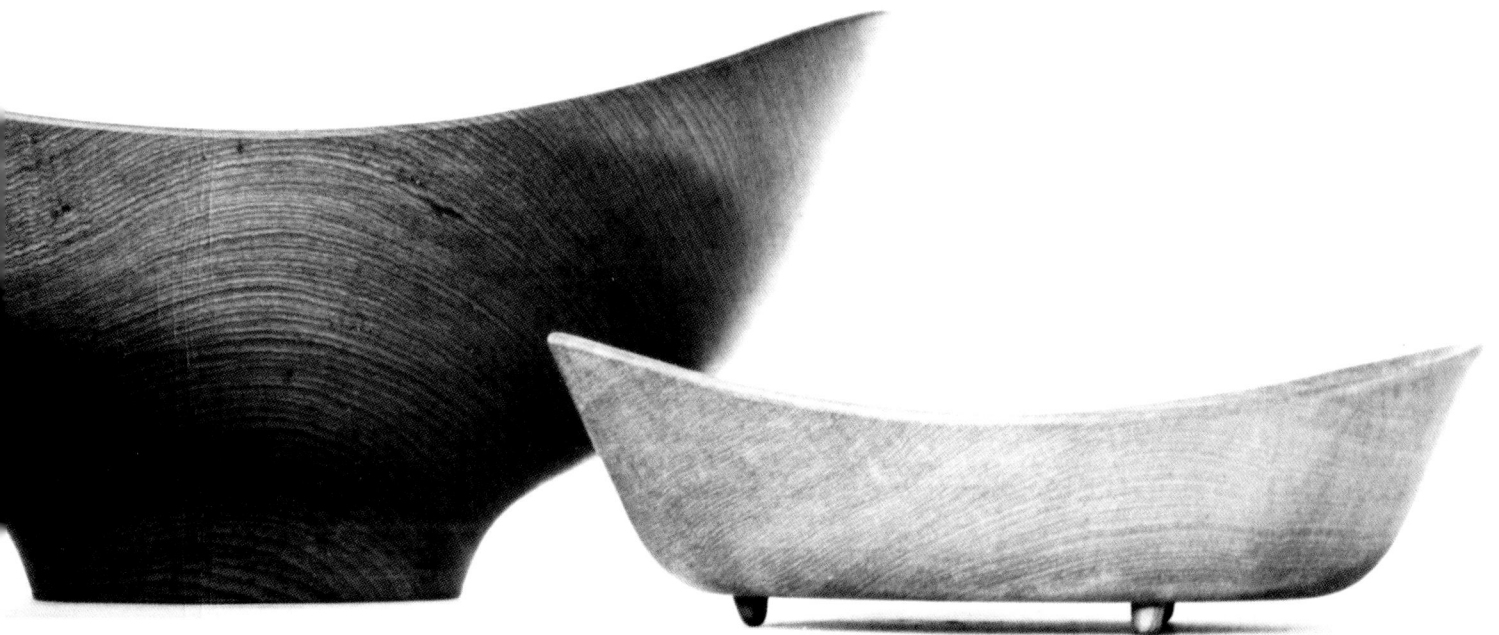

Glove Cabinet for Bedroom Suite

Year	1961
Manufacturer	Ludwig Pontoppidan
Measurements	W 69 cm, H 37/52 cm, D 35 cm
See page	221

In 1961 Finn Juhl participated in his 25th and what would be his penultimate the Copenhagen Cabinetmakers' Guild Furniture Exhibition, presenting a suite of bedroom furniture that he dedicated to his life partner, Hanne Wilhelm Hansen. His longstanding collaboration with cabinetmaker Niels Vodder had been brought to an end, and Finn Juhl's contribution was produced by Ludwig Pontoppidan. The *Bedroom Suite* comprises, first, two low chairs with a broad, sturdy rectangular cushion, covered in Thai silk and resting on a cherry-wood frame. The chairs have straight metal legs and a cylindrical back cushion, also in Thai silk. In addition, there is a box-spring bed in a similar construction, only with painted panels. Likewise a little cabinet – purportedly for the wife's glove collection – is comprised of two cubes on metal legs, which swing open around the axis of a metal pipe. Each of the drawers of the cabinet is painted in a different colour. Cherry wood is used throughout, and the *Bedroom Suite* was exhibited, as usual, alongside works of art, in this case a sculpture by Erik Thommesen and a painting by Vilhelm Lundstrøm. In their article 'Applied Art Going Astray' in the architecture journal *Arkitekten*, the designers Børge Mogensen and Arne Karlsen criticised a handful of their exhibiting colleagues, Finn Juhl among them, for exaggerating the aesthetic aspect of their work at the cost of its functionality. The *Bedroom Suite's* geometric forms were seen as a silly pastiche of the Bauhaus School's then 30-year-old ideals. "Has religious war broken out?" responded Juhl in jest, but there is little doubt it pained him that his colleagues took him to have spurned the lessons of the experiences he had gained through his finest designs. Instead they felt he had given himself up to 'the perfumed', which in their opinion had always threatened to overpower his expression. The *Bedroom Suite* was never put into production, but House of Finn Juhl later relaunched the *Glove Cabinet*, and parts of the suite can be viewed in the bedroom at Juhl's own house in Ordrup.

Lamp for Lyfa

Year	1963
Manufacturer	Lyfa
Measurements	W 18 cm, H 43 cm, D 25 cm
See page	256

In the 1960s, Finn Juhl designed several items of furniture, but only very few were put into production. He moved his design studio back to his house at Kratvænget, and his commissions grew increasingly scarce. That did not mean, however, that he stopped working. Among his surviving drawings there are proposals for craft utensils in wood, glass, textile, porcelain, and silver. In recent years, some have been put into production, including a *Turning Tray* in wood and melamine for Ørskov & Co., where each tray has two colours. Likewise, a series of lamps Juhl designed in 1963 for the lighting company Lyfa, which were in fact manufactured by Lyfa at the time, but without commercial success. The series uses lacquered metal and comprises a desk lamp, a wall lamp, and a pendant. The first two have a lampshade that can be tilted.

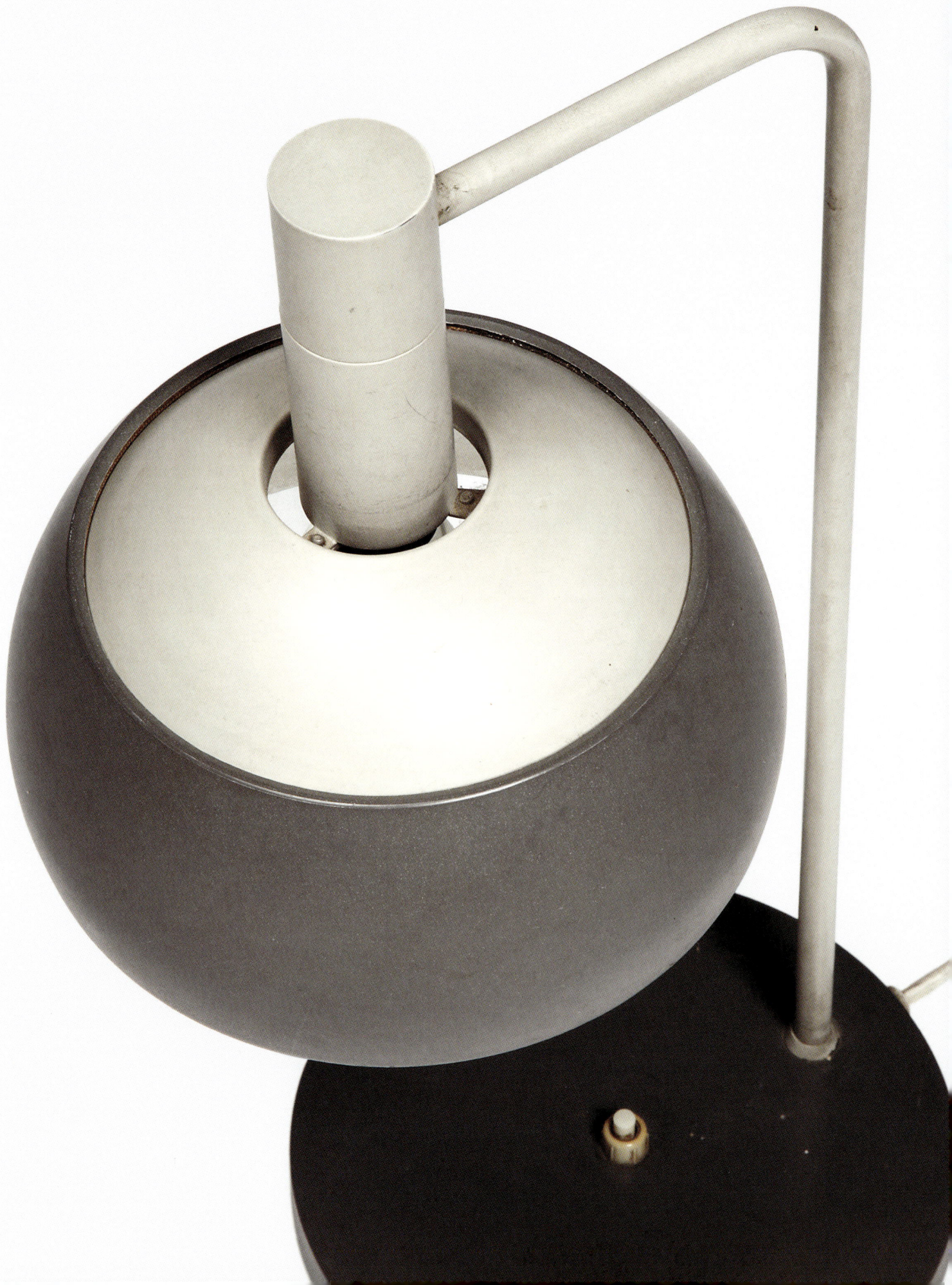

1950 ——— 1959

The Journey
to America

Edgar Kaufmann Jr. and Juhl striking a Schiller-and-Goethe pose. Life-long friends, soulmates, workmates – but also client and designer.

'Further than Aunt Lise in the country'

The Danish poet Christian Winther's children's poem 'The Flight to America' tells the story of a boy who has had a difficult day. He gets awful marks at school, is scolded at home for ripping his jacket, and to top it all he is turned down by the baker's sweet daughter, Rikke. With his little brother Emil he decides to flee to America, for although it is far away, further even than Aunt Lise in the country:

> "it's a venture you'll never regret;
> a towering castle all for free
> and mountains of money you'll get.
>
> Of silver, not iron, are all of our tyres
> and all of our horses' shoes;
> gold will lie plentiful everywhere by us,
> bend down and take up what you choose."[40]

Many Europeans have emigrated to North America throughout the years in search of happiness – and gold – in what had come to be called the New World. Here, one could farm a plot of land in America's great, uninhabited plains or take a job in one of the rapidly growing industries, which would together become the world's largest economy. Between 1860 and 1930, more than 300,000 Danes emigrated to the United States.

After the Second World War, the USA was the only political and military superpower that was also economically strong (in comparison to the Soviet Union and Europe). During the post-war years, when Juhl was just breaking through as a furniture designer, many European countries were experiencing what critics have termed the Americanisation of their economies, consumer practices and culture. During the Cold War, the United States' intelligence services established an extensive propaganda programme aiming to ensure that European populations embraced Western capitalism over the Soviet-dominated communist approach. Thus, the American Marshall Plan, which sought to help to rebuild Western European economies while also increasing the American military presence in Central Europe, was accompanied by an official promotion of cultural exports. It was the young in particular who took to this new 'American way' through film, music, magazines and comic books. They were also attracted to innovative household appliances and novelties like the supermarket, which originated in the United States and was considered an appealing, modern phenomenon.

On the other hand, the prosperous Americans and their vast markets were a dream for European businesses and, of course, for independent actors, including artists and craftspeople. An affluent elite in American society cultivated a sense for alternative, often carefully designed, high-quality European goods, from British sports cars to Danish chairs.

A Guru and an Inspiration

Since his debut in 1937, Juhl had exhibited at 14 of the Copenhagen Cabinetmakers' Guild Furniture Exhibitions and his pieces had won prizes at all of them (taking first prize on four occasions). After the three stylish chairs of 1944, 1945 and 1946, Juhl was awarded the Royal Danish Academy of Fine Arts' Eckersberg Medal in 1947 in recognition of artistic design work. But this was all in a very Danish context, and there were greater breakthroughs to be made overseas.

In 1948 the Museum of Modern Art (MoMA) in New York planned an exhibition of Scandinavian design. MoMA's head of design, the curator Edgar Kaufmann Jr., undertook a research trip to Sweden, Norway, Finland and Denmark. Kaufmann was not just anybody. His father was the wealthy owner of a chain of department stores, and Kaufmann Jr. had studied crafts in Vienna during the 1920s as well as architecture under the American architect Frank Lloyd Wright at the latter's combined studio and architecture school, Taliesin, in Spring Green, Wisconsin. At the close of the 1930s, Kaufmann Sr. commissioned Frank Lloyd Wright to build a summer residence for the Kaufmann family at the Bear Run nature reserve, not far from Pittsburgh, Pennsylvania. The residence, *Fallingwater* became Wright's most recognised work.

Kaufmann Jr. first came across Finn Juhl at 'Den Permanente' (The Permanent), a sales exhibition of Danish design and crafts at Rådhuspladsen (City Hall Square) in Copenhagen. He had already heard about Juhl through Abel Sorensen, a Danish-born architect at Wallace K. Harrison's design studio, which managed the international architecture team that designed and planned the United Nations' Headquarters in New York. Sorensen was responsible for the building's office interiors, and he had met Finn Juhl on a visit to Scandinavia to consider furniture for the building.

Sorensen's positive impression was confirmed. Kaufmann Jr. was immediately excited about Juhl's furniture – this in contrast to his general impression of Danish furniture, which he saw as less modern and less sophisticated than its Swedish counterparts. In return, Finn Juhl admired the American's knowledge of art history, and this was the beginning of a lifelong professional acquaintance and personal friendship. Later they would travel together on several occasions, to Italy among other places. Kauffman visited Juhl in his home on Kratvænget, and Juhl visited Kauffman both at *Fallingwater* and on the Greek island of Hydra, where Kaufmann had a house. Finn Juhl called Kauffman his guru and inspiration, and their meeting was undoubtedly the catalyst for Juhl's international breakthrough[41].

Finn Juhl of Copenhagen

The exhibition at MoMA never materialised, but in November 1948 Kaufmann published a splashy, illustrated article in the American magazine *Interiors* titled 'Finn Juhl of Copenhagen', introducing Juhl to the American public. It ran, "Only occasionally does a master chair designer come on the scene – one in thorough command of comfort, construction, and style. In Copenhagen is such a one, Finn Juhl."[42]

The article refers to the *Fireplace Chair*, *FJ44*, *FJ45*, *FJ46* and a variant of the *Poet Sofa*. Kaufmann accentuates the highly skilled craftsmanship that characterised Danish furniture design and the modern expression brought about in the partnership of cabinetmaker and designer,[43] in this case Niels Vodder and Finn Juhl. In this way he acknowledged that Juhl was not alone in promoting high quality furniture; Denmark had other great designers, Hans J. Wegner among them, but according to Kaufmann, Juhl's furniture was "peculiarly suited to represent the spirit."[44] It was not long after the article's publication that MoMA bought three of Juhl's chairs: *FJ44*, *FJ45* and *FJ48*.

In addition to Kaufmann's warm recommendations and his promotion of Juhl's work, there were two other circumstances that made breaking into the American market easier for Juhl than for many of his compatriots. For one, he had what the Americans call personality; an expression that had sprung up along with the rise of Hollywood stars and the modern advertisement industry, which in large part developed in the United States. In the tough competition of modern society products no longer sold themselves. And when it came to personal products, such as works of art and design pieces, the person behind the product had to sell as well. This seems natural today – as early as primary school we are taught to 'sell ourselves' – but around 1950, this was new, and the salesman became one of most familiar characters of the period. The other reason Juhl found the American market easier to navigate than some of his countrymen is that he spoke English as his stepmother had insisted that it was spoken in his childhood home.

In 1948, the Museum of Modern Art held a competition for a chair that could be mass-produced and sold at an affordable cost. Juhl's participation might be due to his acquaintance with Edgar Kaufmann Jr., the head of the design department. He submitted a polyamide chair with armrests, but the first prize went to Charles and Ray Eames for one of their (later famous) shell chairs.

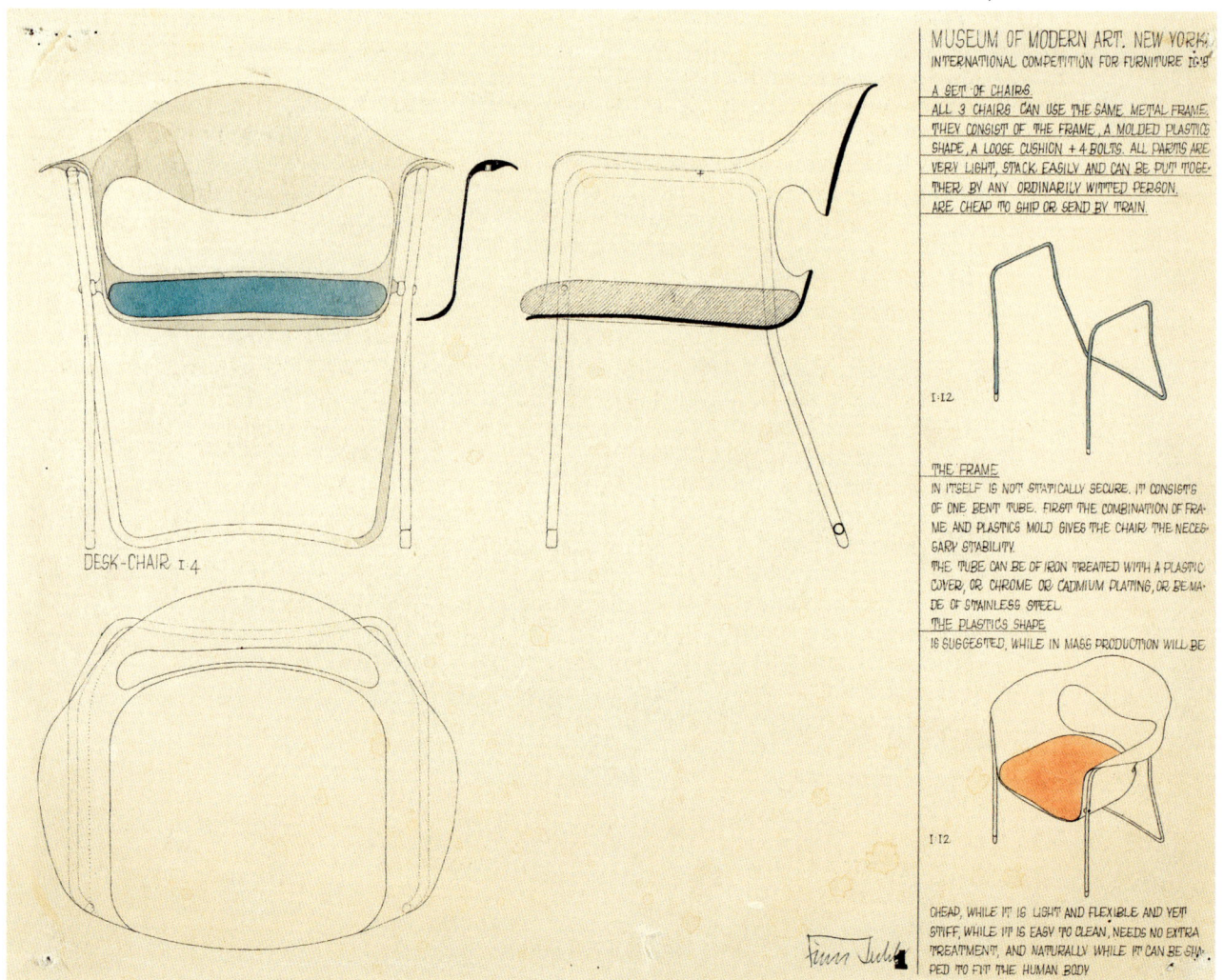

When Juhl's furniture premiered in America it was sold by a Dane, Frederik Lunning, who together with his son, Just Lunning, ran a Georg Jensen store on Fifth Avenue in New York. In 1952 they asked Juhl to refurbish the shop's interior, just as five years later Juhl designed the interiors for the Georg Jensen outlet on New Bond Street in London, and in 1958 for a new store in Toronto.

George Tanier, who was married to a Dane, was the next to import and sell Danish-designed furniture, including Finn Juhl's products for the Danish furniture manufacturer Bovirke. George Tanier was married to Inge-Marie Tanier, who had studied at the School of Interior Design in Copenhagen and worked for Juhl. Further, in 1950, on the American West Coast the Dane Svend Wohlert established the business Pacific Overseas, which specialised in Danish Modern furniture.

Danish Fine Craftsmanship and American Industry

In September 1950, Finn Juhl was again written up in *Interiors*, this time in a 10-page article focusing on his interior projects and his own house: 'Finn Juhl – about the quiet life of a Danish architect'. To a great extent, the article credited the craftsmanship of cabinetmakers, in this case, Niels Vodder, for the outstanding quality that distinguished Danish furniture, such as Juhl's, in comparison to its American counterparts:

"Could Finn Juhl do as well as he does … if he had to rely on the same workmen as American designers? These sensitively moulded limbs; these thin backs and seats, curving plumply in just the right places and covered with leather sewn fine as a glove; this untrammelled contrasting and blending of woods, these sliding shelves and perfectly fitting covers … surely anyone could do this as bravely if he had an extraordinary craftsman like Niels Vodder at his disposal".[45]

The author was of course correct that the demands on quality in American industrial mass production were lower and so could not compete with the demands that Danish cabinetmakers placed on themselves. Nor could manufacturers spend the number of hours on each chair that the cabinetmakers would. But perhaps the author undervalues the aspect that Juhl himself considered the most important: the designer's freedom to experiment and, in the fine joints and daring configurations, push wood to its outer limits. That is, the *freedoms of form* that collaboration with a cabinetmaker allows for.

Of course, such finery was only for the few. And some questioned what value truly lay in this rampant consumer society, in which the market ensured that everyone could get everything they wanted and in multiple varieties. If the wheels could only be kept in motion by producing items of such scant quality that they would quickly have to be replaced, would there not one day be a price to pay? Nevertheless, there was hope among designers that as machinery and technology improved, industrial production would also be able to deliver higher-quality products.

As early as 1951, Juhl had entered into a contract with the manufacturers Baker Furniture in the 'Furniture City' of Grand Rapids, Michigan. They began to produce a collection of his furniture, including chairs and tables, a sofa, a bed and storage furniture. And of course, Juhl designed the company's showroom. This partnership refutes the myth that Danish furniture was exclusively produced in Denmark by Danish cabinetmakers, and by the mid-1950s, Juhl was represented on the American market with both locally and Danish produced industrial furniture. Naturally, there was imported, handcrafted furniture too. Danish Modern had become an established, albeit small and select brand in the United States. Finn Juhl's organic styles in particular facilitated the desire of progressive, well-educated Americans to stand out from the crowd.[46] His furniture paved the way for other Danish furniture designers in the United States.

During the 1950s, Juhl achieved wide representation in the United States with imported, Danish-made cabinetmakers' and industrial furniture as well as pieces made in the United States.

The American-born furniture
manufacturer Hollis M. Baker
travelled to Nyhavn, Copenhagen
and convinced Juhl to let Baker
Furniture in the 'Furniture City' of
Grand Rapids, Michigan, produce
some of his furniture designs.

BENCH OF WALNUT

Most of the Baker Furniture designs
had originally been designed for
and produced by cabinetmaker
Niels Vodder, including the *FJ48
Chair* (bottom). However, the *Table
Bench* (top) is a revised version
made by Bovirke.

SECTION THROUGH LIVING - DINING SPACE

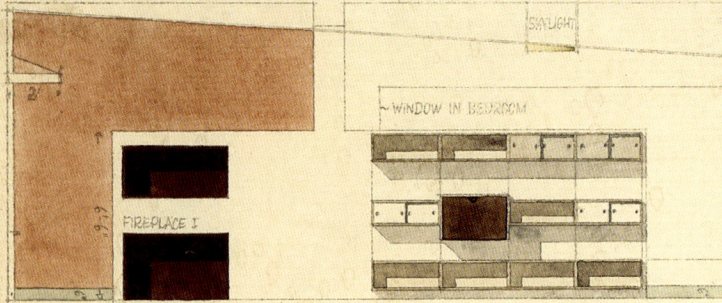

SECTION THROUGH LIBRARY - BEDROOM

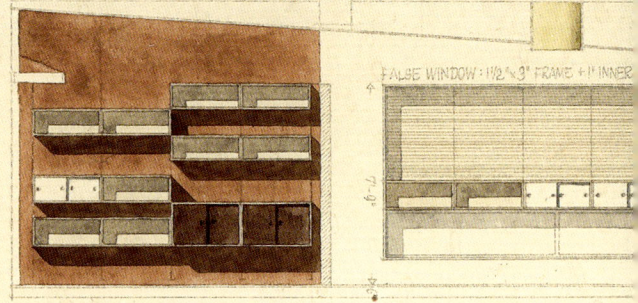

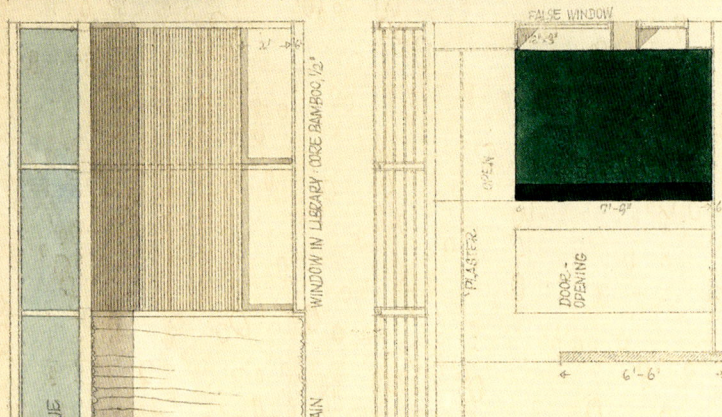

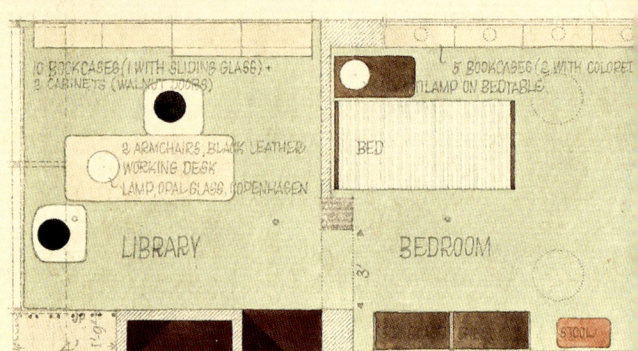

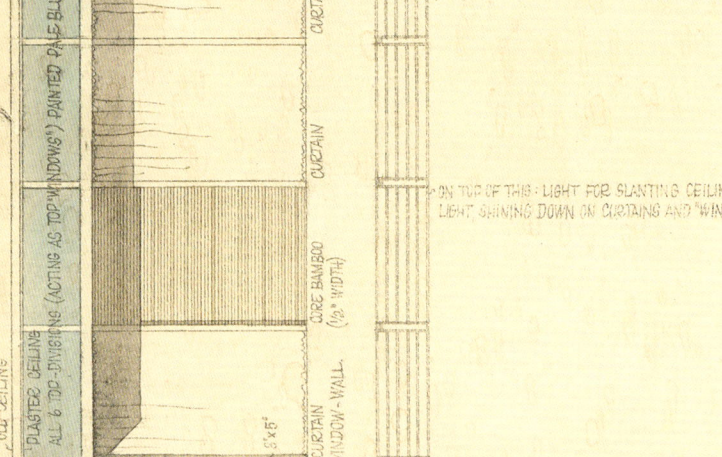

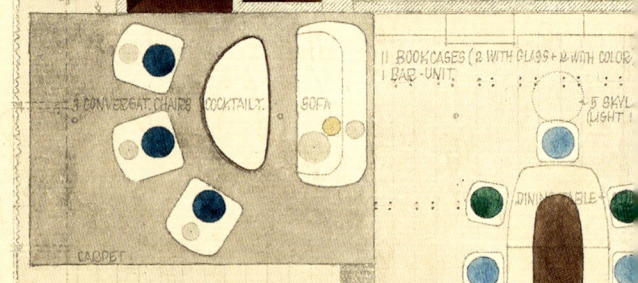

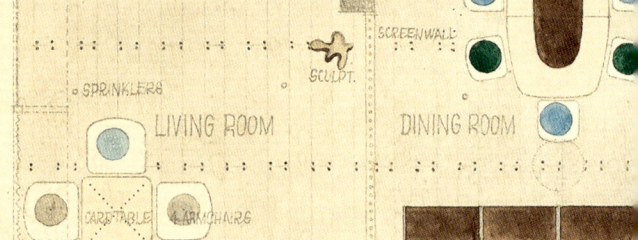

FIREPLACE I

WINDOW IN BEDROOM

FALSE WINDOW: 1½"×3" FRAME + 1" INNER

WINDOW IN LIBRARY: CORE BAMBOO 1/2"

OLD CEILING

"PLASTER CEILING - ALL 6 TOP-DIVIDING (ACTING AS TOP-WINDOWS") PAINTED PALE BLUE

CURTAIN

CORE BAMBOO (1/2" WIDTH)

CURTAIN

WINDOW-WALL

CURTAIN

ENTRANCE

LOWER CEILING

FALSE WINDOW

OPEN

PLASTER

DOOR - OPENING

WALL BETWEEN BEDROOM AND LIBRARY

ON TOP OF THIS - LIGHT FOR SLANTING CEILING + LIGHT SHINING DOWN ON CURTAIN AND "WINDOWS"

PLAN OF LOWER CEILING, MADE OF 6"×1¼" BOARDS PAINTED WHITE. OVER ENTRANCE OLD SPRINKLERS

10 BOOKCASES (1 WITH SLIDING GLASS) + 2 CABINETS (WALNUT DOORS)

5 BOOKCASES (2 WITH COLORED) 1 LAMP ON BEDTABLE

2 ARMCHAIRS, BLACK LEATHER WORKING DESK LAMP, OPAL GLASS, COPENHAGEN

BED

LIBRARY

BEDROOM

11 BOOKCASES (2 WITH GLASS + 9 WITH COLOR) 1 BAR-UNIT

5 CONVERSAT. CHAIRS COCKTAIL T.

SOFA

CARPET

SPRINKLERS

SCULPT.

SCREEN-WALL

LIVING ROOM

DINING ROOM

CARD-TABLE 4 ARMCHAIRS

SCREEN-WALL

SECTIONAL SOFA

COFFEE TABLE

ENTRANCE

SPRINKLERS, TO BE CARRIED SLANTING PLASTER-CEILING

OLD SPRINKLERS

PLAN OF SHOWROOMS FLOORS IN 5 LEVELS MADE IN WHITEWASHED PINE, SCREWS COVERED WITH TURNED TEAK-BUTTONS

SECTION THROUGH BEDROOM - LIBRARY

CEILING OVER ENTRANCE-ROOM

BAMBOO
DTH"

CAGE9

PAINTED
BLUE ON
SIDE

DARK RED

FIREPLACE II

DARK RED

WALL BETWEEN
LIBRARY AND BEDROOM

BEAM

SKYLIGHT

PLASTER

CHINESE MATING

FIREPLACE II

SCREEN OF 1/2" TURNED STICKS
THROUGH No. 25 PLAQUE
NATURAL WOOD DOWELS ETC

ENTRANCE-ROOM WITH LOW CEILING

BAKER FURNITURE, INCORPORATED
Grand Rapids 2, Michigan

SHOWROOMS FOR JUNE 1951

FINN JUHL, architect m a a
Nyhavn and Gothersgade, Denmark
Telephone: Palæ 6318 - Ordrup 800

date 25 APRIL 1951   rev.
no.   scale 1/4" - 1'
43

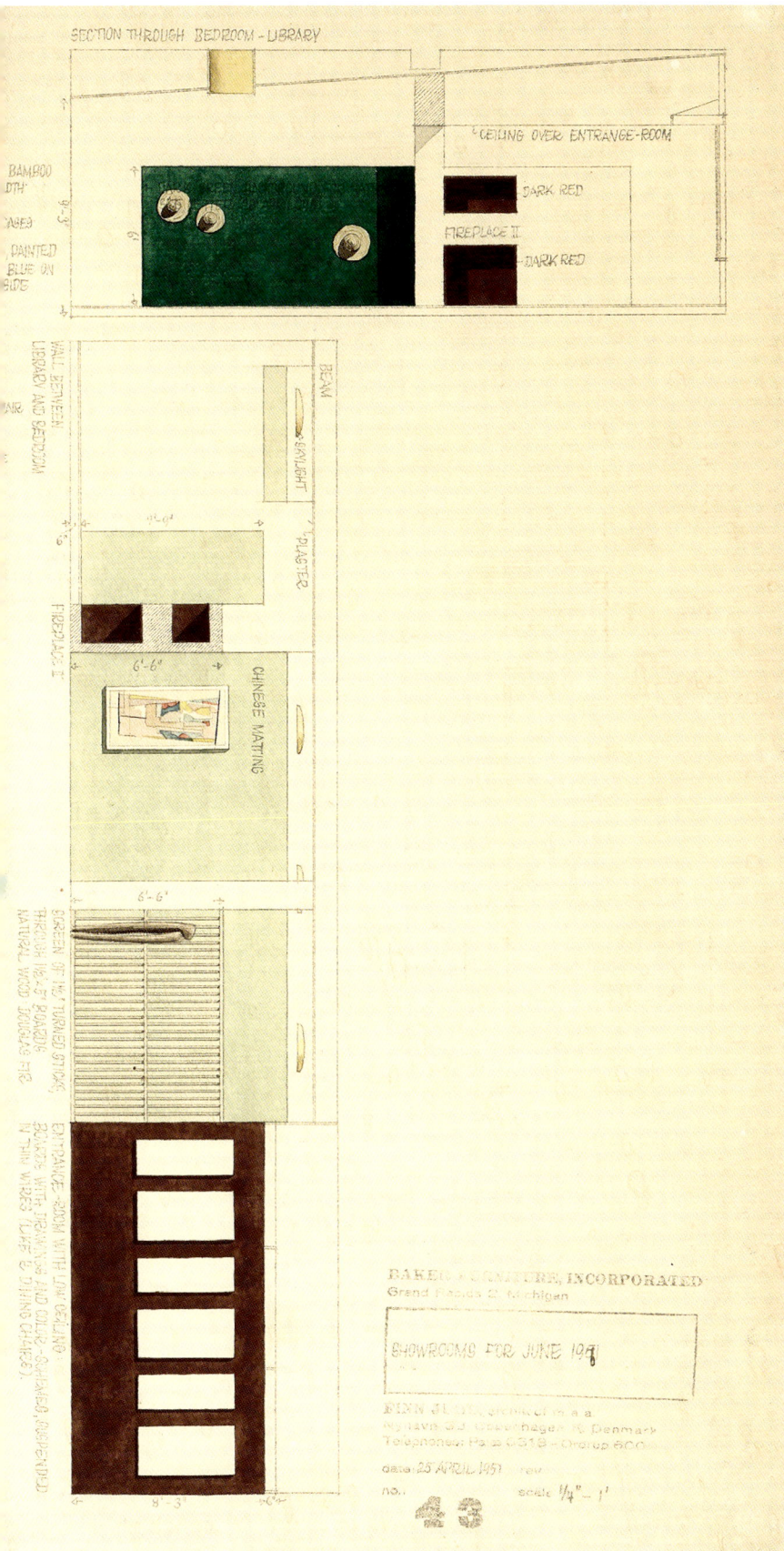

Juhl also designed Baker Furniture's
showroom where his own furniture
and other designs were displayed.
Plan and elevations of the interior
(1951).

Baker Furniture's showroom in
Grand Rapids, Michigan. Danish
Modern in the United States.

The Interior of the Trusteeship Council Chamber at the UN Headquarters

In 1950, after being awarded the Eckersberg Medal, Juhl was selected to design the interior of one of the three council chambers at the United Nations Headquarters in New York. The three Nordic countries each donated a chamber for the new organisation's building complex, which had been designed by an international team of architects including Le Corbusier, Oscar Niemeyer and Sven Markelius under the leadership of the American architect Wallace K. Harrison.

The complex comprises three buildings: a modernistic curtain-wall skyscraper – one of the first in New York – with 39 floors for the secretariat's offices; a trapezium-shaped building that houses the United Nations General Assembly hall; and facing out across Roosevelt Drive and the East River, a low rectangular building with three meeting chambers: the Security Council Chamber, the Economic and Social Council Chamber and the Trusteeship Council Chamber. Until 1995, the latter was the UN's organ for monitoring decolonisation across 11 regions, a task that the UN had inherited from its predecessor organisation, the League of Nations.

Perhaps it was not so bold a decision to commission Juhl to design the interior of the chamber that Denmark was to donate. He was, after all, a rapidly rising star in furniture and interior design and enjoyed a growing status in the USA. By contrast, however, Norway and Sweden selected two experienced and well-established architects. The Norwegians chose the 68-year-old Arnstein Arneberg, who had designed Oslo City Hall, and the Swedes opted for the 61-year-old Sven Markelius, one of Sweden's most renowned architects, who was also a member of the architecture team behind the entire UN complex. Finn Juhl had designed furniture and the interior for the Bing & Grøndahl porcelain manufacturers' boutique, and he had headed his own design studio for five years. There was also *Radiohuset*, although outwardly at least, that had been Vilhelm Lauritzen's responsibility. And so, while Edgar Kaufmann and Abel Sorensen may have pulled some strings and whispered in the right ears, the commission was still a great show of confidence and a fantastic opportunity for Finn Juhl.

The international team of architects behind the United Nations Headquarters in New York. On the far left, the head of the team, the American Wallace K. Harrison and (second left) French-Swiss Le Corbusier, who designed the high-rise tower in the UN complex. In the middle, the Brazilian Oscar Niemeyer, who designed the General Assembly Building, and just behind him, the Swedish architect Sven Markelius.

The United Nations Headquarters in New York with the General Assembly Building and the tall Secretariat Building. Ensemble of the three original UN buildings that houses the low Conference Building with the three Scandinavian halls in front – viewed from across the East River.

Coloured drawing of the Trusteeship Council Chamber at the UN Headquarters in New York with the large glazed-in section facing the East River, the colourful ceiling decoration and the petroleum-coloured *Delegates' Chairs* on the floor.

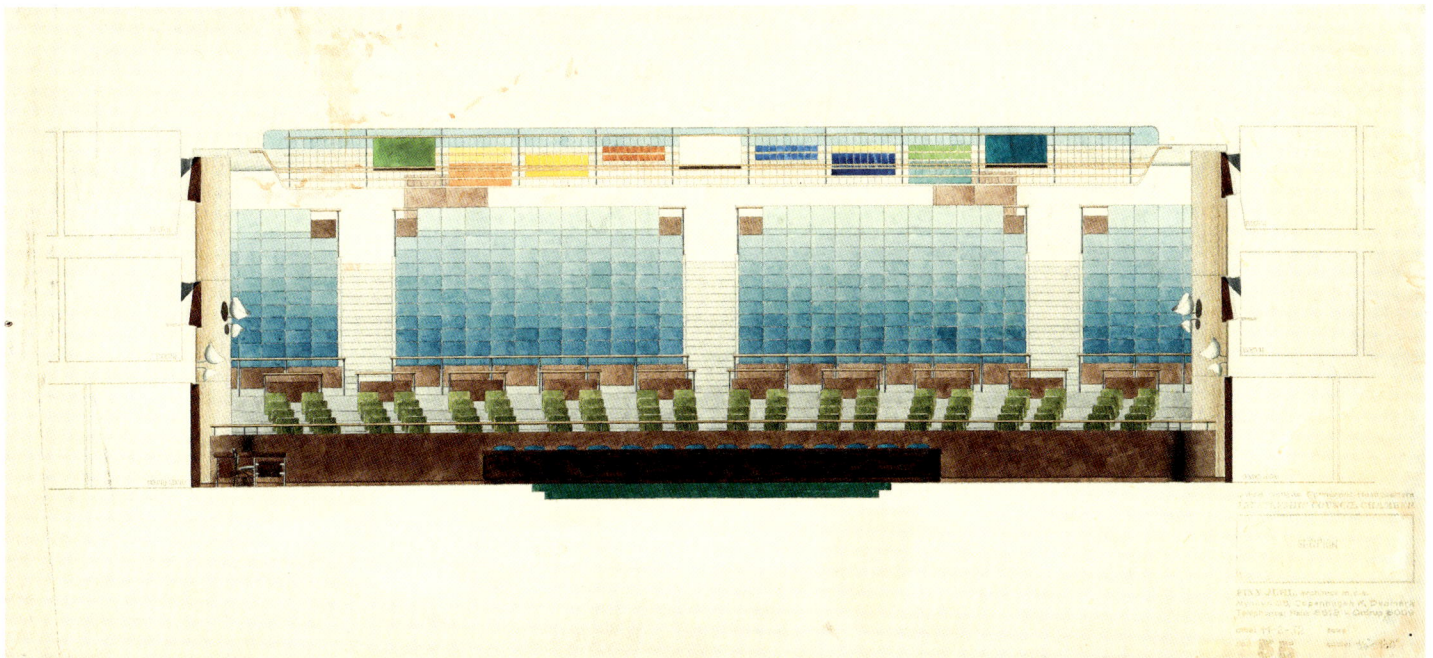

For the three Nordic countries, this was an opportunity to present Scandinavian modernism to both the international community and the United States. And it was not just the three chambers that received the Nordic touch. Quite apart from the fact that the first two secretary-generals of the UN were from Nordic countries, the Norwegian Trygve Lie and the Swede Dag Hammarskjöld, the lobby of the building that houses the General Assembly hall borrows from modern Nordic architecture. The architectural historian Michael Sheridan has pointed out that the cantilevered balconies are in all likelihood inspired by Alvar Aalto's Finnish pavilion from the New York World's Fair in 1939 – where the lead architect for the UN building, Wallace K. Harrison, had designed the two signature structures – while the long flight of stairs and the concave pillars recall Gunnar Asplund's work. Sheridan suggests that the Nordic expression helped to mediate between the UN as a Western project and as an enterprise whose very success depends on its being perceived as genuinely international by future member states: "Nordic Modernism offered an architectural language that was free of traditional symbols, such as the columns and pediments that had come to represent political power in the West. Rather than representing power, modern Nordic architecture offered a vision of reconciliation: between nature and technology, between tradition and change, and between different ways of understanding the world. As such it was ideally suited to the interiors of a global parliament."[47]

A Human Interior

The interior of the Trusteeship Council Chamber (1951) at the UN Headquarters is Finn Juhl's masterpiece as an interior architect. The chamber is a large space, over 1000 m², and both oblong and relatively low.

Even at first glance, this was no simple task. Juhl certainly did not think so. He was concerned about the height of the ceiling and noted after first inspecting the hall that "there is no sense or definition of space whatsoever".[48]

The light sources were also unevenly distributed and difficult to manage. As shown in photographs from the time, there were 8-m-high panoramic windows facing out onto Roosevelt Drive and the East River, with Long Island City's high-rises in the background. The light streamed in through a thin curtain that suggest the contours of the buildings on the far side of the river. Although this might be regarded as a genuine Nordic touch, it did raise the problem that everyone facing away from the window was turned to silhouettes in the powerful backlighting.

So much the more is Juhl's accomplishment in rendering the space comfortable and inviting, while also carrying through a distinctive and elegant design. The chamber is neither imposing nor anonymous. It is perhaps precisely human scale, human understanding and human reconciliation that Finn Juhl incorporates into the chamber. His point of departure was clearly the notion of a meeting, in the sense of a face-to-face conversation in mutual respect and in a light, warm, cordial atmosphere. Stepping into the chamber, one's first impression is of being welcomed. The intention is not to make people feel small in order to impress them – one is immediately an equal of the space.

Juhl drew the initial sketches for the Trusteeship Council Chamber and the *Delegates' Chair* during a summer holiday in Italy. Later the individual elements were elaborated, with for example the two-directional lamps.

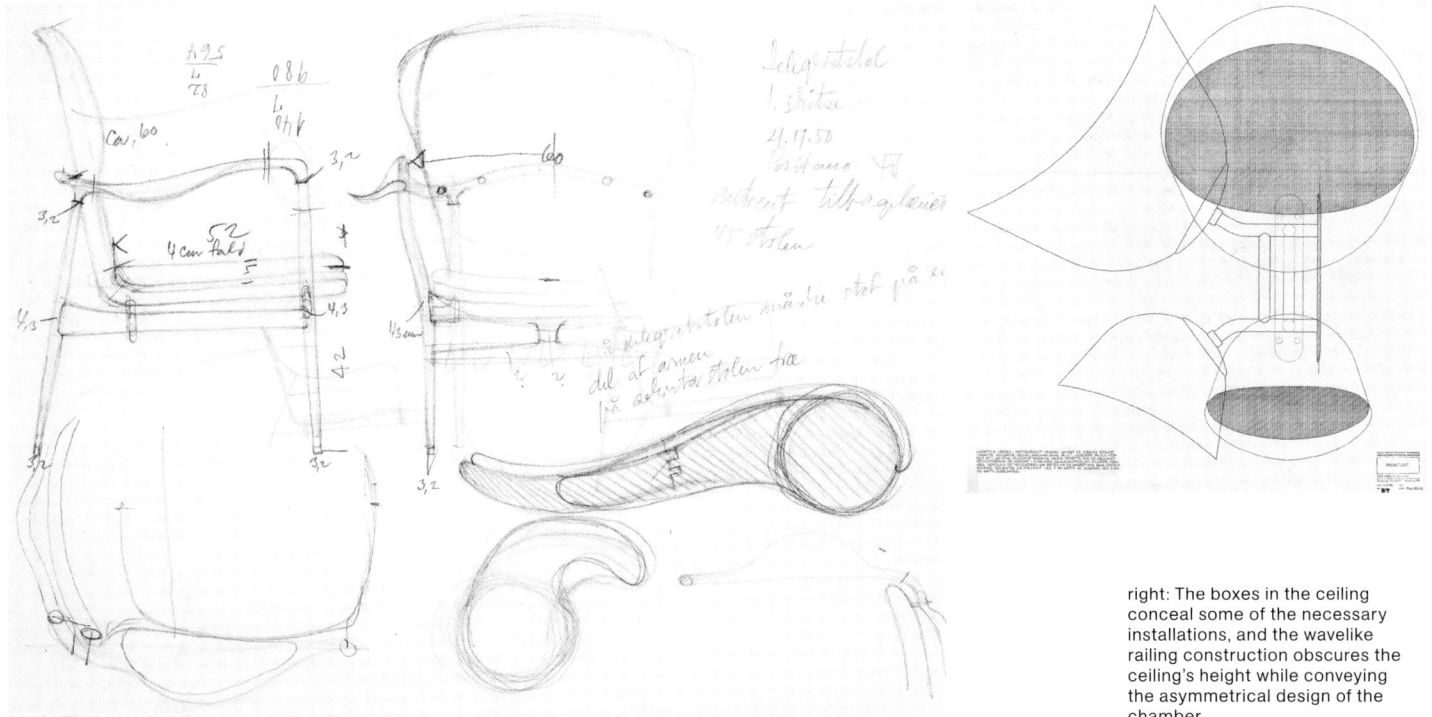

right: The boxes in the ceiling conceal some of the necessary installations, and the wavelike railing construction obscures the ceiling's height while conveying the asymmetrical design of the chamber.

When the Trusteeship Council Chamber at the United Nations Headquarters in New York opened in 1952, it was clear that Juhl had resolved the project with a masterly total design. Every detail, colour and piece of furniture was part of the larger whole, entering into a unique interplay with the ceiling elements and the pattern of the carpet. The photo shows the renovated chamber (2013).

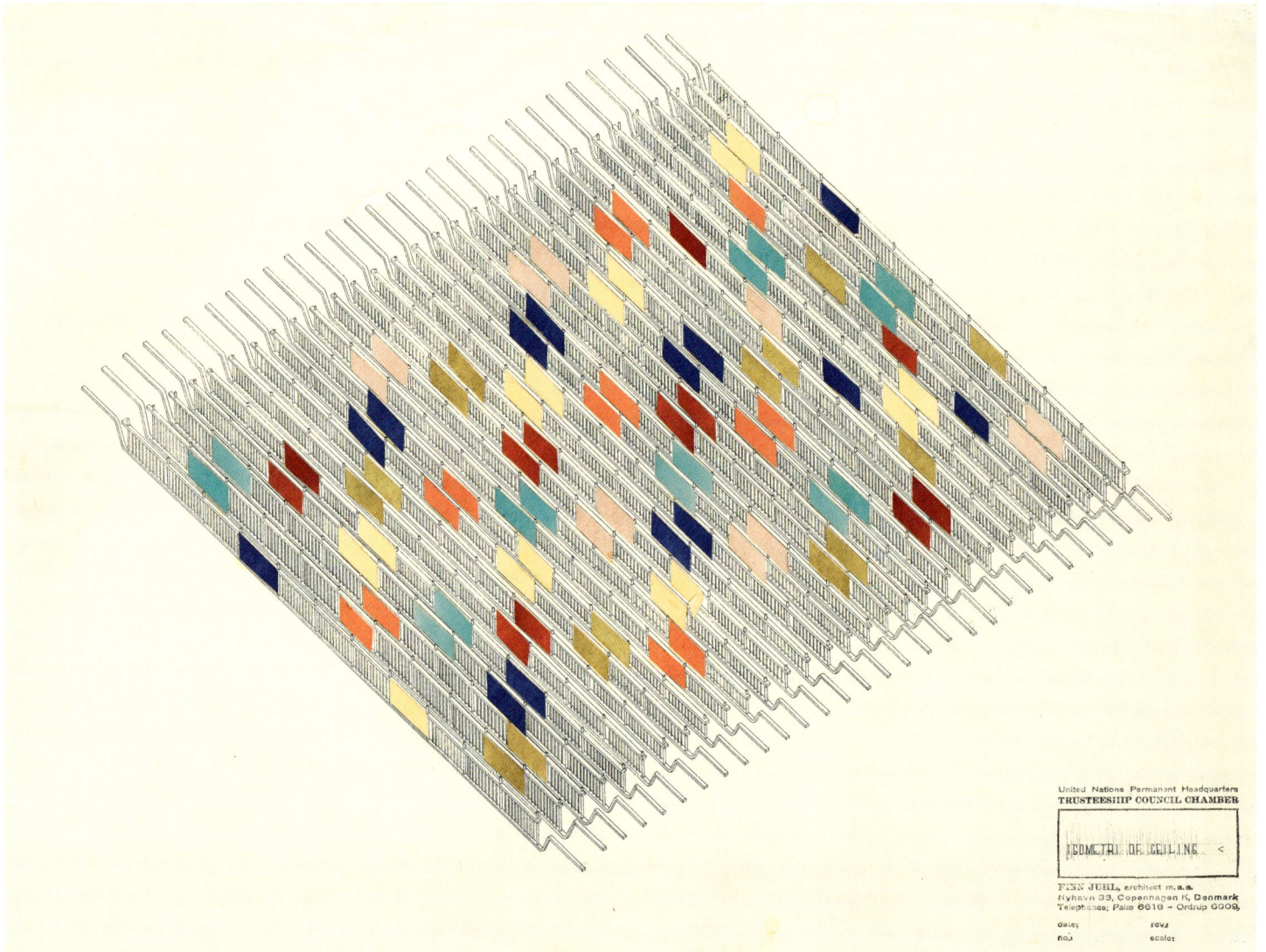

United Nations Permanent Headquarters
TRUSTEESHIP COUNCIL CHAMBER

ISOMETRI OF CEILING

FINN JUHL, architect m.a.a.
Nyhavn 33, Copenhagen K, Denmark
Telephones: Palæ 6618 – Ordrup 6009

date:
no.:
rev.:
scale:

The colour scheme in the ceiling decoration in the Trusteeship Council Chamber presented the biggest challenge to Juhl, as he wanted to create the illusion of a high-ceilinged room.

United Nations Permanent Headquarters
TRUSTEESHIP COUNCIL CHAMBER

DELEGATE'S CHAIR

FINN JUHL, architect m.a.a.
Nyhavn 33, Copenhagen K, Denmark
Telephones: Palæ 6618 – Ordrup 6009

date: 25.8.1950 rev.:
no.: 5 scale: 1:5

Juhl designed a chair for the delegates that Niels Vodder produced. Not happy with how it came out, however, Juhl redesigned it, altering the overall design and reducing the height of the back.

From Holiday Sketches to a Masterpiece

Finn Juhl sketched out the interior of this challenging space while on holiday in Italy. The first sketches, which are remarkably close to the final design, are dated *Positano, 12th July 1950.*[49]

Juhl covered the lengths of the walls in lightly curving, S-shaped ash panels in order to lend them more character and so create a more defined sense of space. Juhl would have preferred teak, but that was beyond the budget. The wall panelling surrounds the doors – unadorned planes of teak that sit flush with the walls and have large flat embedded panels of aluminium to push as one exits. The panelling also encircles horizontal rows of windows into the interpreters' lodges. The warm wooden strips and the lightness of the pale grey carpets inscribed with coloured strips, in combination with the theatrical ceiling construction, underscores a living atmosphere.

In autumn 1950, while his studio worked to carefully set the colours for the ceiling, Juhl wrote to the contractor: "Soon I'll send the first drawings of the ceiling, which has been and still is my biggest concern."[50] In order to avoid the impression that the chamber was low-ceilinged, Juhl decided against a conventional dropped ceiling, which would have concealed the lighting and ventilation fittings. Instead he raised most of the ceiling by almost 80 cm where it was possible, that is, the two areas between the exposed beams. He painted these fields sky blue. From this height he suspended a structure of teak railings supported by metal pipes. The railings varied in height, creating a wavelike motion across the ceiling. Between the rails were placed 49 rectangular metal boxes in an unsystematic, asymmetric design. The lighting and ventilation systems were built into the boxes, which were painted in one of six colours along their lengths, so that they resemble children's building blocks and are reminiscent of waving banners. In order to complement the wave-motion, the base of each box was cut diagonally at an appropriate angle.

The three-dimensional, floating installation is without doubt the most atmospheric component of the space. It works to negate the issue of the ceiling's height, while the light blue colour lifts the ceiling towards the heavens and beyond. Juhl got the idea for the boxes at an exhibition in Switzerland where a sea of flags were hung such that they formed a roof or a canopy of large vertical banners. The colours of the boxes were not meant to suggest national flags, however, as this might have been a little too obvious in this building for all the nations; instead, they were intended to give a ceremonial or celebratory feel.[51] Finn Juhl commissioned a model of his ceiling so that he could study the play of light, and in developing the lighting for the chamber he was assisted by Mogens Voltelen, who lectured in lighting at the Royal Danish Academy of Fine Arts, School of Architecture.

In order to give the Trusteeship Council Chamber a coherent expression, Juhl created a board with fabric swatches and colour studies to aid design decisions for the interior and furnishings of the chamber.

With and Without Armrests

The central feature of the chamber is its horse-shoe layout. In a Nordic, egalitarian manner, it stands in contrast to the hierarchical, auditorium arrangement that is otherwise typical of large committee rooms. Juhl designed two types of chairs for the chamber. The conference tables had already been determined. Abel Sorensen had designed a table fitted with microphones, speakers and electrical sockets for use throughout the UN Headquarters. He had also designed a fixed-position chair for the press- and public-seating areas, as well as for the advisers, who were seated in the meeting area behind the delegates.

What remained for Finn Juhl was to design a chair for delegates and a chair for secretary staff. He struggled to integrate the UN furniture with his own chairs and the interior design of the chamber overall. In his opinion, the UN tables were too short and too high, not leaving enough space for the chairs he had sketched. "It will be your task to design a chair with specific dimensions and maximum comfort," was Juhl's brief from Harrison's design studio.[52] He was also instructed to include a clear difference in comfort and stature between the delegates' chairs and those of the secretaries. In short: with and without armrests, thanks.

As with the overall design of the decor, Juhl had already sketched the *Delegates' Chair* while on holiday in Italy. On his return, the drawings of this initial *Delegates' Chair* were sent immediately to Niels Vodder, who produced a prototype, which was exhibited that autumn at the Copenhagen Cabinetmakers' Guild annual furniture fair.

Watercolour of the chair for the secretariat staff made by Niels Vodder in walnut.

Juhl's drawings of *FJ51* with the clear indications of material transitions that are seen in the final version of the *Delegates' Chair*.

Faces Turned Towards the Empty Space

The horse-shoe arrangement of the tables and chairs was likely part of Juhl's brief. In the centre, however, the secretariat tables are positioned in a sunken area, which means that all of the delegates in the chamber face in the direction of an empty space. This could be interpreted as the premise for all negotiation: the as of yet open possibility of agreement. It is a subtle combination of form and function that is typical of Juhl's interiors and was undoubtedly his own idea. Overall, the interior in the chamber is oriented towards the centre, and the sunken section alludes to egalitarian and Nordic ideals, since all delegates find themselves on the periphery in relation to the empty space above the secretariat tables, which becomes the central point of intersection".[53] This parity, ironically, forces the delegates to focus their attention on the invisible ones – the ones without armrests – who *serve* the people who are responsible, in turn, for reaching the consensus that is needed to save the world. Quite literally.

The Trusteeship Council Chamber just after the inauguration in 1952, seen from the audience seats. Over time it was necessary to make room for representatives of new member countries, and the furniture was therefore turned 180 degrees in 1964–1965. A subsequent renovation in 1977–1980 changed the chamber radically. Today, the chamber has been restored and recreated as a total design.

Renovating an All-Too-Popular Hall

The United Nations had 51 member states when it was inaugurated, compared with 193 today. Hence, the horse-shoe formation had gradually to be given up as the UN grew, and the chamber came to seat more delegates. Likewise, the slope of the floor was adjusted and the general decor changed, so that the chamber became quite removed from Juhl's original intention. Moreover, the chamber became increasingly run down, for after the Trusteeship Council's work ceased, the chamber became one of the most frequently used meeting spaces in the UN complex, in part because of its excellent acoustics.

Between 2007 and 2013, the entire UN complex was renovated. With state support from Denmark as well as funding from the Danish philanthropic association Realdania, the renovation succeeded in both restoring and renovating the chamber. The horse-shoe formation was restored. At the same time, a design competition was set up in Denmark to develop new tables and chairs for the secretariat. It was won by two young Danish designers, Kasper Salto and Thomas Sigsgaard. Their upholstered shell chair in laminated oak clearly nods to Arne Jacobsen's the *Swan*. The matching conference table, also in laminated oak, effortlessly updates the chamber's expression for the 21st century while maintaining a clear thread running back to the tradition and Juhl's generation.

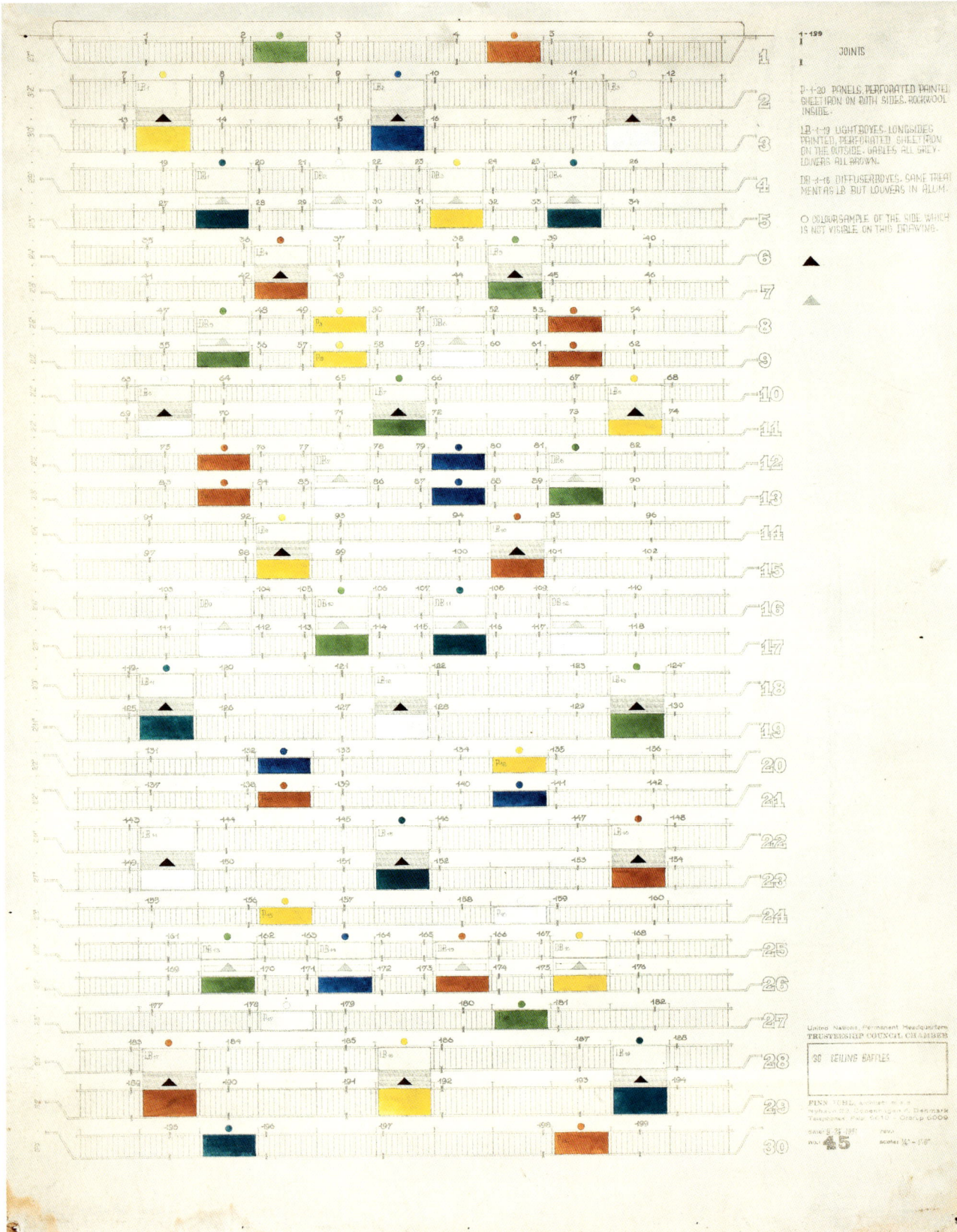

The early sketches of the carefully composed ceiling installation with multi-coloured lighting boxes show several shades of blue, white, green, yellow and orange scattered across the ceiling.

Principal Work

Finn Juhl himself regarded the Trusteeship Council Chamber at the UN as his principal work. And the decor is thoroughly 'Juhl-ian' down to the smallest details and formal components. For those familiar with *Radiohuset*, the chamber has many reminiscent features. Are the outstanding acoustics really a coincidence? After the efforts of a few years previous, working on *Radiohuset's* concert hall, with its panels and curving walls? Hardly. The lamps. Even the clock with its teak plate is a cousin of the clock in *Radiohuset*, and the chamber in New York shares many of the same qualities. But in the ceiling's box-kites there is also something playful and witty, which is different, less strictly modernist and less finished than *Radiohuset*. The decor represents Juhl 'gone solo', and on the international stage, to boot.

Juhl made no secret of finding neither Arneberg's traditional, monumental interior for the Security Council Chamber nor Markelius' overly cautious 'Asplund-ism' in the Economic and Social Council Chamber particularly accomplished. That said, in the appropriate contexts he expressed himself diplomatically. Michael Sheridan, as mentioned, sees Nordic modernism as having provided a conciliatory and understanding framework for the coming together of people and thought in the UN building's three Scandinavian chambers. By contrast, in a review from 1951 in the American magazine *Architectural Record*, the critic Henry Stern Churchill remarks on the chambers' more individual expressions: "All three … are the expression of personal ideas of decoration, not the expression of an underlying and common culture."[54]

Finn Juhl had designed lamps previously, among others for *Radiohuset* at the close of the 1930s, while he was working for Vilhelm Lauritzen's design studio. The lampshades of the two-directional lamps in brushed brass amplify the chamber's organic atmosphere.

Exhibitions in the United States

From the middle of the 19ᵗʰ century and right up until the advent of the Internet in the 1990s, exhibitions played a vital role in informing the public about new products. This applied in particular to the spheres of arts and crafts, and design. One exhibition that contributed hugely to promoting Danish and Scandinavian design in the United States was the touring exhibition *Design in Scandinavia*. It visited more than 20 American cities and was seen by at least 650,000 members of the public. Both Juhl's furniture and a collection of his teak bowls were exhibited. In fact, exhibition work became some of the most important commissions for Finn Juhl and his design studio during the busiest years of the 1950s and well into the 1960s. And quite a few of the exhibition assignments either originated in or toured the United States.

In 1951, the same year that Juhl was in full swing with the Trusteeship Council Chamber, Edgar Kaufmann asked him to design the *Good Design* exhibition in Chicago. Kaufmann had taken the lead on this annual exhibition series that had been established in a collaboration between MoMA and Merchandise Mart (or simply the Mart) – the world's largest trading house, a famous and still-standing 400,000-m² trade fair site in Chicago. It was the first time that a museum and a wholesale trade fair had exhibited together, and the goal was to present the best in modern design for the home. Charles and Ray Eames had designed the first exhibition in 1950, and in its second year the task was entrusted to Juhl.

Sketch for the exhibition *Design in Scandinavia* from 1953, where Finn Juhl drew a proposal for an adjustable panelled wall. The exhibition visited more than 20 cities and was seen by ca. 650,000 visitors, who were able to view several of Juhl's furniture pieces and bowls.

In 1954, the world-famous Danish silversmith Georg Jensen's company celebrated its 50ᵗʰ year, and Juhl was on hand to design the jubilee exhibition at the Danish Museum of Art & Design. Juhl adapted something of the visions of abstract painting to the monochrome silver in the cool, grey museum. He used coloured stands for the display pieces, while suspended banners, sisal runners on the floor, and a vaulting, fabric baldachin hung from the ceiling, brought warmth to the space. That exhibition also found an audience in the United States, where Georg Jensen's silver was already well known. *Fifty Years of Silver* was shown in Washington, Dallas and Saint Louis, among other places. Juhl returned to the baldachin-motif for *The Arts of Denmark* at the Metropolitan Museum of Art in 1960-1961, which presented Danish craftwork through the ages.

Finn Juhl was ambivalent about mass production, probably not least provoked by what he experienced in the United States, where industry scale was not always conducive to 'good design'. On the anonymous market, a piece of furniture was no longer a part of that broader whole he had been trained to search for as an architect – first with Kay Fisker at the School of Architecture at the Academy of Fine Arts and then in practice at Vilhelm Lauritzen's design studio. Juhl had made a name for himself in doing so. When a design is no longer a part of a whole, it becomes a thing in itself, imposing its ego onto its surroundings. A strong, personal expression will always dominate, refusing to content itself with being decoration. A natural example is Juhl's own *Chieftain Chair*.[55]

Even when reflecting on his first serious commission as an exhibition designer, and while in the midst of his biggest, international interior commission, Juhl seems to have recognised that a work of art cannot be placed into an exhibition room or a beautiful home or a design work without something being lost. To Juhl's credit, he fought on, insisting on approaching art from design and design from art, until he bravely positioned himself right there, where the unruly and impractical collides with the commercially marketable.

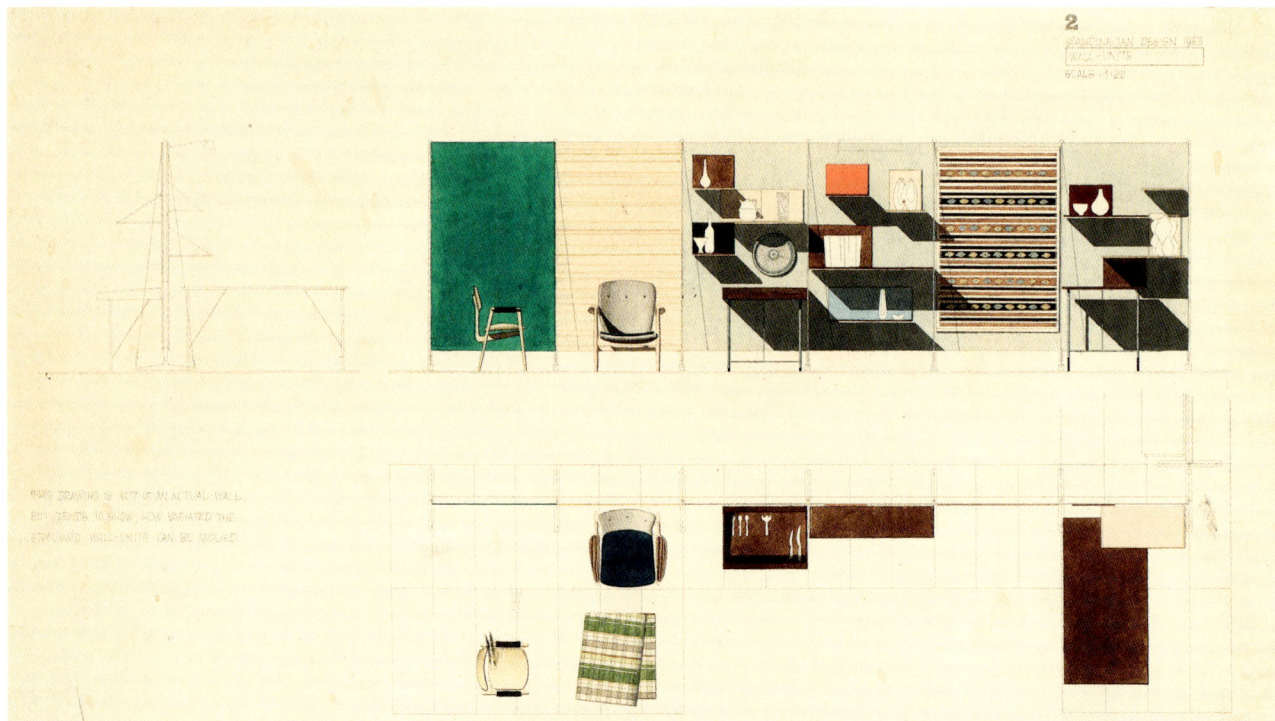

Finn Juhl standing at the entrance
of the Merchandise Mart exhibition
Good Design in Chicago, 1951.
This was the first of Juhl's many
commissions as an exhibition
designer.

WIRE

STANDARD-WALL UNIT (DRW.2)

PASSAGE

← STANDARD-BOARDS FROM WAL

PLATFORM FROM ABOVE ➡

"CEILING" OVER PASSAGE

BELOW IS SHOWN, HOW THE GABLE OF
A SHOWCASE CAN BE FILLED WITH A PHO-
TO. (COULD BE GLASS OR A COLORBOARD).
THE LONGSIDE-FRONT-IS A SLIDING
GLASS-PANEL. THE LONGSIDE-BACK-
CAN BE LEFT OUT, IF AGAINST A WALL,
OR GLASS-PHOTO-, COLOR-PANEL.
SUPPORT, SAME AS USED FOR TABLES,
SHELVES, ANY SIZE, GLASS OR WOOD.

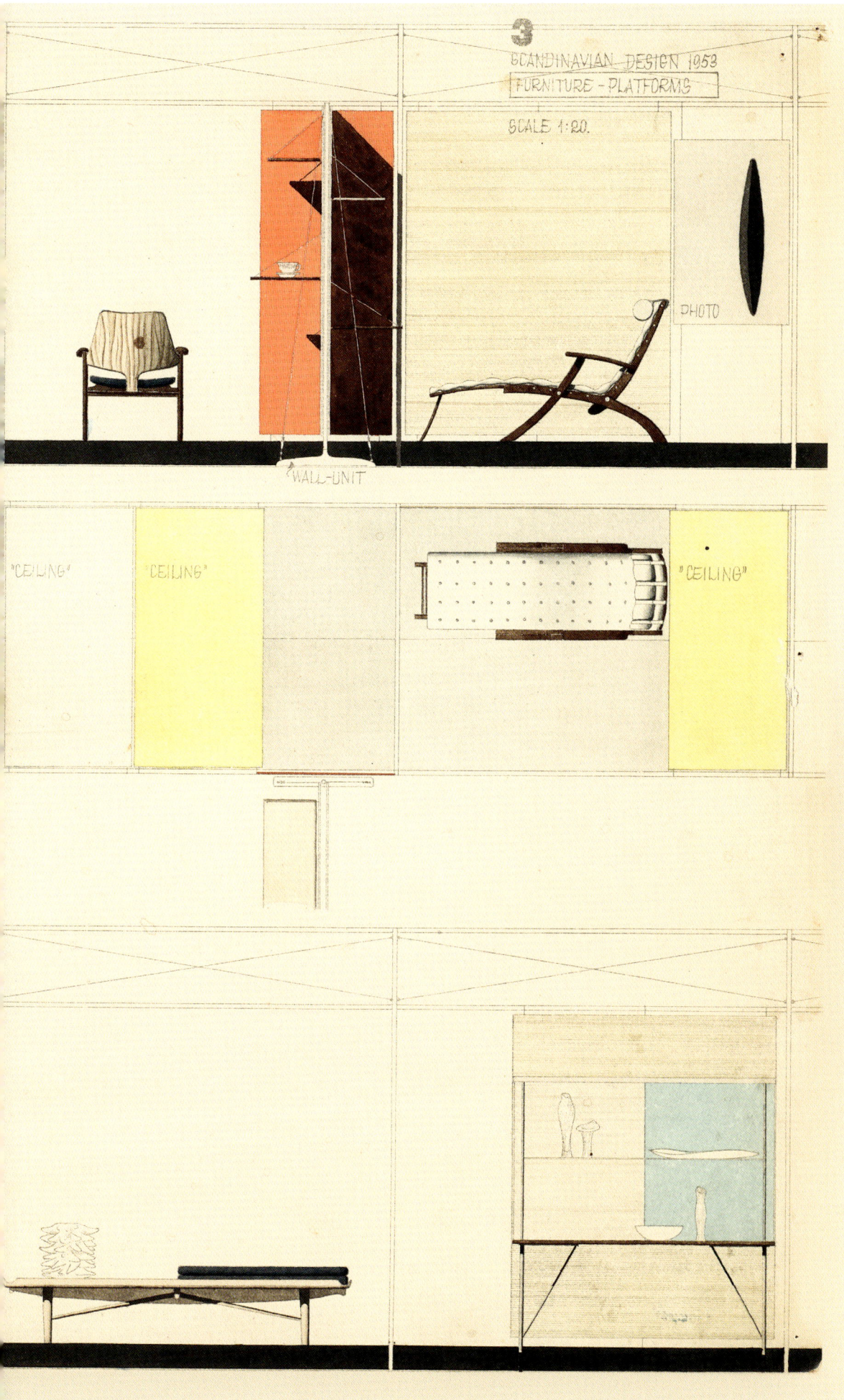

SCANDINAVIAN DESIGN 1953
FURNITURE - PLATFORMS

SCALE 1:20.

PHOTO

WALL-UNIT

"CEILING"   "CEILING"   "CEILING"

The exhibition *Design in Scandinavia* in the USA, 1954-1957. Neither Finn Juhl nor Danish furniture could ask for better marketing. Among the exhibits, one sees Kaare Klint's *Deck Chair* from 1933 (far right) and, on the lowest level, both Bruno Mathsson's easy chair *Eva* from 1941 and Juhl's own *Table Bench*.

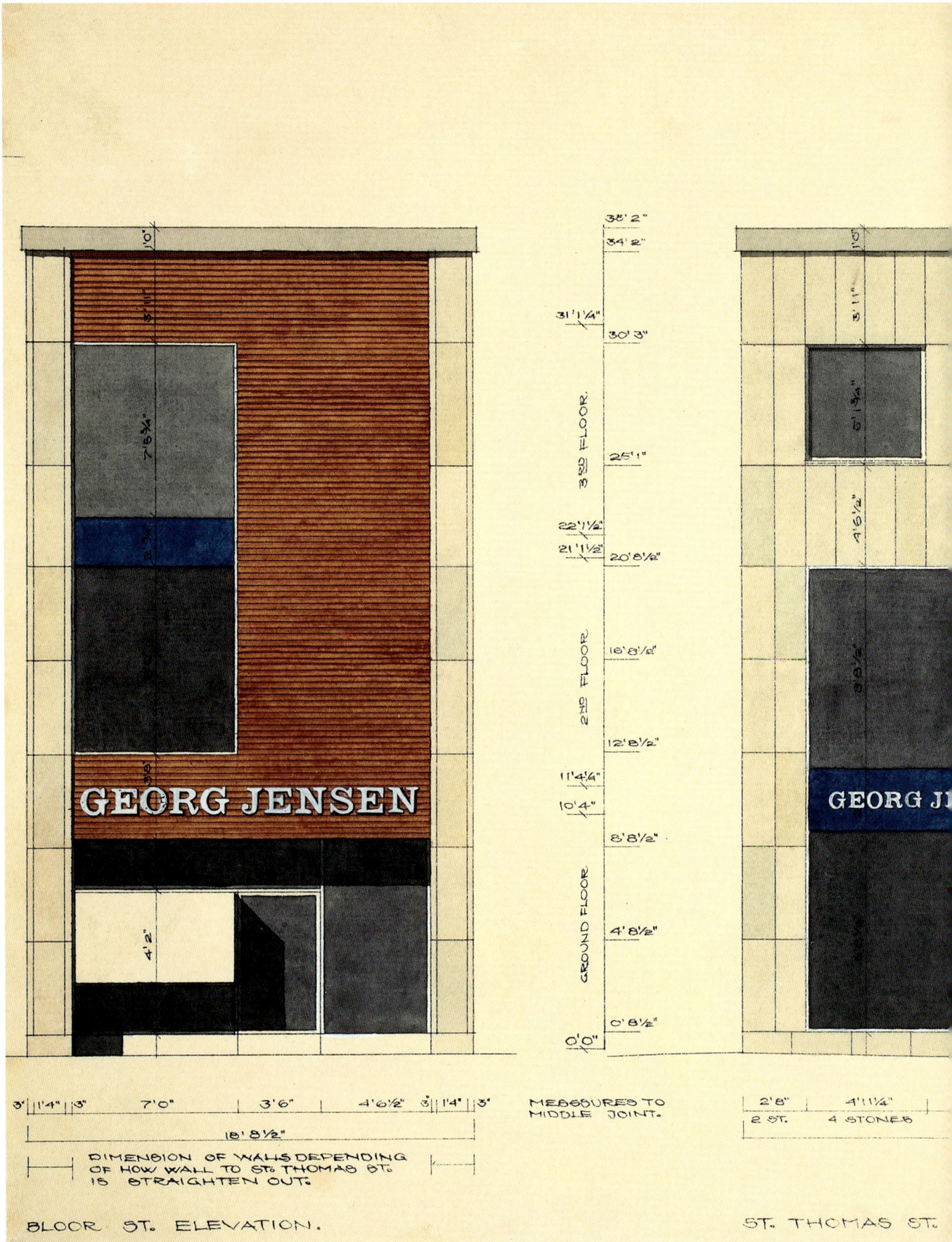

GEORG JENSEN

GEORG JI

MEASURES TO
MIDDLE JOINT.

3" 1'4" 3" 7'0" 3'6" 4'6½" 3" 1'4" 3"

18'8½"

DIMENSION OF WALLS DEPENDING
OF HOW WALL TO St. THOMAS St.
IS STRAIGHTEN OUT.

BLOOR ST. ELEVATION.

2'8" 4'11¼"
2 St. 4 STONES

ST. THOMAS ST.

Georg Jensen Inc. was the
first company to display Juhl's
furniture in North America. Juhl's
watercolour from 1956 depicts the
shop facades of the Georg Jensen
silversmith store, at the junction of
St. Thomas Street and Bloor Street
in Toronto, Canada.

GEORG JENSEN
GEORG JENS
2'8"
2 ST.
4'11¼"
4 STONES
5'11¾
5 STONES
2'8"
2 ST.
4'11¼"
4 STONES
5'11¾"
5 STONES
2'8"
2 ST.
4'11¼"
4 STONES
95'11"
8'6¾"
7 STONES

In 1952 Georg Jensen Inc. commissioned Finn Juhl to renovate their shop on Fifth Avenue in New York, and in 1957 Juhl renovated their shop on Bond Street in London (in collaboration with the English architect Trevor Dannatt). The following year, Juhl furnished a new store for Georg Jensen in Toronto, Canada, with his own wall unit as well as Danish furniture and Danish crafts. In the photograph of the ground floor interior, one can see Wegner's *Papa Bear Chair* to the left, and Finn Juhl's own *FJ45*.

Furnishing of Terminals and DC-8s for Scandinavian Airlines

Kay Fisker had designed the interiors of Danish ferries, and in the 1950s Finn Juhl designed the interiors for a string of Scandinavian Airlines' (SAS) flight terminals across the world, from Jakarta to Prague. The first was the SAS office in Gothenburg, which opened in 1958. SAS asked that Juhl design the interior of their combined ticket office and check-in terminals, which airlines then had in all major cities. The task involved giving the offices across different countries a uniform character, which at the same time set them apart from other airlines' images, as we would say today. If his experience of America was a foretaste of the working conditions of modern designers in an industrial and commercially driven market, then this commission for SAS had more to do with standardisation, design manuals and the requirement for all international collaboration: mastering the art of the possible.

The combined ticket office and check-in counter received a uniform, Nordic touch with light woods and a cabinet-maker's finish. Juhl went about the task in the same way as when he designed furniture and exhibitions, applied art and houses: his departure point was the best kinds of wood, employing the careful craftsmanship of cabinet-makers and a singular, human, architectural language. While developing a set of standard furnishings to accommodate all of the necessary functions including ticket purchasing, baggage check etc., Juhl also had to make a number of quick, off-the-cuff decisions as many of the offices were to be put to use right away.

Juhl worked methodically to ensure consistency and coherence across his design expressions, something that is taken for granted in companies and organisations today. When the Gothenburg terminal, the first, was decorated with the new furnishings, Juhl proposed that the knowledge of this office's function should be collected into a manual for 'an ideal SAS office'[56], complete with diagrams and instructions. This would form the basis for the interior design of future offices. Juhl's proposal of compiling design manuals, which would have contributed to establishing SAS's signature and brand, was ahead of its time – they are now used by many corporate groups. In the late 1950s however, they were something new, and the proposal came to nothing.

Scandinavian Airlines office in Paris, 1960. Finn Juhl furnished 33 SAS offices across the world, chiefly using his own furniture. Here *FJ45* is placed centrally, beside the spiral staircase.

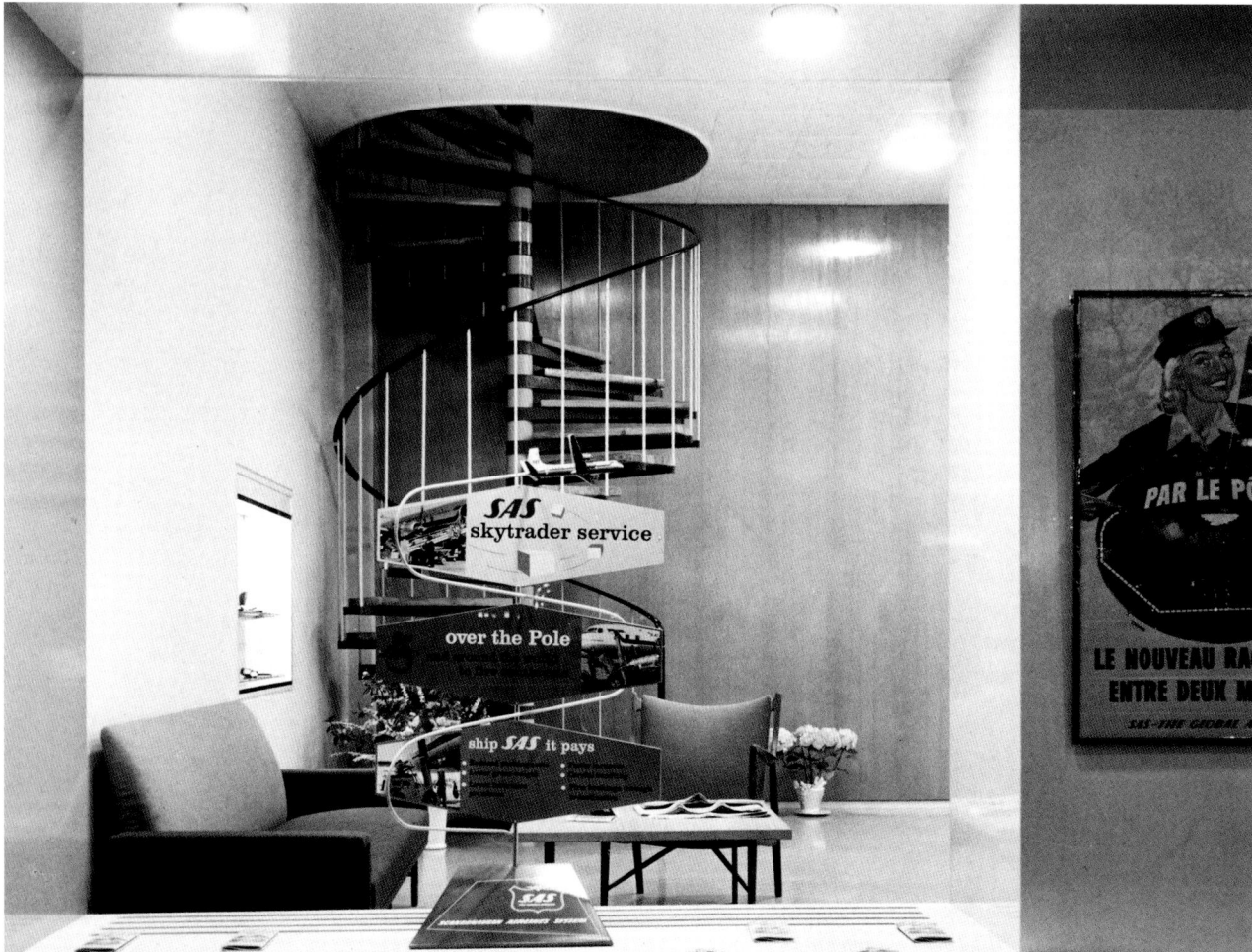

The first SAS office opened in Gothenburg in 1958, and Juhl was commissioned to give the offices a unified character the world over. SAS and Danish Modern went hand in hand. The SAS counter in Gothenburg (top) and a sketch proposal for an SAS office in Amsterdam (bottom).

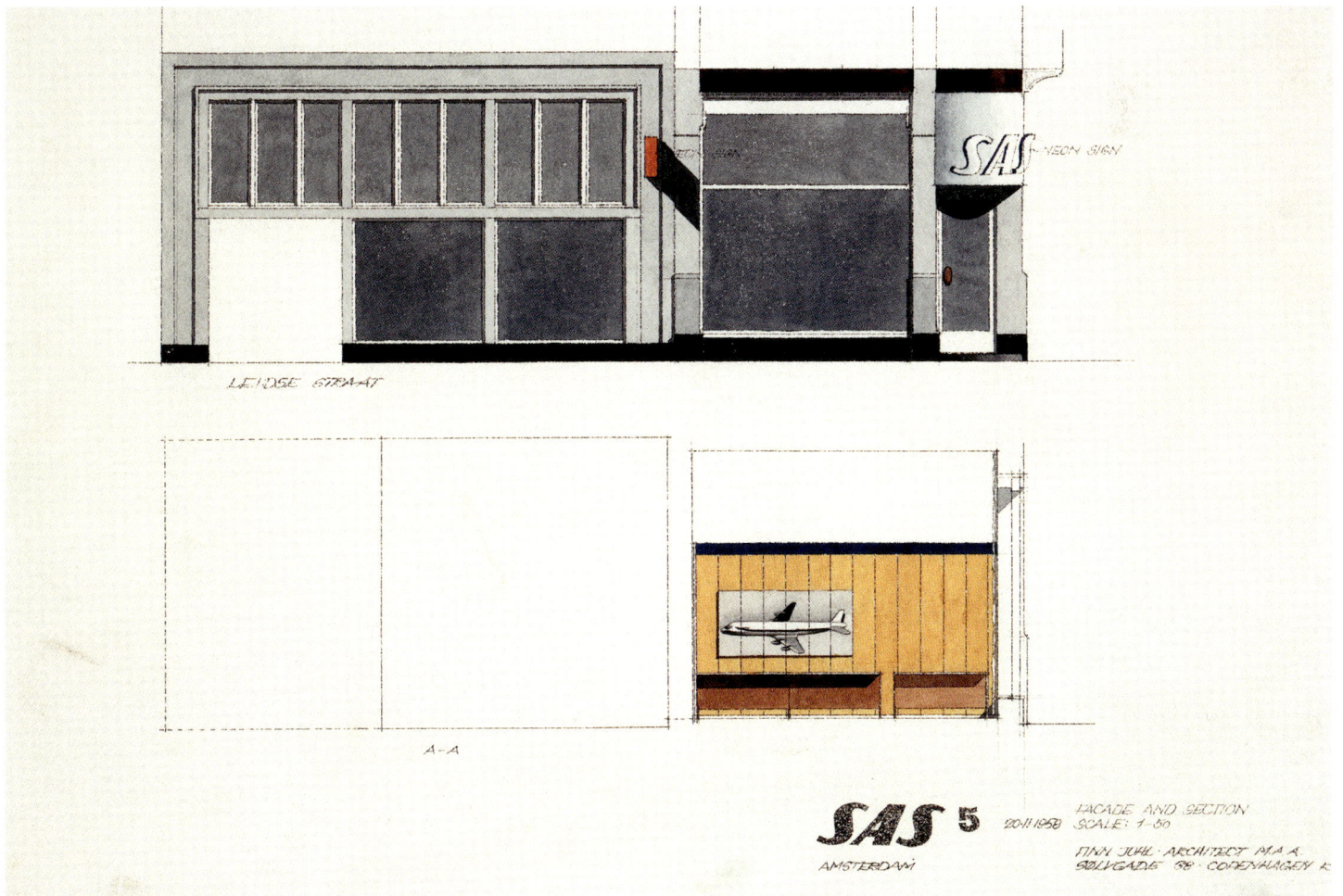

In any case, the offices were furnished one by one. To judge from black and white photographs from the time, the SAS offices were unmistakably Nordic, modern, functionalist and typical of Juhl. And this in Alexandria and Jakarta, Tokyo and Prague, Tehran, Johannesburg and a string of other international cities. Today, unfortunately, all of the offices are gone. Otherwise, it would be a great attraction to be able to check in at a Finn Juhl interior in Budapest or Kolkata.

For economic as well as practical reasons, Juhl had to collaborate with local furniture manufacturers and architects across the world, and so could not retain complete control of the execution and quality. Yet, he did what he could, travelling intensively during this period in order to supervise construction. His design studio's monthly reports to the SAS head offices in Stockholm evidence Juhl's frustration. On the 1st of May 1958 for example, when the office in Vienna was apparently nearing completion: "It has been quite surprising to note the many deviations that have occurred in relation to drawings, specifications and agreements. Architect Becvar has, for instance, carried out revised drawings for the expedition table with drawer fittings etc. that deviate completely from the agreed standard tables that Finn Juhl designed."[57] This is the kind of annoyance that most architects will be familiar with. And although the commission included many free flights when it was necessary to keep the local teams in check, it will doubtless have been a struggle to ensure that a sense of holistic uniformity and quality were accommodated within the structural and economic demands.

If this work on the SAS terminals gave Juhl air beneath his wings, things became even more interesting when Juhl was asked to design the interiors of seven new DC-8 jet airliners, which SAS had ordered from the Douglas Aircraft Company in the United States.

In December 1956, Juhl travelled to the United States to see a mock-up of the cabin and to trial a new chair type that the manufacturers had developed. The new model was to be used in the cabin – as Finn Juhl was repeatedly told. 'The reminders almost have the form of threats,' Juhl noted in his journal[58]. But typically of Juhl, he was not prepared to let even the near-impossible pass by without giving it a go, and so he sketched a proposal for an arrangement in the first-class cabins with revolving seats that were to be mounted. His idea was that these would be arranged a little offset from one another to ease access for passengers with window seating. However, it proved too ambitious in the timeframe to develop an entirely new chair, complete with lighting, oxygen mask, ventilation, ashtray, life vest, tray table etc. Had it been feasible, SAS would still have needed approval from the international aviation authority to deviate from a set-up where the passengers are permanently placed in the direction of flight. Instead, Juhl designed the galley, cloakroom, toilets and a lounge in first class. Likewise, he chose the cabin's colour scheme and designed its textiles and lighting.

Although Juhl had to give up his vision of revolving chairs in the first-class cabin, his colour and textile choices were by all accounts highly regarded. Juhl's watercolours depict the decor of a classical plane from a time before low-cost airlines transformed air travel from an exotic experience to an airborne bus trip. "You felt very comfortable in SAS's DC-8," wrote the Juhl expert Esbjørn Hiort, adding, "In the opinion of many, this was one of the most beautiful machines in their air during those years."[59]

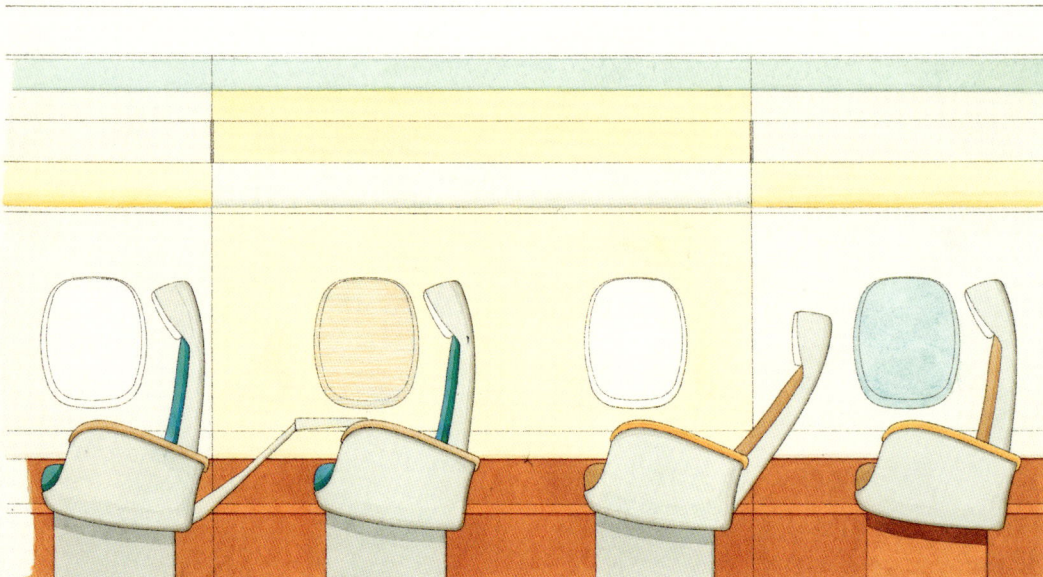

This watercolour from 1957, which depicts the colour scheme of a DC-8 plane, is typical of Juhl, who gave detailed specifications of the colours, textiles, and lighting of his interior designs.

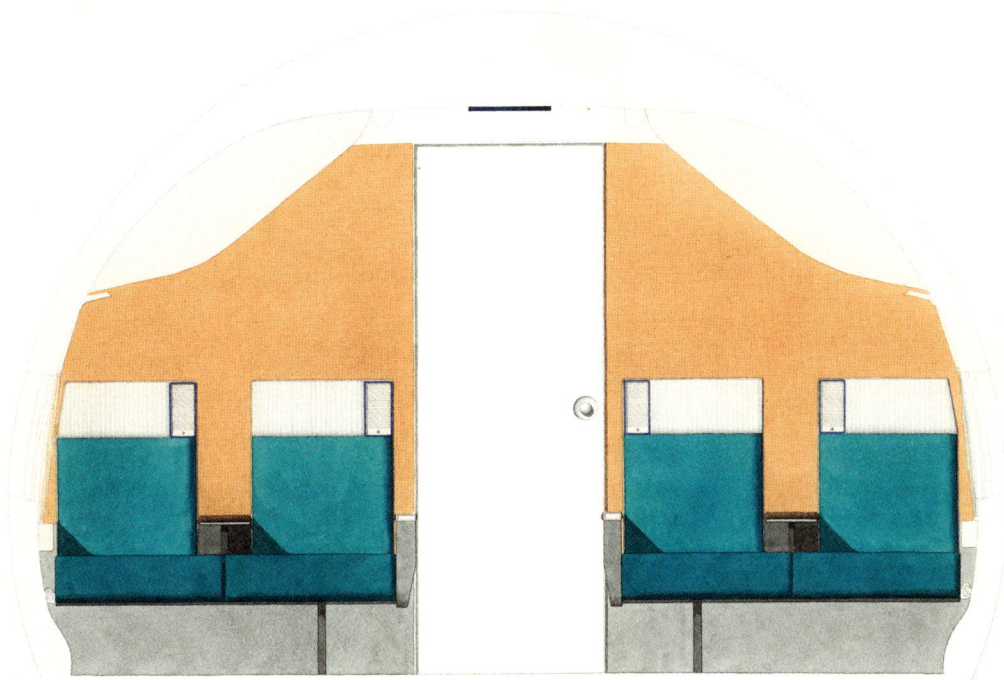

Finn Juhl proposed to SAS that the first class section should be fitted with revolving chairs that were not mounted in the standard arrangement, as is shown in the (top) picture. Eventually, the proposal was rejected, and SAS opted for a standard chair. A watercolour (bottom) from 1957 by Finn Juhl, showing a cross section of the tourist class section in an SAS DC-8 plane.

Perspective drawing of the cabin in the DC-8 jet plane, where the welcoming interior is marked by a colour scheme with good contrasts.

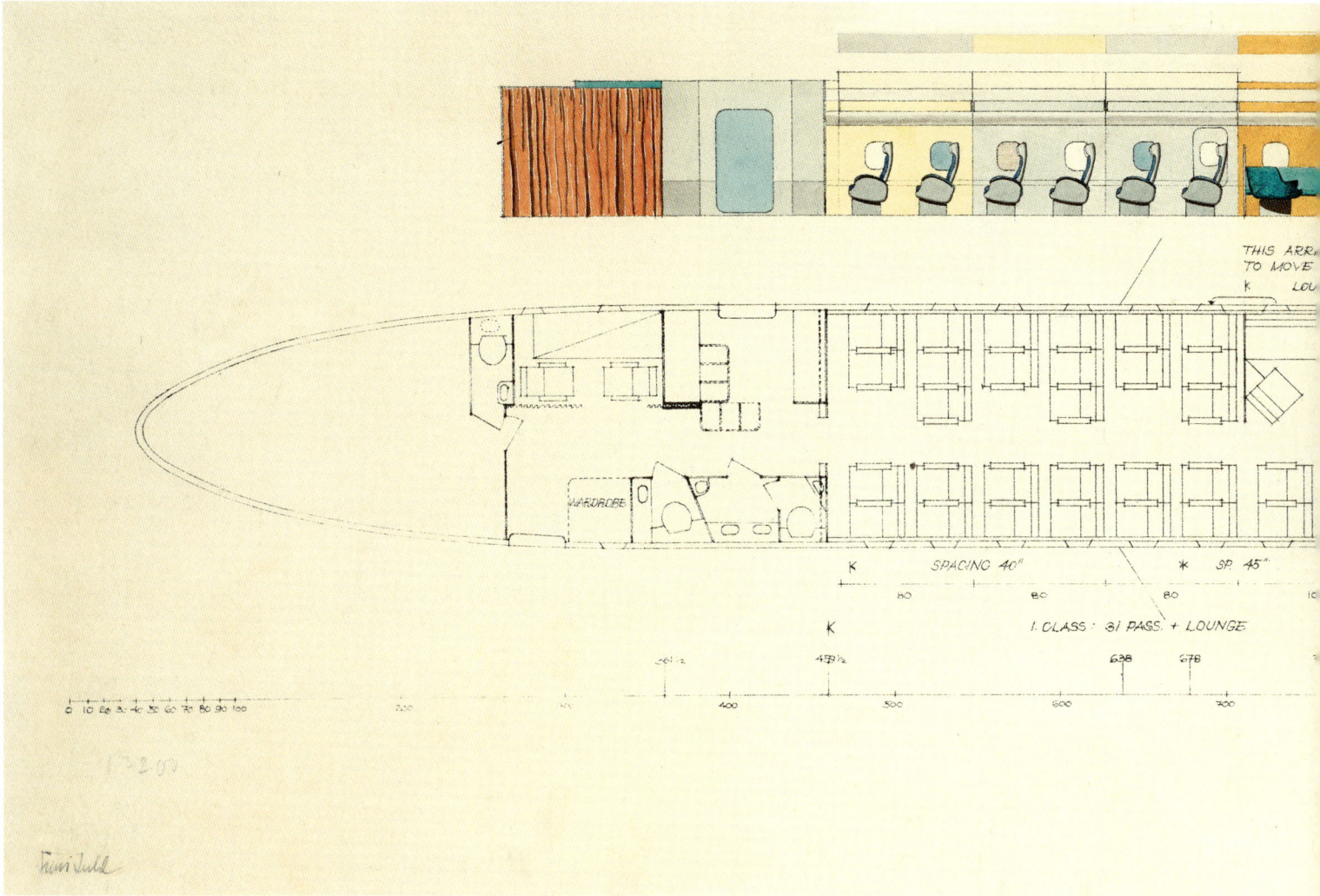

THIS ARR.
TO MOVE
LOU

WARDROBE

K SPACING 40" ✳ SP. 45"

80 80 80 10

1. CLASS: 31 PASS. + LOUNGE

0 10 20 30 40 50 60 70 80 90 100 200 400 500 600 700

1:200

Finn Juhl

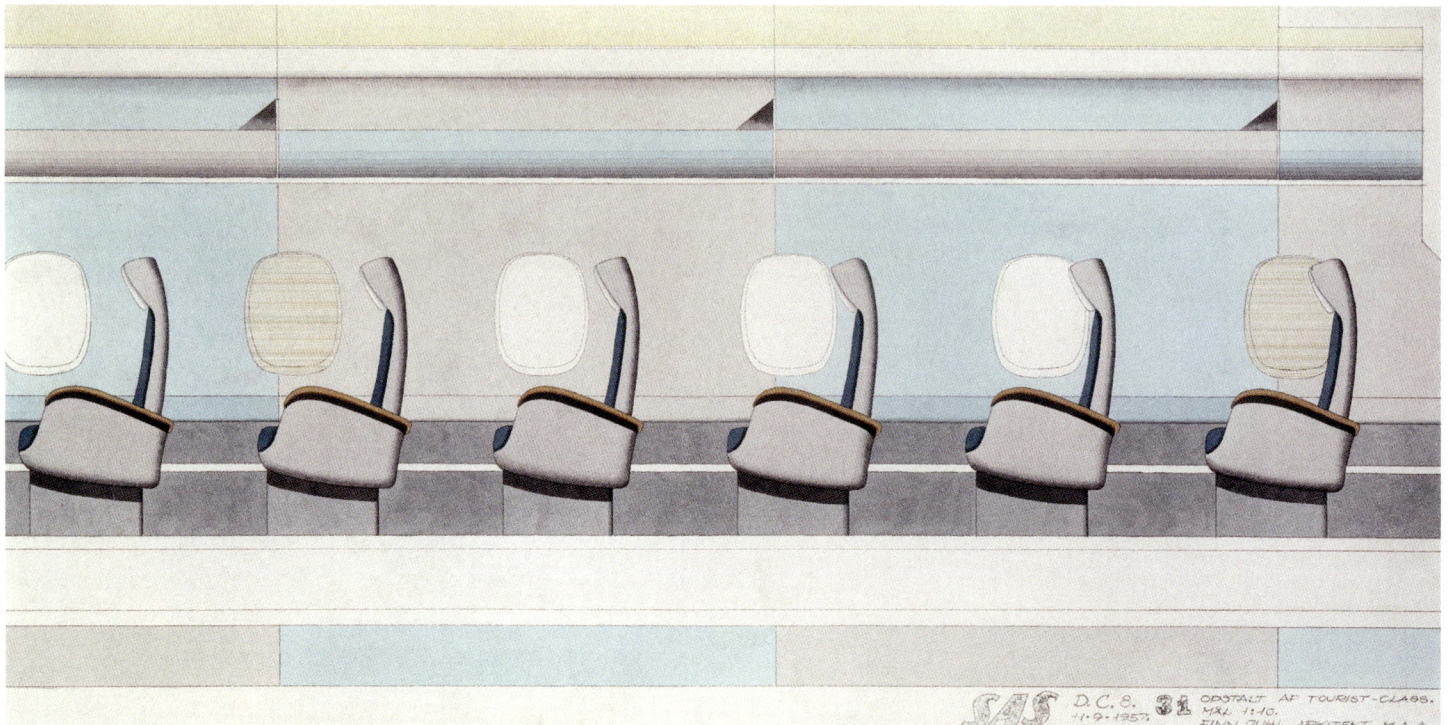

SAS D.C.8. OPSTALT AF TOURIST-CLASS.
11·9·1957. MÅL 1:10.
FINN JUHL, ARKITEKT M.A.A.

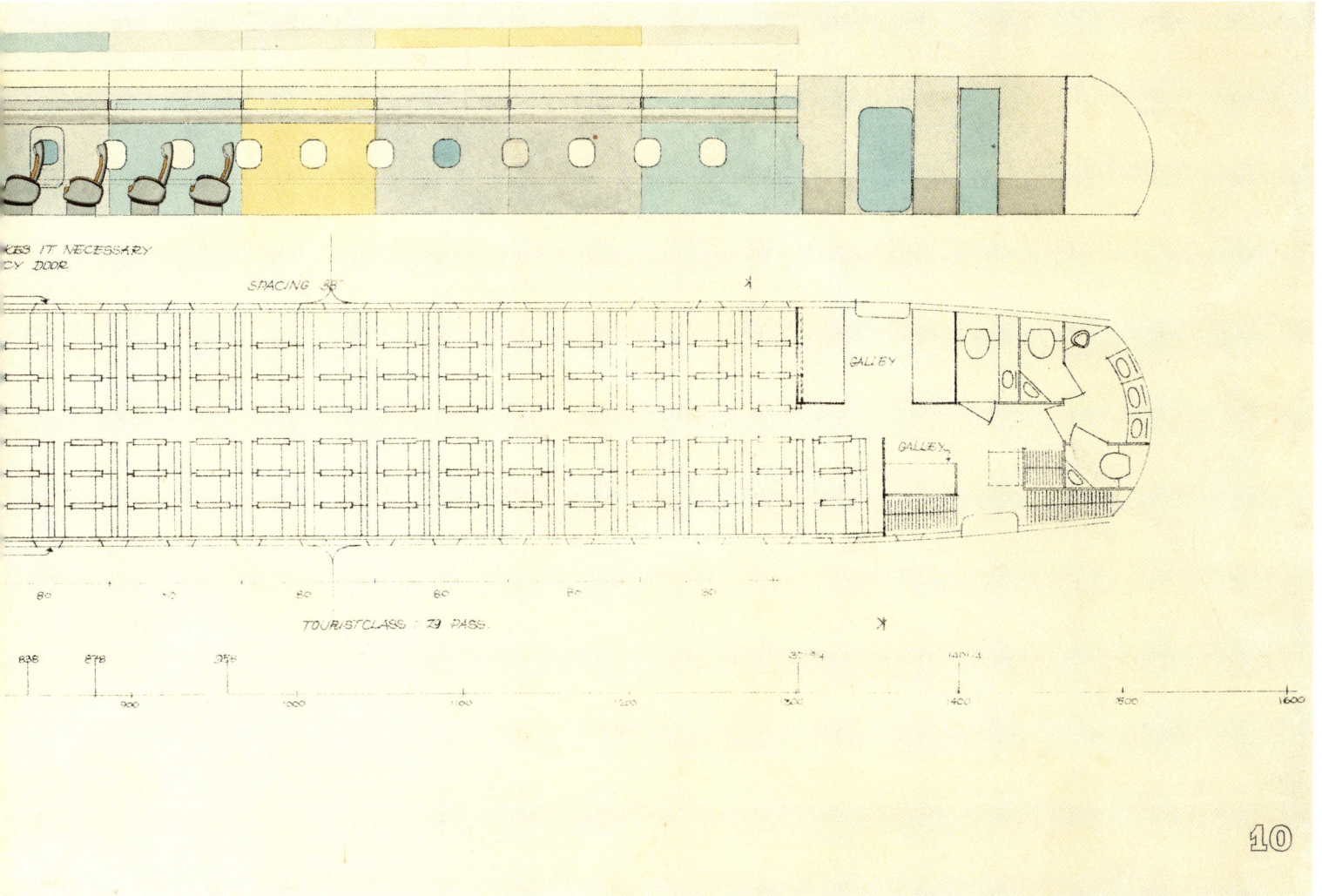

GALLEY

GALLEY

TOURISTCLASS : 79 PASS.

10

SAS had ordered seven new DC-8 jet planes, which replaced the DC-7 propeller-driven aircrafts, from the Douglas Aircraft Company factory in Cleveland, USA. Finn Juhl hoped to have a more elegant chair accepted than Douglas' rectangular standard chair, but he was not successful. Juhl's proposal (top) for a revolving chair in the first class section in the middle of the cabin. The watercolour (left) is from 1957 and shows the plan and elevation of the interior of an SAS DC-8.

1950 —— 1982

The Right
Form

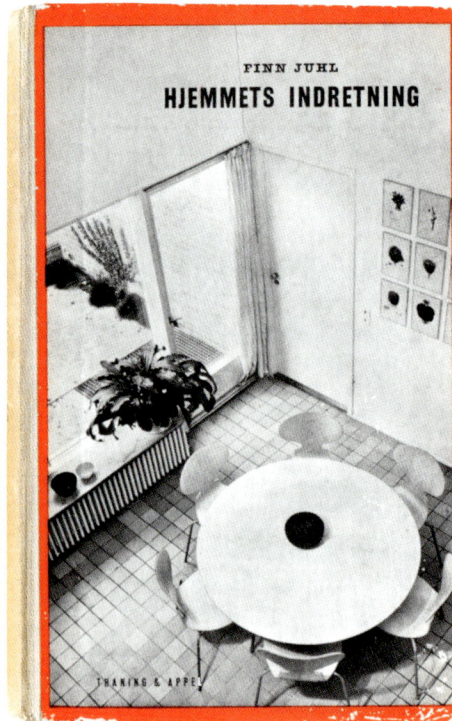

In 1954 Finn Juhl presented his experiences and points of view in the book *Hjemmets Indretning* (Furnishing the Home). The earliest known written text of Juhl's is a review of the book Acceptera (Accept!), a modernist manifesto written by the Swedish art historian Gregor Paulsson, the architect Gunnar Asplund and others who had taken part in the *Stockholm Exhibition* in 1930. Architecture encompasses all scales, from urban planning to the furnishing of kitchens, and all levels require a modern, analytical approach based on the requisite functions and the right form. Gunnar Asplund and the other Swedish functionalists had in 1930 called on architects to accept these modern challenges, in a book with precisely that title.

A Sharp Young Man

Already as a 19-year-old architecture student, Juhl called 'functionalist' an idiotic concept. This speaks to the brazenness of youth but also a more mature awareness, given it was just 1931. The occasion was Juhl's review of *Acceptera* (Accept), Nordic functionalism's manifesto penned by the Swedish art historian Gregor Paulsson, architects Gunnar Asplund, Sven Markelius and others. The manifesto grew out of the *Stockholm Exhibition* and the thrill of modern architecture's arrival in Scandinavia. What should be accepted, the authors claimed, was everyday life and the challenges it poses for architects. Rather than applying arbitrary historical styles to arbitrary buildings and furniture, the goal should be to define these objects by analysing the needs they meet. In this way, architects could develop the most rational possible designs so that form would always follow function. This might then be termed functionalism, but, as the young Juhl observed, the term was inappropriate for "the modern search for the right form".[60]

But what was the right form? If it was inappropriate to call modern architecture and design functionalist, it was because pure function (the solving of a problem) does not have a single form. Nature abounds with ingenious, functional solutions, but they find expression in a variety of ways. The same applies to human artefacts, which are largely modelled on the laws and methods of the natural world. The early functionalists in the 1920s and early 1930s believed that *the machine*, as an almost purely functional object, could be a model for all other constructions, including architecture and design. Machines, like all tools, have an inbuilt rationality, based on economic, structural and social factors. They are economically and structurally streamlined to meet their purpose, and because they can be utilised by anyone who needs them, they serve a democratic and social purpose. However, the aesthetic aspect of design remains unresolved unless one assumes that the appearance of a thing is fully determined by what it is, its design reflecting only its application. In short, that a thing *is* its function. The same function can of course be achieved by different aesthetic expressions, otherwise there would be no such thing as design. But could the aesthetic appearance of an object be streamlined in the same way as its utility? This is the basic hypothesis that functionalism puts forward, and which underlies the aspiration of finding 'the right' form.

Furnishing the Home

With his background and interest in art history, Finn Juhl could never quite give himself to functionalism's ahistorical admiration for machine aesthetics. Indeed, this may well explain his early, thoughtful scepticism about the very concept of functionalism. In his 1954 book *Hjemmets Indretning* (Furnishing the Home), Juhl set out his own views of how the modern search for the right form should be understood. It is a manual for modern architecture and design, viewed, as it were, from the inside. From inside a home, an inhabitance with its decor and furniture; from inside the Danish housing industry during the 1940s and 1950s; and from inside a sensibility: Juhl's own experiences as an architect, furniture designer and, not least, a teacher at the School of Interior Design, a position he left the following year. The book collects a series of articles from the journal *Hvordan. Hjemmenes raadgiver* (How. The Home Advisor) and was likely also intended as a collection of textbook examples, based on considerations from his teaching. It might also have been intended as a job application. Kaare Klint had died in March 1954, and a successor was needed for the Chair of Furniture Design at the Royal Danish Academy of Fine Arts, School of Architecture. Finn Juhl applied. So did Klint's students Ole Wanscher and Børge Mogensen. In the end, Mogensen withdrew his application, and Wanscher was instated. It has been supposed that Juhl, not having attended the Furniture School, was considered to stand in such clear opposition to Klint that he could not possibly be offered the position, and that it therefore went to Wanscher, because it was seen as imperative to continue the Klint School at the Academy. However, Wanscher did have teaching experience in furniture design from the School of Arts and Crafts, and he was a thoughtful analyst and historian, as is clear from his 1955 book *Møbelkunsten* ('The Art of Furniture'). Indeed, if one compares Juhl's and Wanscher's furniture, their aesthetic expressions are not so different. What instead might have played a role in Wanscher's appointment over Juhl is that the relationship between the Academy of Fine Arts and commercially successful practising architects – particularly those who had worked in America – could at times be somewhat strained. Finally, interior architecture or design has never had the same professional prestige as 'proper' architecture. Interior design was seen as an American whim, something taught through a correspondence course – in its most condescending description, a pastime for bored housewives. Right into the 1960s, architecture was considered a male discipline, which required a background in other 'masculine' disciplines, such as bricklaying or carpentry. Until recently, it was normal for medium-sized design studios to call in a (typically female) designer to set the colours for their projects. Or for a studio's best illustrator to add a few little sketches of interiors to an architectural rendering as an afterthought. In 1955, perhaps it would not do for an academy professor to be as closely associated with 'interior decoration' as Juhl was.

Finn Juhl with a class of graduating
students from the School of Interior
Design in Copenhagen (1955).

In fact, *Hjemmets Indretning* gives the impression that Finn Juhl had great respect for Kaare Klint and aligned himself with Klint's approach. In the book, Juhl dates the advent of modern Danish furniture design to around the First World War, when Klint designed his *Faaborg Chair* (1914). Juhl describes Klint as a pioneer to whom the times' most talented furniture designers owed their education.[61] He writes of the rational planning that dictated Klint's furniture and describes the many considerations and functions that condition Klint's designs as a technical *tour de force*. He even defends Klint's aesthetic idiom and his affinity for English styles, something Juhl had been critical of in the past. He also mentions other sources of inspiration for the Klint School, in particular the Shaker furniture and traditional, anonymous furniture of the Mediterranean:

"When Klint chose these as models, it was because they so clearly advocate the honest approach that he also strove to reintroduce and fundamentally renew ... anyone must admire the conceptual and artistic force and stringency that characterise his furniture ... It is essential to mention Klint and his contribution, since it is as alive today as when he set out, and because it has preserved its ability to shape new furniture designers through a specific working practice."[62]

Børge Mogensen and Arne Karlsen – Klint disciples who would later criticise Juhl for abandoning their teacher's ideals – would not have put it differently. True to form, however, Juhl also included a subtle quip about his competitor, Ole Wanscher, whose chair is described in a perfunctory caption: "A new attempt from this designer, whose work otherwise rests on a traditional and English-inspired foundation."[63]

The position set out in *Hjemmets Indretning* is clear: in line with the view of the Bauhaus School, modern architecture is a holistic enterprise. Everything is connected, from urban planning and the scaling of housing blocks, through investigations of the number of gramophones in Copenhagen flats or the most rational way to arrange a kitchen, right down to the use of oak in desk drawers to keep them from warping. For Juhl, this honest approach was also a point of departure for exploring new production methods and materials and for establishing a rational, contemporary expression. In a single paragraph, a single breath it seems, Juhl moves effortlessly from an analysis of the new production methods and materials such as moulding in plastic and bending in plywood; to an overview of the various types of wood and their applications; to common-sense advice on furnishing ('Never buy more furniture than you absolutely need') or how best to remove stains from tabletops; to a general defence of modern floorplans with fewer and more flexible interior walls and partitions that better allow a house to meet changing needs or growing families. Juhl concedes that open-plan homes, such as Philip Johnson's *Glass House*, are avant-garde, but at the same time he points out that they are simply the logical consequence of functional analyses: space and furniture should not dictate the way we live but make room for our lives to unfold.

Porcelain service design for Bing & Grøndahl in 1950. Fifty-two of its items are located in the house on Kratvænget. The service was never put into production.

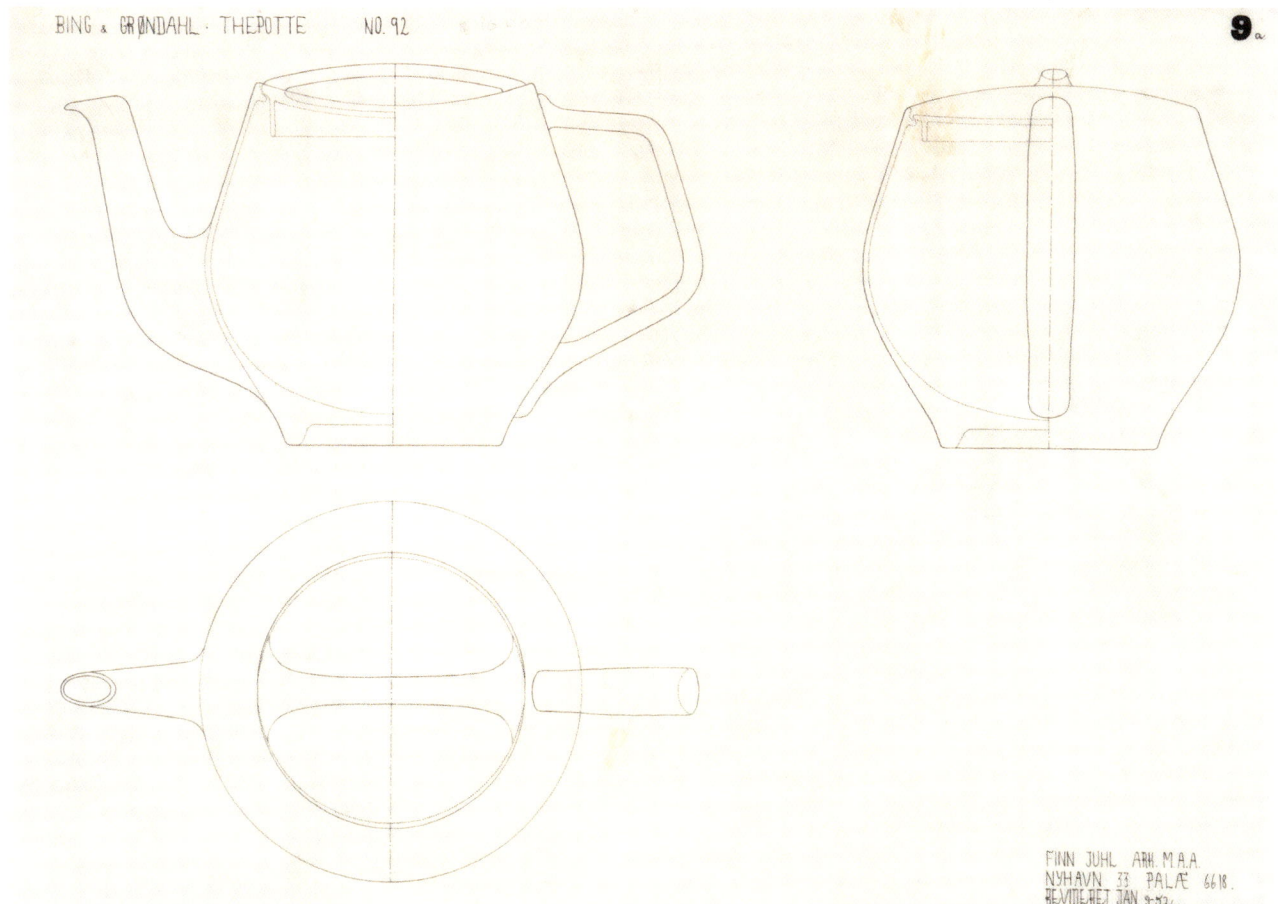

BING & GRØNDAHL : SAUCE KANDE NO. 8   FINN JUHL, ARK. M.AA.   NYHAVN 33 PALÆ 6618   24. 4. 50   7a

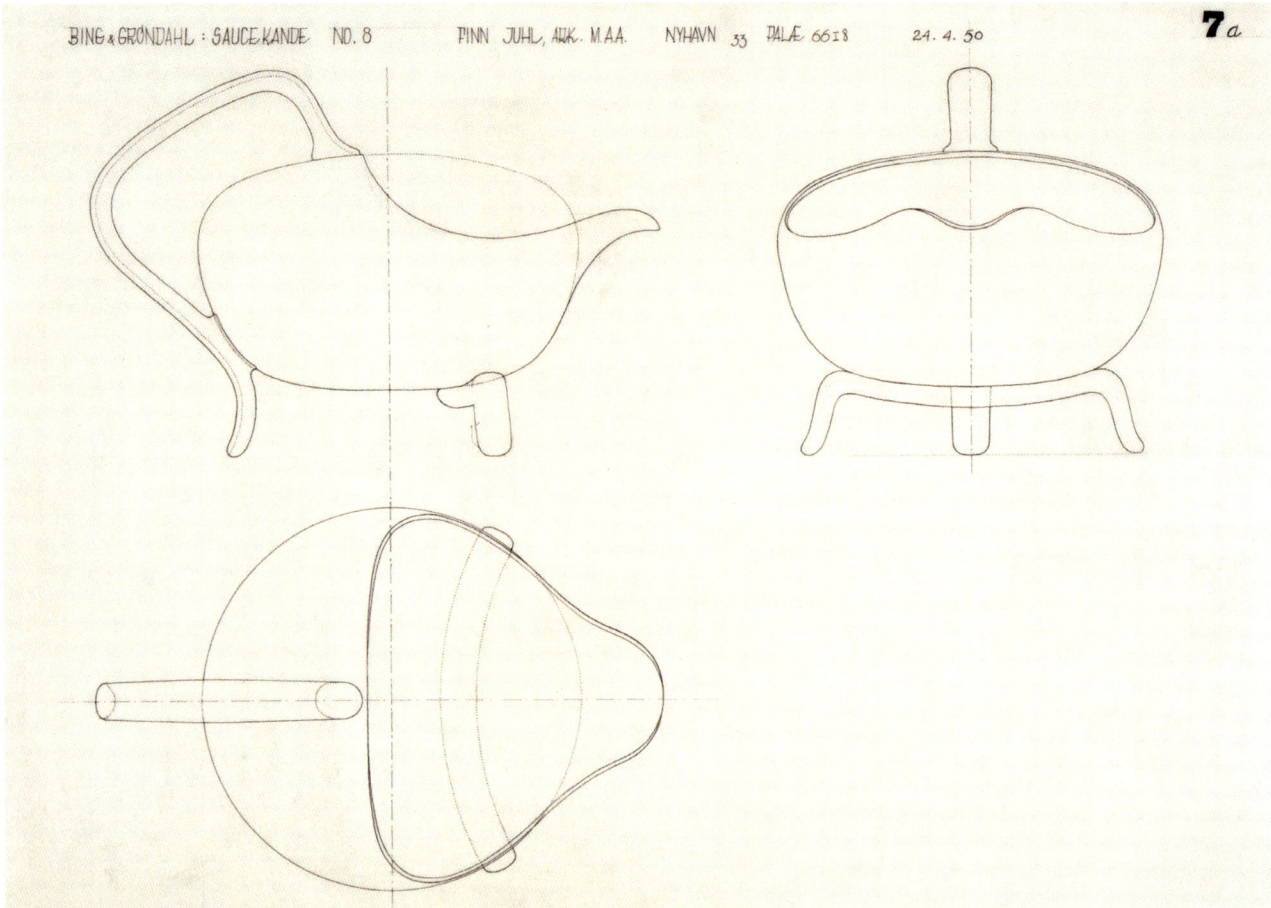

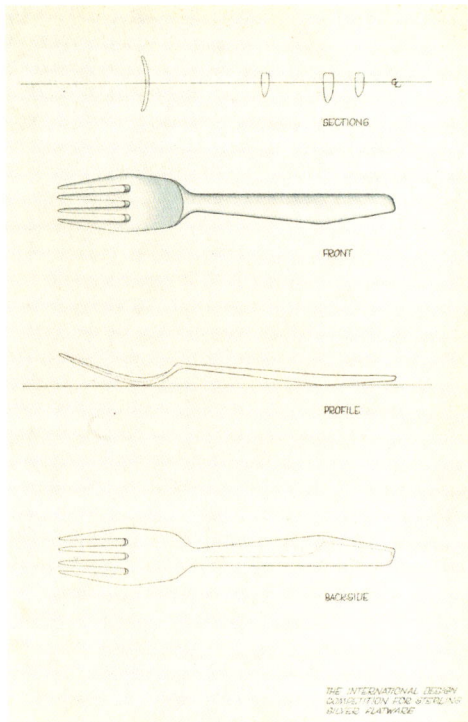

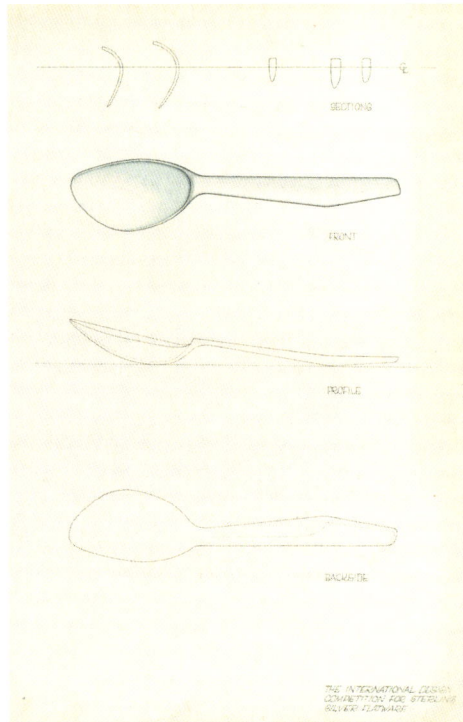

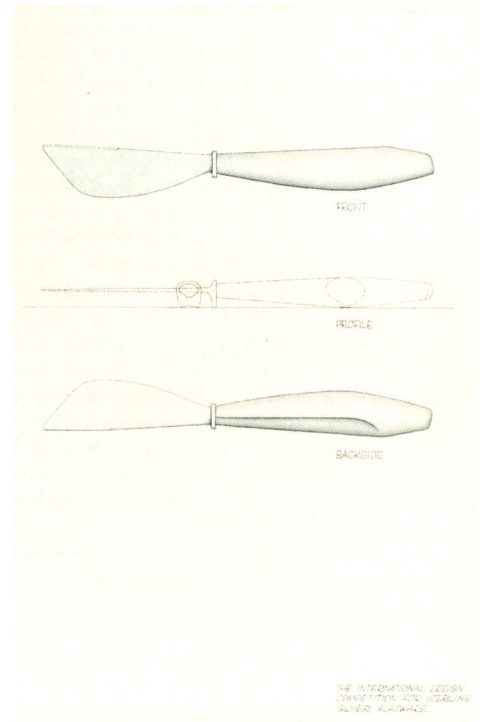

Finn Juhl hoped to be able to fill his
house with objects he had designed
himself. Neither his service for Bing
& Grøndahl nor the silver cutlery
that he entered into a competition
ever made it to production,
however. This was the last time Juhl
tried his hand at that type of design.

Morality versus Fashion

The modern endeavour is thus an attempt to combine a moral idea about honesty, sincerity and naked function with this new apprehension of space, made possible by new means of construction and developed in step with new habits and structures of daily life. It is perhaps typical of Juhl's sensibility and sense of synthesis that he describes this new apprehension of space as though it were a release, an almost artistic experience in which we ourselves inhabit the work of art. Space is no longer an "easily comprehensible volume of air but becomes moveable, dynamic … People's free bodily movements, not following a geometric formula, appear to be symbolised by this free space, as are their imaginings and ideas".[64]

In his considerations of how architects and designers can collaborate with industry to achieve this modern synthesis, Juhl draws on his personal, ambivalent experiences from the United States, voicing a worry about fashion trends that was shared by many of his colleagues and indeed the wider circles of polite society in the 1950s:

"While we [in Denmark] have in many areas improved the quality of our mass-produced products, ensuring that people with lower incomes can buy reasonable and decent furnishings, the Americans produce everything cheaply and are only slowly on their way to improving its quality. *We*, because we want to improve our homes and create something of lasting quality. *They*, while having lost both the respect and the desire for durable possessions. It is questionable how long we can maintain our attitude. It is valuable because it strives for a moral quality in contrast to a purely commercial, fashion-driven interest in competition."[65]

The cinema Villabyernes Bio in Vangede, north of Copenhagen, is a good illustration of Juhl's ability to create a high-impact space, using only low-cost materials. After the opening the press wrote that the acoustics in the auditorium were "fantastic". Perhaps Juhl drew on his experience of the Trusteeship Council Chamber at the UN Headquarters in New York, which has also often been praised for having outstanding acoustics. In the 1970s Villabyernes Bio was closed down, and in 1980 it was demolished.

As a building architect Juhl was influenced by the unpretentious modernism he had learnt from Kay Fisker and Vilhelm Lauritzen. The summerhouse Juhl designed in 1962 in Rågeleje, north of Copenhagen, for the CEO Anders Hostrup-Petersen illustrates this well. It has a simple, open plan with a blurring of the transitions between inside and out as well as low, Japanese-inspired furnishings. Naturally, Juhl used his own furniture, as here in the living room with an open fireplace. The painting is by Lundstrøm.

The bedroom at Kratvænget before
the extension that added, among
other features, a larger bedroom
with access to the garden.

Plan of a Bovirke exhibition that shows Finn Juhl's careful work with the interplay of surfaces, textures and colours (above). Plan and elevation of Juhl's contribution to the Cabinetmakers' Guild Exhibition of the same year, *An Art Collector's Study* (right).

OPHOLDSSTUE FOR EN KUNSTSAMLER. IDÉEN ER AT VISE MODERNE MØBLER OMGIVET AF LIGESAA MODERNE FREMBRINGELSER INDEN-
DE FRIE KUNSTARTER. DET FORUDSÆTTES, AT DER ER ANDRE OPHOLDSRUM I VILLAEN, HVOR MERE FEMININE SYSLER KAN UDFOLDE SIG.
PAA REOLFORSIDERNE ANBRINGES MESSINGKROGE TIL STUDIEOPHÆNGNING AF BILLEDER FORAN BØGERNE.
KAMINVÆGGE OG VINDUESVÆGGEN BIBEHOLDES SOM DE ER. REOLERNE KAN PAA UDSTILLINGEN UDFØRES SOM STIGEREOLER.
DEN FORESLAAEDE TRAPPE GØRES SAA BRED, AT KAMINKROGEN IKKE GENERER GANGLINIEN. GANGLINIEN FØRER IGENNEM RUMMET,
SOM MAN DERFOR FORNEMMER OMKRING SIG, ISTEDET FOR AT PASSERE LANGS KANTEN, SOM PROGRAMMET FORUDSÆTTE (KØJESY-
STEMET. DETTE RUMS STØRRELSE SKULDE MOTTIVERE DENNE VARIATION FRA TRADITIONEN PAA UDSTILLINGERNE.
PAA KAMINVÆGGEN 2 MALERIER AF LUNDSTRØM, ØVRIGE MALERIER AF EGILL JACOBSEN, BILLE OG RICARD MORTTENSEN. SKULPTURER AF
ROBERT JACOBSEN, BILLE OG THOMMEGEN. KERAMIK AF VAGEGAARD OG MUNCH-PETTERSEN (SAMT BLANC DE CHINE FRA DEN KGL.). GLAS
AF AALTO.
TRAPPE OG REPOSE I ASK. KAMINFLISER FRA HASLE. RESTEN AF GULVET HELST ASK, I NØDSFALD; MUSEETS FLISER. HVIDLAK. PERSIENNE.

UD

KAMIN

IND   BLENDET

Morality versus fashion. This was in many ways the everyday drama beneath the shadow of the Cold War. Although there were, of course, outstanding American designers such as Eames, Johnson, Wright and the naturalised Mies, who Juhl admired, and whose work he often returned to, in an international context America represented a fascination with the new but also with the commercial and the superficial. According to Juhl and many of his contemporaries it would pay for designers to look eastward instead, to Japan. Juhl describes how the Japanese home is designed around its basic unit, the traditional Tatami mat:

"You would not say of a space that it is so many square metres, but that it is three, four, six or more mats. A floor mat is a standard unit. The wall posts have a fixed distance that also shares in the mat measure. It is a purely mathematical architectural style, which at the same time has created romantic housing forms in the best sense of the word. Our architecture's natural setting, with a garden area, is something we have learnt from the Japanese, who are masters at incorporating their houses into beautiful open spaces."[66]

Juhl adds that the aesthetic sensibility of the Japanese has left a lasting imprint on Western European and American architecture.[67] From our present-day perspective, we notice this when we look back to the 1950s. The striking flexibility at play in Japanese homes, where the furniture that is not in use is tucked away in cupboards, was a welcome influence on the Western apprehension of space. Indeed this is not unlike the homes of the Shakers, who hang their chairs up on racks on the walls.

Architect-Designed Inhabitance

In 1952, the National Museum of Decorative Arts and Design in Trondheim, Norway, commissioned Juhl to design a permanent interior for exhibition. It was to be a model of Scandinavian interior design. The museum already had a William Morris room, presenting the Arts and Crafts movement's style from around 1850, and a Henry van de Velde room with Art Nouveau decor from around 1900. The Finn Juhl room was to typify a well-designed, modern, mid-20th-century interior.

The exhibition room Juhl was provided with was long and narrow, so he persuaded the museum to extend it with a broad bay the full height of the room, providing both light and a view over the city and the fjord. In addition, he had a narrow window installed, perpendicular to the entrance door. Juhl furnished the room with his own furniture as well as an Eames chair, stools designed by Aalto and a small, very slender rosewood table by the cabinetmaker Peder Moos. To complement these, a striped carpet by the Swedish weaver Barbro Nilsson, "light woollen curtains by Paula Trock",[68] Kay Bojesen's complete silver cutlery set *Grand Prix*, porcelain by Tias Eckhoff, stoneware by Axel Salto and, of course, an Erik Thommesen sculpture.

The CEO's office at the furniture manufacturer France & Søn in Ørholm, Denmark, with an ensemble of Finn Juhl furniture that the factory produced: the *Spade Chair*, a coffee table, the *Wall Sofa* and the *Table Bench*.

Plan and elevation of the interior
of the museum room *Interior-52* at
the National Museum of Decorative
Arts and Design in Trondheim,
Norway. *The Panel System, Chieftain
Chair, FJ48, Kaufmann Table, Wall
Sofa* and *Baker Sofa* are all featured
in the interior.

Interior-52 with the *Wall Sofa*, *FJ45*, a coffee table by the Danish cabinetmaker Peder Moos and Erik Thommesen's sculpture *Two People* as the element that ties them together.

The living room in Finn Juhl's own house in Ordrup. The *Chieftain Chair* is seen from behind and the *Table Bench* stands beside the window. The woman depicted in the well-known Lundstrøm painting is Finn Juhl's second life partner, the music publisher Hanne Wilhelm Hansen. After Juhl's death in 1989, she instituted a prize in Finn Juhl's name. It is awarded annually to architects and designers who in Juhl's spirit have made a special contribution, particularly in the field of furniture design.

The room is called *Interior-52*. Juhl examines it thoroughly at the close of *Hjemmets Indretning*, describing it as an illusion of a study for a person interested in modern decorative and industrial art.[69] This person seems at once to be the museum guest, Finn Juhl himself and also an ideal spirit of the times, somebody who feels at home amid the harmonious, subtle workings of the space, all achieved with as few elements as possible. Light, view, materials, lines, colours, combined spatial effect: illusions. Creating something that seems bigger, more interesting, more inviting than a slightly different selection of objects, combined in a slightly different way. Juhl apologises for his detailed description of the abstract, but explains that he thought it vital to share all these "deliberate little feelings and deliberations".[70]

Like other modern architects, Finn Juhl had discovered that across all of its scales, from urban planning to interiors, architecture had the capacity to make modern society more habitable. More habitable, certainly, than industrialisation had done, with its accompanying social inequality, alienation, pollution, overcrowding, housing shortages and superficial, decorative styles. Architects could do what they do best: interpret the break with the past, the new technology, the new living and working arrangements spatially, in terms of the formation of space, the usage of space, the sense of space. By finding ways to fulfil human needs that draw closer to the core of those needs, architects could contribute to the liberation from habit that Juhl called for in *Hjemmets Indretning*.

Nonetheless, it was a widely held view that in an 'architect-designed' home, people would no longer be allowed to enjoy their own (possibly dreadful) personal taste. Carl Jensen's wonderful drawing *Der gik en arkitekt gennem stuen* ('An architect went through the room') from the annual satirical publication *Svikmøllen* in 1943 captures exactly ordinary people's resistance to professionals telling them how to decorate their homes. Also during this period, the American interior design magazine *House Beautiful* repeatedly attacked international modernism for not being cosy. And although Juhl wrote in *Hjemmets Indretning* that he expected that the magazine editors would eventually relent, the debate raged on. Not least in relation to the concrete tower blocks hastily erected in the 1960s. These comfortless structures resembled modernism, but in truth they were devoid of the modernist aspiration for holistic architecture.

In 1981, the American author Tom Wolfe described in *From Bauhaus to Our House* how those poor unfortunate people living in clean, white, empty torture chambers designed by insensitive architects might try to sneak a couple of cosy, colourful Thai silk cushions onto their white sofas, but alas, "the architect returned ... as he always does, like the conscience of a Calvinist ..."[71] and threw the cushions out. Oddly, no one ever seemed to question why the architect's work should stop at the front door. From urban planning to housing plans and down to the very last brick, most people were happy to leave the tasks to professionals. Finn Juhl did not accept this division of labour, and his own interiors are really continuations of his furniture, just as his own house combines all these aspects and scales into a dynamic whole that is a platform of liberation.

Finn Juhl established his own design studio in Nyhavn, Copenhagen, in 1945. In the 1950s, as he was receiving more and more commissions, he and his staff moved to a larger premises, an old wine cellar at Sølvgade 38. The homely feel in the workplace, as seen in the photograph, became even more pronounced in 1961, when Juhl moved his studio back to his own house in Ordrup.

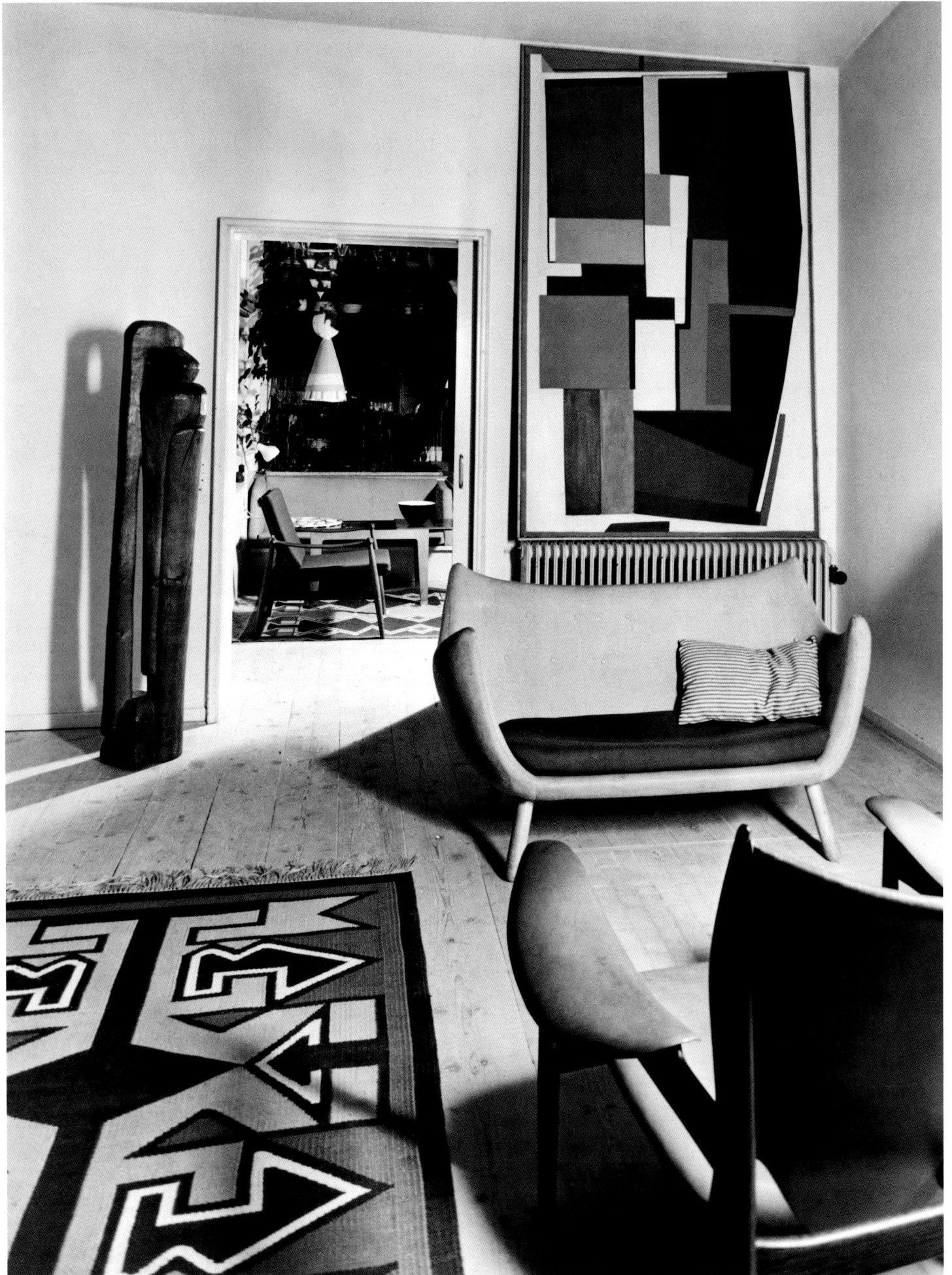

Industrially Produced Furniture

In the 1950s, Juhl began to move away from only designing furniture that would be handmade by cabinet-makers in limited numbers and towards industrial production. In fact, his collaborator, the cabinetmaker Niels Vodder, had already arranged for many of Juhl's works to be factory-made, *FJ45* among them[72].

Juhl likely saw through functionalism's somewhat naive ideas about the ability of designers to influence the industrial production of everyday objects, but he was undogmatic when it came to the cabinetmakers' monopoly over the Danish furniture industry. The modern designer's obligation to stay contemporary implied the need to be open to the new technologies, materials and collaborations that lay in industrial production. In a contribution to the British *Architects' Year Book* of 1949, Juhl describes how he sought to create forms that seemed more natural for people in the 20th century, though he was also of the opinion that "these shapes really should be looked at as experiments, to train oneself for the work on a quite new type of furniture: *mass-produced furniture*."[73]

In *Hjemmets Indretning*, Juhl presents the Finnish-American architect Eero Saarinen's *Womb Chair* and Charles Eames' chairs in bent laminated wood as examples of industrially manufactured, international models that could compete, both aesthetically and functionally, with the Danish cabinetmakers' products. In Denmark, Arne Jacobsen's *Ant Chair*, inspired by Eames, had moulded itself into a future classic. It was clearly developed through an experiment with materials and an aesthetic minimalism, both of which had their basis in the new technical and industrial possibilities of the time. In 1953, Finn Juhl designed a dining chair for the furniture manufacturer Bovirke. Today known as the *Reading Chair*, it meet a very typical need in a way that is perhaps more tongue-in-cheek than pleasing on the eye. If one sits on the chair in reverse, the top rail becomes a support for the sitter's arms.

Among his industrially produced furniture from the 1950s, Juhl's *Spade Chair* from 1954 and his *Japan Chair* from 1957 have all of his characteristic trademarks: originality, innovation, an organically shaped central supporting element, a floating supported element, select but precise detailing, friendly ergonomics and, above all, comfort. Both models were designed for the furniture manufacturer France & Søn. The company had originally been a mattress factory called Lama owned by the Englishman C.W. France. At some point they began to produce sofa and chair cushions and so found their way into furniture production.[74]

The *Bwana Chair* and one of the wooden bowls that Juhl designed for Kay Bojesen, in an advertisement by the Danish furniture manufacturer France & Søn (left). the *Spade Chair* in an advertisement by the American furniture retail chain John Stuart Inc., which was a considerable buyer of France & Søn-produced Finn Juhl furniture.

Photograph from early in the 1960s, showing a corner of Finn Juhl's own house. It attests to the fact that Juhl substituted the furniture in his home gradually, as he designed new pieces. However, he held on to the *Chieftain Chair* and the *Poet Sofa* throughout the years. The sculpture is by Erik Thommesen.

The furniture manufacturer Bovirke was strictly speaking a furniture retailer, but in 1947 the company contacted Finn Juhl and began by making variations of the models that Niels Vodder had produced. In the photograph is the *Reading Chair* (*BO62*) and the sofa *BO77*, both of which were designed for Bovirke in 1953.

For the most part, Juhl's industrial chairs were originally devised and designed as handcrafted pieces and then subsequently simplified for machine production, for instance with less complex joints and with visible screws. However, as evidenced by many of Juhl's manufactured models, from France & Søn's pieces to the *Fireplace Chair* (Bovirke's lightly revised version of *FJ45*) to, not least, Baker Furniture's production of *FJ48* and the *Chieftain Chair*, it did not take long before the manufacturing industry achieved a very high standard. Naturally, it irritated the cabinetmakers to see the industrial manufacturers reaping the profits from their experiments. Juhl was aware of the problem and recognised the risk that industry might take on the more fashionable products while leaving the high-quality work to the cabinetmakers. In fact, however, large-scale mass production never really materialised – apart from a few really successful designs, including the *Ant Chair* and Wegner's *Wishbone Chair* – and in many cases, industrially produced designer furniture was actually able to measure up to the cabinetmakers' own standards of quality.

This conflict of interest between cabinetmakers and industrial manufacturers spilled over into a dispute concerning Den Permanente, a well-known showroom and long-standing tourist attraction. The exhibition space on Vesterbrogade in Copenhagen had always sold furniture exclusively by cabinetmakers. Den Permanente did not keep industrially produced furniture, just as, conversely, the large Copenhagen department store Illums Bolighus did not stock handcrafted furniture. That was the deal that the cabinetmakers had made, and which they stuck to, even when it was clear that the future belonged to industry.[75] In 1953, when Bovirke asked Den Permanente whether they would stock their industrially produced Finn Juhl furniture, the request was declined. Not because Den Permanente was not interested, but because the cabinetmakers put their foot down. In the first of two strongly worded articles on the previously illustrious partnership between designers and cabinetmakers, Børge Mogensen and Arne Karlsen compared the dispute between the cabinetmakers and the industrial manufacturers to the Cold War between the Eastern bloc and the Western powers. The authors argued that both parties needed to realise their joint interest in promoting quality furniture.

The conflict was all the more absurd, given how much the cabinetmakers and the manufacturers were coming to resemble one another. Some cabinetmakers had many more employees than manufacturers, their tasks and production methods were close to identical, and only their sales strategies really distinguished the two. The cabinetmakers continued to sell directly to the public or through Den Permanente, while the furniture manufacturers traded through furniture outlets. The Copenhagen Cabinetmakers' Guild should instead focus its efforts on a particular clientele, the new upper-middle class. This was a generation brought up on quality furniture, who had both spending power and fine taste. As examples of the sort of furniture that appealed to this demographic, Mogensen and Karlsen highlighted Juhl and Vodder's interior from the 1944 edition of the Guild's annual furniture fair.

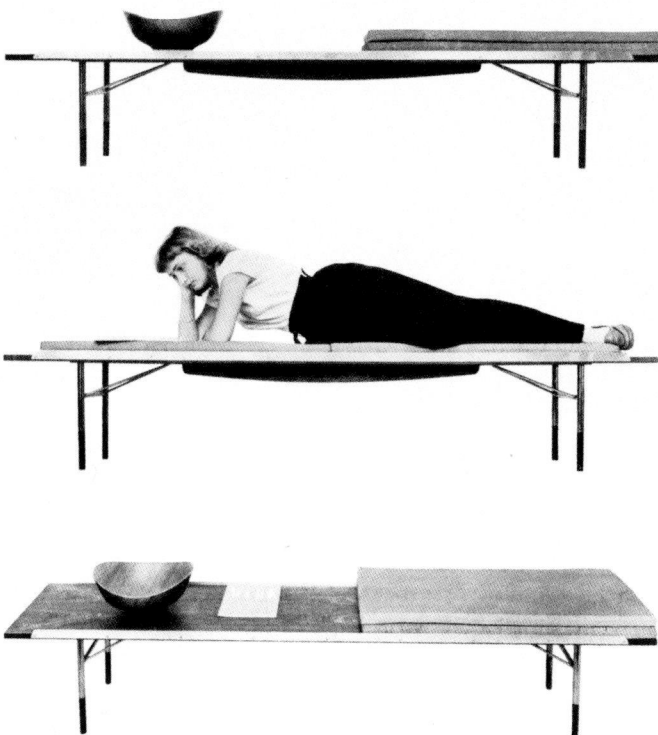

BORD-BÆNK

220 × 45 × 40 (h) cm, med bruneret metalstel og matslebne messingkanter. Pladen leveres fineret med palisander, teak eller formica. – Leveres også 112,5 cm lang eller i mål efter opgave. Puder af skumgummi. – Møbeltypen er fra en ny serie, tegnet arkitekt m.a.a. Finn Juhl.

BO 101

BOVIRKE

FALKONER ALLE 46 , TELEFON NORA 8777 , KØBENHAVN F

Foto: Keld Helmer-Petersen

Bovirke's advertisement for the *Table Bench* in 1953 demonstrates its dual function as both a table and a bench to sit or lie on. A brass trim prevents the cushion from sliding off.

An exhibition stand where the furniture company Bovirke displayed industrially manufactured Finn Juhl furniture, which used cheaper types of wood, were less delicately produced and had much less complicated joinery.

Teak, Honesty and Plagiarism

Finn Juhl often worked with teak, admiring both its physical expressiveness and its finish. Teak is a hard, tropical wood with many attractive properties, among them that it is self-oiling. In Juhl's eyes, its compact structure, fine-grained growth rings and deep glow made it ideal for hand-crafted furniture such as his own, with soft, flowing curves and sophisticated joinery. Moreover, by working in teak Juhl distanced himself from the practice of staining European woods darker in imitation of finer, more exotic types of wood.

Juhl detested the practice of staining wood, probably because he felt, like many modern designers, that all attempts to alter a material's natural, authentic expression were inherently dishonest. As with the use of lacquer, wood staining prevents the furniture from developing a natural patina over time. The wood is suspended in an artificial, eternal after-life, so to speak, not allowed to age in the manner of all living things, including human beings and trees. Børge Mogensen, who had cultivated the conception of an authentically Nordic expression, thus worked almost exclusively in light Nordic woods, such as oak, beech and pine. However, when Juhl began his collaboration with France & Søn he persisted in his affinity for teak. That led to a problem in production. Teak contains so much resin that factory cutting tools quickly blunt against it. The cabinetmakers addressed this issue by regularly sharpening their tools, but that was not cost-effective in industrial production. However, the resourceful Mr France came up with a solution. He had read that aluminium was often cut using rotating blades made from a tungsten carbide alloy with a high melting point. It struck him that the same method could be transferred into industrial woodwork. This lead to teak furniture coming into fashion and all but flooding the market, while the technical breakthrough was quickly picked up by other manufacturers, who now had the tools to plagiarise designer furniture. Not least Finn Juhl's. His manufacturers responded by taking their models out of production when they had been plagiarised and watered down too extensively.[76]

The photograph is from Finn Juhl's presentation of the Future Home in 1954. He designed a house in an open plan, where the different areas could be separated from one another with sliding doors. The furnishing includes the *Spade Chair*, the first chair that Finn Juhl designed for France & Søn in 1954.

The Last Experiment

In 1945, Erik Herløw – who went on to become the first professor of industrial design at the Royal Danish Academy of Fine Arts in 1959 – reviewed that year's Cabinetmakers' Guild Exhibition for the journal *Arkitekten*:

"The most interesting work at the exhibition was probably Finn Juhl's, especially as we see here so clearly the mature result of many years of experimentation. Unlike Wanscher, whose work is founded in refinement of the tradition, Juhl has broken each project down into its functions and created the forms from that basis. During his early years, these attempts felt exaggerated, at times far fetched, but all the more interesting now to view the results that this man has reached along his own path."[77]

Finn Juhl's watercolour from 1949 shows the plan and elevation of a sofa bench that has been known as the *Double Chieftain Chair*. It also shows a coffee table produced in teak and Oregon pine, which has an inlaid plate for hot items.

This was the year when Juhl exhibited one of his most successful chairs, *FJ45*. Herløw's brief portrait could scarcely be more precise. Experiments within the social, ethical and aesthetic aspects of design and architecture were a crucial component of the modern pursuit of the right form; the venture that the 19-year-old Juhl had known to be definitive of both himself and his times.

Like many contemporary alternative movements, the Bauhaus School became an expression of social experimentation *en miniature*, albeit with big, idealistic ambitions. Indeed Bauhaus' own internal divisions – between the artistic-contemplative and the scientific-technological, the handcrafted and the industrial, the traditional and the innovative – were typical of the modernist dilemma more broadly. In a scientific sense, experimentation is a working method, a means of testing hypotheses; thus, it is not necessarily an aim in itself when it is associated with technological development and industrial production. Artistic experiments, on the other hand, are often works of art, and any unfinished aspects are allowed to stand as an important part the expression and, thus, the outcome. As practical, technical and artistic disciplines, architecture and design belong somewhere in between the two approaches. It is interesting, then, that Herløw praises Juhl's ability to do both: In line with a scientific experiment, Juhl has 'broken each project down into its functions', and with an artistic approach, he has 'created the forms from this basis'. That some of the experiments failed, creating results that were exaggerated or far fetched, is an inherent aspect of experimentation: things can go either way. The issue, then, is whether to present the process itself. Whether to take the revolution-arily innovative path by involving the public in the dialogue. Or opt for a more evolutionary approach, utilising the experiments as part of one's own process. Wanscher and the Klint School focused on locating the essence of a design task and finding their forms in the tradition, rather than creating them anew. In truth, Juhl's experiments were hardly revolutionary either. He too preferred the slow, meticulous work with wholes and details to the more fashionable or sensational shortcuts to public attention. And neither did Juhl seriously stray from wood as his material.

In fact, Wegner went much further when in 1950 he suddenly came out with his *Flag Halyard Chair*, made of stainless steel and 240 metres of halyard rope. And Wegner was happy to flaunt his experiments. In a 1964 interview with the newspaper *Politiken* on the occasion of his own and Børge Mogensen's 50th birthday, Wegner admitted that every once in a while he could not resist "dropping a bomb" just to see what happens. He continues, "We never know when we're finished with something. One may want to exhibit something that's really just an attempt. For one's own sake. To understand oneself and gauge the reaction. Otherwise, it gets too boring." Børge Mogensen had the opposite view: "It's nonsense, all this talk about experimenting. An artist who is serious about his work will never exhibit anything he considers an experiment. He presents things that he can answer for. And then it's *the result* of an experiment. Sure. But a result."[78]

SOFABÆNK, 1:5, UDFØRES I IMBUJA OG MED OKSEHUD-BETRÆK. KONSTRUKTION SOM HVILESTOLENS.
KLAPBORD, 1:5, UDFØRES I TEAK OG OREGON-PINE MED BESLAG OG PLADE AF MATSLEBET MESSING.
PLADEFORM OG BENPLACERING GIVER NEM ADGANG 'INE SOFAEN. 'FRI' FORM DA INGEN FUNKTION STIL-
LER. BINDENDE KRAV.

When Juhl, a little nonchalantly perhaps, threw himself into a final and radical experiment, he seemed to be deliberately searching for a completely new expression, and he got a kicking for it. His assailants were Børge Mogensen and Arne Karlsen in their two reviews of the 1959 and 1961 editions of the Cabinetmakers' Guild Exhibition. They castigated both their designer colleagues and their cabinetmaker partners for what they exhibited: the designs were superficial, the cabinetmakers had failed to object and the finished products lacked both artistic and artisanal gravity.

In the first article, 'Illusion and reality. Reflections on the Copenhagen Cabinetmakers' Guild Furniture Exhibition 1959'[79], Mogensen and Karlsen surveyed a long list of exhibited furniture, pointing out structural solutions that were vague or had been made excessively complicated for aesthetic reasons; construction and joints that paraded as one thing when they were in fact something else; materials of different qualities being cobbled together; a thoughtless consumption of materials; superfluous padding; decorative details that undermined function. It was as if all of the childhood lessons of *Danish Modern* had been lost. Indeed, there were so many "affronts to the most natural demands one can make of furniture design and furniture craft", that the self-satisfaction with which the chairman of the Guild had opened the exhibition stood in dire contrast to its reality, which according to Mogensen and Karlsen, called for one thing: self-critique.

What had gone wrong? Mogensen and Karlsen observed a fatal loss of professional community: "These individual artists stand so strangely alone; there is no sense of community among the young nor any kinship between young and old. Each individual works at his own private formalism, whether in expressive forms or rectilinear asceticism."

Finn Juhl continued to provoke when in 1964 he developed his much criticised geometrical chair from the *Bedroom Suite* into a television chair and a television sofa as a direct and mocking polemic challenge to Børge Mogensen's television sofa and its "roly-poly bolster", as Juhl had called the cushion one might use to roll into place in that deep item of furniture.

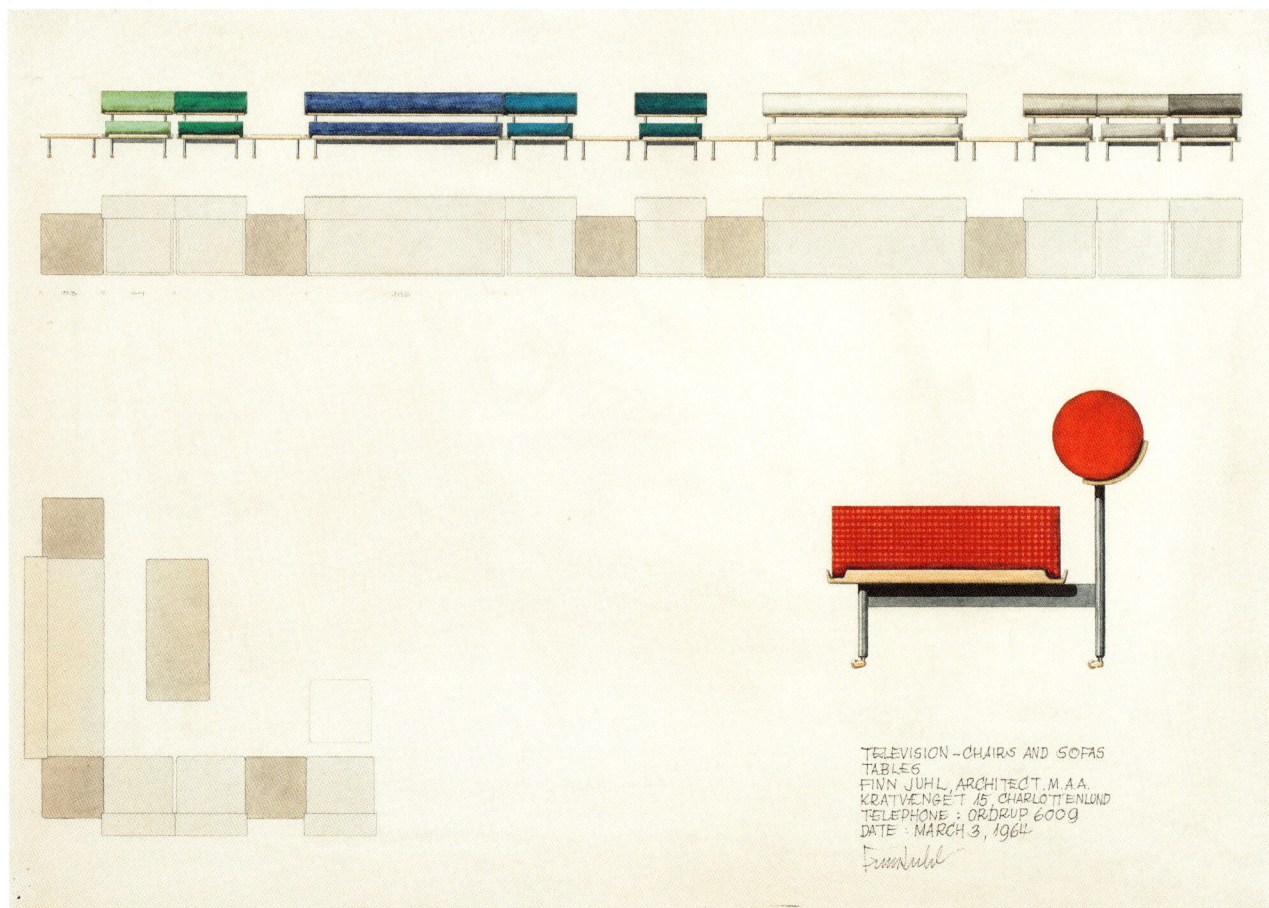

TELEVISION – CHAIRS AND SOFAS
TABLES
FINN JUHL, ARCHITECT, M.A.A.
KRATVÆNGET 15, CHARLOTTENLUND
TELEPHONE : ORDRUP 6009
DATE : MARCH 3, 1964

In the Stocks

In the second article, 'Applied Art Going Astray' from January 1962,[80] their censure is more principled. They argued that Danish design in general, and furniture design in particular, had betrayed its ideals and its professional, level-headed practices in favour of commercial novelty. The younger talents were thus led to believe that they should dabble in a little of everything instead of deliberately limiting their field of work "to make the more careful contribution there". In their hopes of public recognition the young are "thrown unprotected to the publicists" who claim design products should above all have "sales appeal".

It is the age-old story of Socrates, who was charged was corrupting the youth. But in their criticism, Mogensen and Karlsen condemned a handful of their colleagues to the stocks. Although they claimed that the figures they criticised were selected arbitrarily, it is hard to avoid the impression that they were exactly that, *selected*, because they represented the wrong tendency. Finn Juhl was one of them.

Mogensen and Karlsen saw a growing contempt for function and construction. They argued that there had been a shift in mentality, so that designers no longer conceived of their products in terms of a functional typology, as both the Bauhaus and Klint Schools had aspired to. Instead, furniture was conceived only in terms of its outer appearance and each designer's personal artistic expression. Mogensen and Karlsen felt that this arrogant approach to furniture design and an artistic self-assertiveness – at the cost of community and functional analysis – were personified by Finn Juhl. At the Guild's fair of 1961 he exhibited a bedroom he had designed for the music publisher Hanne Wilhelm Hansen, who he had begun to live with earlier that year.

The bedroom was an experiment. It breaks with many of the lessons of Juhl's own practice. The room constitutes a free play with form and material, just as Juhl had played freely with upholstery in the 1930s (see page 33ff). Was it that a lovestruck Finn Juhl longed for a little freedom after the hectic years towards the end of the 1950s, designing Scandinavian Airlines' (SAS) offices and plane cabins, the interiors for shops and exhibitions, furniture for industrial production and handcrafted objects, expanding his design studio and perhaps, truth be told, wearing himself a little thin?

Rectangles, cubes, cylinders and thin steel legs. It looked like Bauhaus formalism dressed up in fine wood and Thai silk. Juhl's colleagues, Mogensen and Karlsen pounced on this: "Although the geometrical structure of Finn Juhl's new furniture bears resemblance to Marcel Breuer's, for instance, it is not as honestly naked as his."[81]

Juhl was channelling the roaring 1920s. The excesses of the period, not its call for clarity and purity. Despite the many jokes about the furniture of that time, it was also admired for its very modern attempt to make form an element of function and for its ambition of drawing furniture design closer to other contemporary art forms, sculpture in particular.

Now, Juhl seemed to have abandoned the analytic experiments he had in common with the Klint School, instead setting out on a misguided artistic mission. For Mogensen and Karlsen, this was the wrong sort of experiment. "The new Finn Juhl furniture does not arise from a new way of life, a new manner of sitting and sleeping …" they wrote, before issuing their *coup de grâce:* "… and this could be said to be the general weakness of all Juhl's furniture, that as types they are conventional, and it is only in a formal sense that they have sought new paths."

Finn Juhl and Queen Ingrid in cubist formalism at the opening of the Copenhagen Cabinetmakers' Guild Furniture Exhibition in 1961. It might be considered appropriate that it is a Lundstrøm painting on the wall.

It was a criticism that must have hit Juhl hard, as it had always been his aim to unite the functional and the formal in a single whole, a push towards synthesis, a leap of inspiration, creating furniture, not sculptures. Hence the need to experiment. In response to the review he appealed, "But why should we take the joy out of everything? It is completely wrong for these two stern critics to warn the young against using their imagination – and pointless too, by the way, for they will probably do so, no matter what."[82]

Juhl did agree with Mogensen and Karlsen's reproval of the fashion-driven and commercial in design. In an interview shortly after their review, Juhl argued that the export potential of Danish furniture depended on maintaining the technical and formal quality. "It is always dangerous when something becomes fashionable, as has happened with Danish furniture in the United States."[83] Juhl had himself come of age alongside an idealistic functionalism and had learned as much from Kay Fisker and Vilhelm Lauritzen as he had from Wegner and Arne Jacobsen. Juhl pointed out that he was well aware of the differences between furniture and sculpture, but insisted that in either case, the artistic expression was the same: "An artisan's ability to create forms, surely, is the same as a sculptor's. A chair is not just an applied-art product positioned in a space, it is a form and a space in itself."[84]

For the next three years, Juhl did not exhibit at the Guild fairs, and it was discontinued after its 1966 instalment.

Character Assassination of a Perfume Seller

The dispute might have developed into fruitful dialogue were it not for a tone of envy and a hint of character assassination that coloured the rest of the review. The authors suggested Juhl was far from the design messiah he had been proclaimed to be. Rather, he was a decadent charlatan, a weathervane, his furniture in all the world's most fettered museums while he stood, cocktail glass in hand, a conceited smile upon his lips. The bedroom Juhl exhibited, they suggested, was not even fit to stand as an artistic experiment. Clean, geometric forms had been seen before, and dressing them in silk was just seedy. Their longstanding suspicion that Juhl was no more than a 'perfume seller', had been confirmed. Finn Juhl and Børge Mogensen never returned to speaking terms.

Because this line of criticism pulled the rug from beneath Juhl's achievements and attacked his professional integrity, it doubtless hit him harder than he immediately let on. He returned to their criticism often in interviews, and in a letter to Kaufmann in 1982 Juhl referred to himself as a perfume seller,[85] a slur that was then being levelled at the new Danish Prime Minister Poul Schlüter.

Sæder og skikkelser På snedkerlaugets udstilling hænger en af de udstillede stole, der er udbygget med en højst utraditionel pølleryg, vakt opmærksomhed.
—En mand med Deres fortvivlet traditionelle formgivning skal overhovedet ikke sidde i stole...
(Tegning: MOGENS JUHL)

Mogens Juhl's satirical cartoon in the newspaper *Politiken* on yet another modern design idea: Finn Juhl's *Bedroom Suite* at the Cabinetmakers' Guild Exhibition. In the journal *Arkitekten* Børge Mogensen and Arne Karlsen are depicted as the valiant knight and his faithful squire, who made the heads of their colleagues roll in the furniture feud of 1961–1962.

Juhl had received a copy of Mogensen and Karlsen's review before it went to press. He had written a response but never submitted it. Later, however, it was published alongside other contributions in the journal *Mobilia*: "Has religious war broken out? The angry, pent-up Arne Karlsen has harnessed Børge Mogensen to his soapbox cart and is shooting like Thor across the vaults of heaven, dishing out blows with his hammer to dissenters. Thunder and lightning, with the stench of sulphur."

Sarcastically, Juhl commented on Mogensen's and Karlsen's own exhibits at the fair. In Mogensen's case, "a very deep sofa with roly-poly bolster cushions to keep their victim in place," so deep in fact that it would draw the hem of modest women's dresses up to their shoulders. And who really needs a sofa with room for a football team? In Karlsen's case it was a wardrobe "whose hinges are constructed so that the doors need all of the tolerance of a union of bricklayers if they are to be opened." How functional, well-designed or elegant was that?

Juhl responded with humour, but he had a more serious aim: to mount a defence of experimentation – artistic and practical. He added a postscript: "Is the Cabinetmakers' Guild Exhibition not a place for experimentation, a place where one can hope for impartial critique? What is it for otherwise?"[86]

The combination of the didactic, the moralising and the malicious in Mogensen and Karlsen's tone led many others to weigh in, Poul Henningsen (PH), Svend Erik Møller, Axel Thygesen and Gunnar Aagaard Andersen among them. The furniture manufacturer P. von Halling-Koch defended Juhl and experimentation indirectly, arguing that making mistakes was a wonderful thing, as it was a condition of progress. He hoped that in the younger generation there were some who were not just dreaming about Kaare Klint and times gone by: "I have produced Verner Panton's *Cone Chair* and the one you call his *Mickey-Mouse Chair*. I don't know if it will stand the test of time as a brilliant piece, it may just be a fad, it may disappear, an experiment on the way forward – to making something even better, it may just be a hint at other forms, it may move things along by just a hand's breadth – but isn't that a lot?"[87]

When the tabloid newspaper *B.T.* asked that Finn Juhl review the Cabinetmakers' Guild Exhibition in 1962, Juhl gave Mogensen and Karlsen a taste of their own medicine, writing for instance, that Karlsen ought to give up furniture design and stick to journalism. In the end, however, it was Juhl who packed it in. His commissions became fewer and fewer, and he moved his design studio back to his home on Kratvænget. In 1977, Juhl summed up his situation in a letter to an American friend, writing that for nearly five years, he had only been offered minor projects: "…there is absolutely nothing to shout about."[88]

Børge Mogensen's television sofa, which Finn Juhl mocked in his response to Mogensen's and Karlsen's criticism of his *Bedroom Suite*.

Finn Juhl had seen the writing on the wall, and in 1968 he designed this easy chair with canvas upholstery, loose cushions and a 'gunmetal grey' steel frame. It never reached production. The triangles that hold the cushions in place continue Juhl's experiments with pure geometric forms, which he had begun in the 1960s.

It was easier said than done for Juhl to keep to his own principle: that designers should create furniture appropriate for their times. Indeed, this chair, from 1969, was not put into production.

POLSTRET ARMSTOL 1:5 . 27.5.1969.

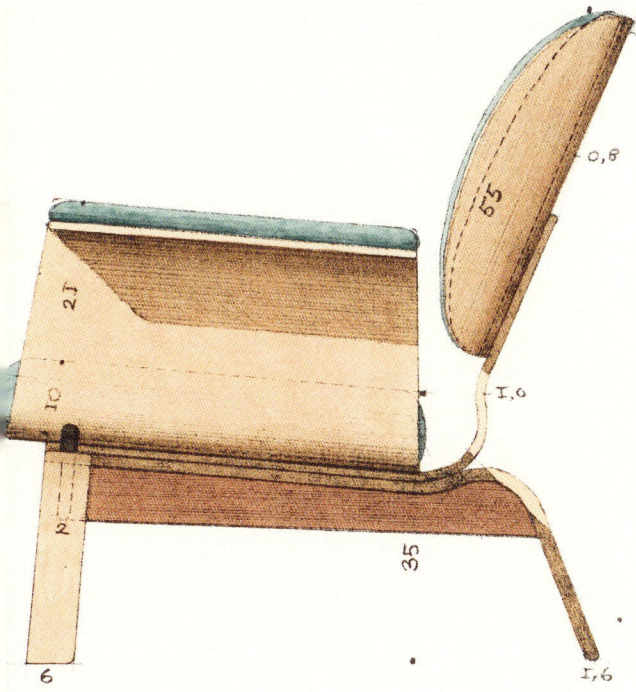

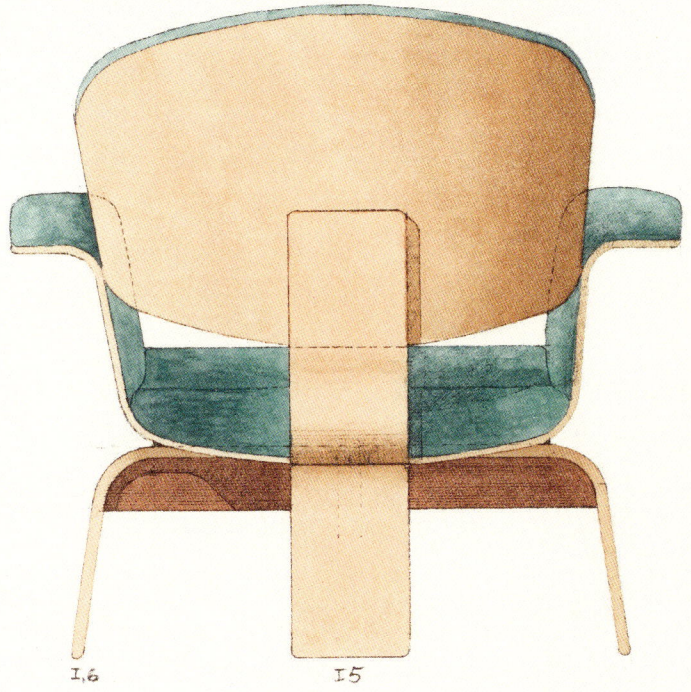

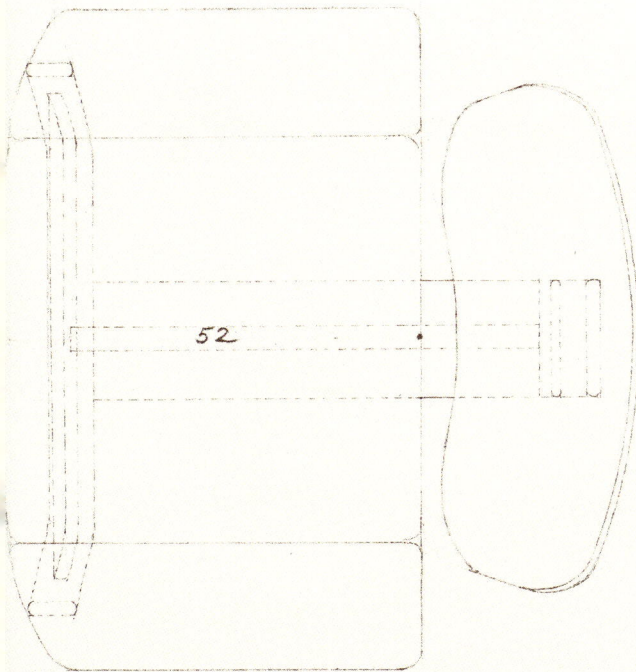

KRATVÆNGET 15
CHARLOTTENLUND
DENMARK
FINN JUHL
ARCHITECT M.A.A.
ORDRUP 7721
ORDRUP 6009

New Practices, No Furniture

Throughout the 1960s and 1970s, Juhl designed less and less furniture, and few of his designs made it to production. This may in part be a consequence of his artistic approach to his craft. Perhaps his talent burned out, inspiration ran dry, the artistic compulsion faded – or however else one might want to put it. But on top of this, in a broader context, the golden age for Danish furniture design was over.

Not least because the mission had been accomplished. Modern design had conquered the market and popular taste. It was no longer only the avant-garde who thought in terms of function. The entire machinery of Denmark's emerging welfare society was influenced by forms which came and went with the changing fashions, while the growing economy and bureaucracy, international trade and development, intense marketing, surging consumption, the proliferation of Western values and Western goods were all deeply functionalist in industrial, technological, political and cultural terms.

In wealthy Western countries, such as Denmark, consumption exploded, accompanied by a similar growth in advertising. In combination with the forces of fashion and countercultural movements, this wrested consumer choice from those authoritative voices that had extolled the moral value of quality designer furniture. During the 1960s, there was a younger generation who were listening to beat music, fighting for women's rights and joining student protests. They furnished their homes as they liked, often with just a couple of wooden beer crates and a mattress on the floor. And they had no interest whatsoever in their parents' handcrafted furniture. A growing environmental awareness also played a role in this shift in values. Ideally, one should live in a hut in the forest, like Thoreau, and build one's own furniture. Either that or go without.

More than many, Juhl had insisted that modern furniture should reflect its times and the lifestyle of its public. But neither Juhl nor his colleagues Wegner or Mogensen had an answer to this new period's demands on function and form. It was another three designers who managed both to hit upon the zeitgeist and find the right form: Arne Jacobsen, Verner Panton and Poul Kjærholm. Instead of collaborating with cabinetmakers they worked closely with the manufacturing industry, using alternative materials such as steel and plastic, and individually they each found a novel, contemporary way to be exclusively modern.

As early as 1948, Finn Juhl was experimenting with a moulded plastic chair, when he took part in a competition at the Museum of Modern Art in New York. In the 1960s he attempted – perhaps halfheartedly – to design with new materials, in this case a chair with a fibreglass shell, foam rubber padding and a steel frame. The chair never made it to production.

In 1966, the year of the final instalment of the Cabinet-makers' Guild Exhibition, Juhl wrote to his old collaborator Niels Vodder. Perhaps in a fit of desperation, Juhl complained quite unreasonably that Vodder had sold too few of his models. In his sad and resigned response, Vodder wrote:

"I think we have worked together 30 years. You designed interesting furniture in forms that were difficult to produce and with unconventional joints. I thought it a good task to take on, and I went about it as best I could … The earnings were scant for my part, and I assume that you didn't profit much either. But we stuck to our task and lived life in the process … If you think, as I do, that I have your best models, I can understand why you might think that they would command the highest fee. To my mind, that would be misguided. Georg Jensen Inc., New York was a disappointment. Baker, who attempted the easy chair *45* didn't make much from it either, and they gave up on *46* … I think I was late in understanding the merciless force of fashion. I will now incur further losses, for last year I built up an excessive stockpile in order to keep the production going …
At present, I have suspended production of all of your models except the dining table … I am not selling enough to take it up again."[89]

Home of
Finn Juhl

KRATVÆNGET 15
CHARLOTTENLUND
DENMARK
FINN JUHL
ARCHITECT M.A.A.
ORDRUP 7721
ORDRUP 6009
DATE

Kratva

1982 —— 2017

Legacy and
Renaissance

Finn Juhl built the house in Ordrup
as a young architect in 1942,
using the money he inherited from
his father, the textile merchant
Johannes Juhl.

From Inside and Out

Even before Juhl made his breakthrough as a furniture designer he had the chance to take on a task that most architects think hardest of all: designing one's own home.

Juhl's father had died in 1941. The year after and with the inheritance he received, Juhl and his first wife built a house at Kratvænget 15 in Ordrup, a little north of Copenhagen. It is a beautiful site, neighbouring the art museum Ordrupgaard to the west and fringed by the Ordrup Krat beech woods. The house is spread across a single storey and comprises two parallel buildings. They are like two musical notes, one short and one long. The short building is a front-gabled house that contains a large living room and a smaller study. The long contains the dining room, kitchen, bedrooms and bathroom. These two buildings are connected by a lower passage containing an entrance hall and a conservatory, which opens onto a terrace sheltered by the surrounding buildings. The site was originally level but Juhl used the earth left from digging the foundations and the cellar to position the house on a slight slope, so that from within one can see more of the lawn. A low crop of wild roses ensures privacy while preserving the view out.

Page from *Das Haus des Arkitekten* (1955) shows the south-west gable with a light, fibre-cement coating, awning, whitewashed brick wall and a terrace made of bricks laid sideways.

Sitting area in the lobby   Sitzplatz in der Halle   Coin du hall

Garden sitting area in angle between two sections
Gartensitzplatz im Winkel zwischen den beiden Bauten
Terrasse à l'angle des deux ailes

Blick in den Garten   Le jardin   View to the garden

FINN JUHL
Architect MAA, Charlottenlund, near Copenhagen
Denmark

One-family house, built 1941/42
Size of lot 1650 m²
Volume 1045 m³
The splitting of the site into two zones is clearly visible from the shape of the house; it consists of two wings connected by a small intermediate building. In contrast to the usual arrangement with living-rooms in one part and bedrooms in the other, the everyday rooms (kitchen, dining-room, bedrooms and the master's bedroom which serves as a music-room) are here grouped together, while the living and guest rooms are grouped apart.
In the connecting building are the porch, cellar steps and hall with the garden sitting area.
The two main sections of the house stand at right angles to each other and are at different levels (4 risers). The roof ridges of the two buildings run parallel to each other, the connecting building has a flat roof. In spite of its cubic appearance, the house leaves a modest impression and convinces by its simplicity. Only the horizontal wing at higher level is cellared. The garage is joined to the main building by means of a pergola. The architect, known throughout Denmark as a furni-

128

The design of the house is thought through from inside and out. This is characteristic of Juhl's feel for space but also of modernism's rational planning, where light sources and doors are placed where they are most needed and not simply where they best accord with symmetry or style. The outer walls were rubbed down and white-washed, and both the gables and the roof with its hanging eaves are coated in light grey fibre-cement. The overall impression is clear-cut and lightly, inter-mittently rhythmical; dancing notes in a little melody, white structures against the woodland's dark.

"We wanted it rural and simple,"[90] Juhl said to a Swedish newspaper, describing his home as "a mixture of a summerhouse and a bit of legitimate elegance."[91] Juhl only designed a handful of other houses: a villa in the town of Nakskov, the cinema Villabyernes Bio in Vangede, two summer houses – in Asserbo and Rågeleje – and two houses commissioned in the town of Klelund close to Varde. His own house gives expression to his dream of furnishing *an existence* (just as in *Interior-52),* designing everything from the teaspoons to the house itself. Juhl did not quite achieve his dream with the house on Kratvænget, but he came close. He furnished it with his own furniture, in part with his own lamps and applied-art objects and with textiles, paintings and sculptures by his favourite artists, just as he would have, were he designing an interior on commission.

In March 1949, the Danish newspaper *Politiken* visited Juhl at his home in Ordrup: "There are armchairs as sharp in the seat as a dried-up virgin, with long, acutely angled grasshopper legs, each one an oversized insect with exposed muscles and tendons but no flesh to their bodies. The writing desk – which in other homes is intended to convey a weighty impression of the intellectual life of the head of the household – is here slender and clean in its lines, its surface wafer-thin and its legs without ornamentation. The dining table feels unsuitable for heavy meals or thick gravy, it is a large, glossy oval on four slender legs. The silversmith Kay Bojesen has strewn the tabletop with silver ducats. Architect Juhl concedes they have an aesthetic effect but adds that they also serve a function in indicating where the plates should be set, depending on the number of diners. The floor is of exposed wooden boards with only a single rug shrunk into a corner. The walls are large, light surfaces that seize and reflect the sunlight; the few paintings are abstract works: Egill Jacobsen, Egon Mathiesen og Vilhelm Lundstrøm. The vases and dishes are created for and complemented by the interior, a white dish is as arbitrary in its form as a puddle. Arbitrary by design, one hastens to add. The lighting is conveyed by porcelain domes that make even PH lamps look like antique curiosities."[92]

This colourful description gives an impression of how provocative a modernist house could be. This may seem bizarre today, but there was a time when abstract art, for instance, could actually make people furious. Indeed, it is still possible to keep drug addicts and drunks away from train stations by playing them opera over the tannoy system.

Today, Juhl's house is a museum, thanks to a private enthusiast, Birgit Lyngbye Pedersen, who in 2007 bought the house outright from the Wilhelm Hansen Fund, which in turn had inherited it from Juhl's life partner, Hanne Wilhelm Hansen. Pedersen entrusted the house to its neighbour, Ordrupgaard Museum, which was well placed to preserve it as a museum. As Pedersen saw it, the situation demanded only "so to speak, a hole in the fence".[93] As Finn Juhl designed new pieces of furniture, he gradually replaced the furniture in his home with those works he was more satisfied with. The house as it stands today is a careful averaging of these different periods and also a pleasant compromise between an exhibition of his furniture and interiors and a semblance of a private home, as though the inhabitants had just stepped outside for a moment.

Spatial Art

Were it not enough that Finn Juhl's furniture is now permanently exhibited, and in his own house, an exact replica of the house has been constructed in Takayama, Japan. Juhl's museum status suggests that his story does not end with Mogensen and Karlsen slating his contribution to the Cabinetmakers' Guild Exhibition in 1961 and the next two decades' wanderings in the wilderness. In fact, Finn Juhl received a fine, personal epilogue, and his furniture underwent something of a renaissance.

It began in 1982. In January that year Juhl turned 70, and in *Politiken* the journalist Henrik Sten Møller described Juhl as the most prolific talent Denmark had ever had in the spatial arts. He wrote that Juhl had long since assumed his rightful place in the *Chieftain Chair*.[94] The members' journal for the Association of Furniture and Interior Designers in Denmark, *Rum og Form* (Space and Form), devoted an entire issue to Juhl. The editorial praised him as one of the first to educate interior designers and employ them within his own studio. It also underlined Juhl's remarkable ability to manage proportions and materials in a way that was both holistic and experientially rich, without losing the human touch: "We hope that this issue of *Rum og Form* will broaden familiarity with Finn Juhl, both as a person and an architect, whose contribution absolutely deserves attention even today."[95]

Juhl was thrilled with the publicity. He immediately bought 100 copies and sent them to friends and acquaintances, writing in one letter that, "naturally, this vain old man is delighted with a magazine like this; one thrives on fuss and it has been fading".[96] The phrase 'spatial art' must have pleased Juhl especially. It positioned him closer to the architectural profession and further from the lower status of interior design while also subtly associating his practice with sculpture – at the time, the school of sculpture at the Royal Danish Academy of Fine Arts was called The School of Walls and Space.

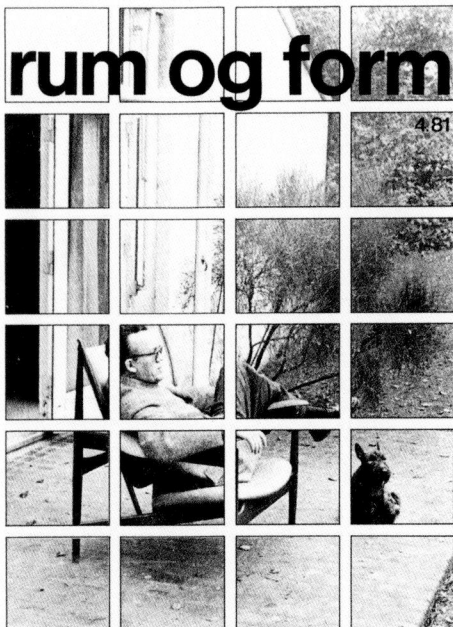

Prior to Finn Juhl's retrospective exhibition at the Danish Museum of Art & Design in 1982, the members' magazine for interior designers *Rum og Form* ('Space and Form') published a special edition dedicated to Finn Juhl. He bought 100 copies of the issue to send to family and friends.

Cover photo of the journal *Rum og Form* ('Space and Form'), in which Juhl demonstrates one of the many sitting styles accommodated by the *Chieftain Chair*, on the little terrace by the south-west gable of the house. Before his death, Finn Juhl just managed to experience the beginning of the renaissance that many of his pieces have undergone.

Finn Juhl's house neighbours the
art museum Ordrupgaard. Ever
since the house was donated to the
museum it has been open to the
public. These pictures date from
around 1950, from the garden side
of the house with a statue by Erik
Thommesen (left) and a view of the
driveway (right).

Juhl replaced the furniture in his house in Ordrup when he had designed something new. The photograph shows the furnishing as it was in 2007, when it was handed over to Ordrupgaard Museum.

Visitors to Finn Juhl's house experience his furniture in the coherent unity of objects, lighting, colours, and textures that Juhl sought to achieve. At the same time Juhl created a house that functioned as both a home and a workspace.

Throughout his life, Juhl had sought to promote interior architecture and to encourage his colleagues, housing associations, private clients and the broader public to recognise that even the most carefully designed blueprint for an apartment – or an exhibition space, for that matter – would fall flat if the project were finished without a thorough furniture plan, which considered both function and form, balanced lighting, textures and colours and a choice of objects that had been tried and tested across a variety of everyday situations. It would not do to simply go out and buy furniture as a casual afterthought, as though this latter part was not an architectural concern. Juhl was well aware that architects were bound to encounter resistance if they overstepped the threshold and entered the interior of the home. As early as 1949, he had written in the article 'The Furniture on the Furnishing Scene', that the "basis for interior decorators is gaining familiarity with the 'human material', who have a legitimate need for assistance. Definitely, this calls for the utmost tact. The public buys into the idea that the individual home should express the inhabitants' (the wife's) personality, and the resident therefore shies away from assistance. That in most cases, each resident's individual personality is similar, to the point of confusion, with all of the neighbours', is clear from the endless rows of *identical*, 'personal' and absolutely individual homes that *Tidens Kvinder*, for instance, present in their documentary reports."[97] *Tidens Kvinder* (Women of the Times) was a Danish weekly magazine marketed primarily at housewives.

Juhl's smarting, ironic critique of 'weak', feminine personalities combing through fashion and interior design magazines in a materialistic search for identity – people who ultimately end up living like everybody else – may have been lacking that excess of tact that he himself had called for. Moreover, it is clearly sexist in a manner typical of the period. But the cause that Juhl championed – spatial art – ought to have spurred more of his colleagues to the battlefield. A famous exception from his contemporary architects' more opportunistic tactfulness, whereby the client is always right, was Arne Jacobsen, who once demanded that people at least refrained from hanging scalloped curtains in his meticulously modernist new builds. Juhl would have nodded in recognition at the complaint voiced in an editorial of a Danish national newspaper as late as May 2017. The article concerns a new, high-end, state-of-the-art housing block in Nordhavn in Copenhagen, a renovated corn silo now called The Silo. The editorial lamented that the residents had not taken the trouble to understand the period or the atmosphere in which the building was first constructed and so failed to decorate *with* the building. Instead they introduced double doors and panels befitting the traditional luxury flats that perhaps they ought to have bought instead.[98]

If Finn Juhl's cutting irony and pointed observations might offend women of the self-important middle-classes, Martin Hartung of the national newspaper *Berlingske Tidende*, in the paper's birthday portrait of Juhl, hints at why Juhl was bound to clash with Børge Mogensen, Arne Karlsen and the popular Danish ideals of equality, common sense and the need for *hygge* (cosiness): "In his furniture, his chairs especially, Juhl expresses himself in a language of form that people had never seen before … In truth, his furniture did not seem typically Danish nor did it particularly seem to address ordinary people. On the contrary, it is refined, sometimes on the knife edge of being fashionable. As such, it reflects the personal traits of its creator, Finn Juhl, the elegant man of the world."[99]

The authentic and desirable in the popular ideal of equality is often conceived as standing in opposition to the excessive, elitist, pretentious or stilted, the un-Danish influences that come in from abroad, and hence, novelty, experiments and developments that defy comprehension will be treated with hostility. Of course, such a reaction is not exclusive to the Danes. The world over, there was good reason for treating modernism with scepticism, because it held out a promise that was not fulfilled. People living in modernity had reason to feel cheated, as they had abandoned the tradition that had provided a sense of identity and security without receiving in return the freedom they had been led to expect.

Finn Juhl, presumably in 1982, beneath Vilhelm Lundstrøm's portrait of his life partner, Hanne Wilhelm Hansen.

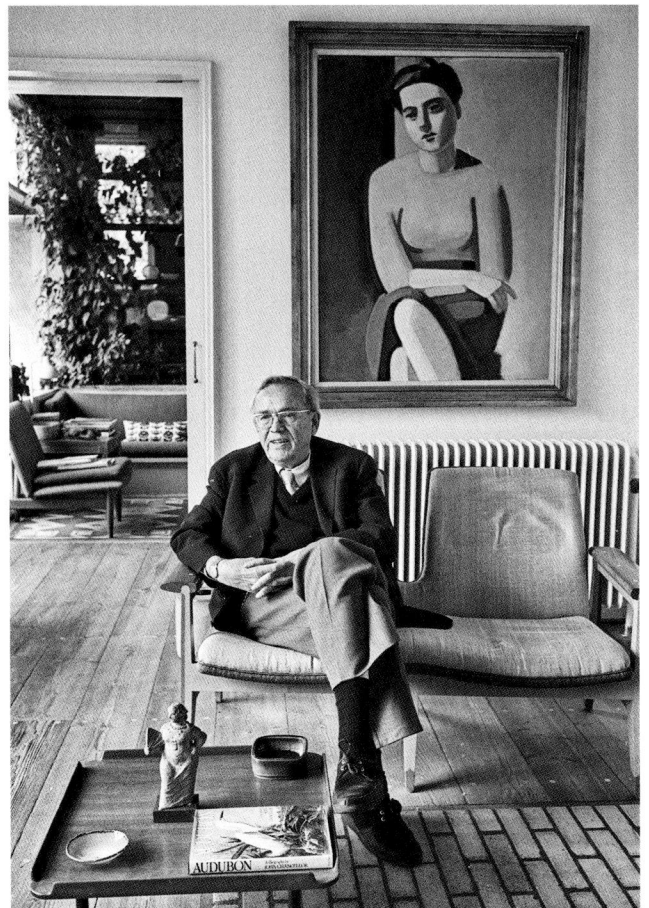

In Denmark this antipathy was particularly evident because the historical homogeneity of the population is closely tied to a down-to-earth egalitarianism. This deep-rooted mentality was not lessened during the 1970s, when the anti-authoritarian rebellion found its cultural and political expression, stressing the value of the collective over the individual, the socially relevant over individualist aesthetics and communal traditions over modern elitism.

Folk high schools blossomed, folk music was re-discovered, pottery workshops cropped up across the country and the political Left was larger and more diverse than ever before. Crafts were more honest than art, which in any case ought really to be political. How could refined furniture design possibly fit into this discourse?

Retrospective Exhibition

It might just have seemed that everything in Finn Juhl's life had happened already. But he received a birthday present that must have delighted him even more than the newspaper and magazine portraits. It was a letter from Erik Lassen, the director of the Danish Museum of Art & Design, who proposed a retrospective of Juhl's work to be opened before the year's end. Naturally it would be curated by the exhibition designer himself.

The Danish Museum of Art & Design on Bredgade in Copenhagen – today Designmuseum Danmark – was for many years a rather distinguished and conservative institution. It is housed in what was once the Royal Frederik's Hospital, a beautiful, grey plastered rococo building, much in keeping with the style of the *Frederiksstaden* district of Copenhagen. Indeed, the hospital was designed in 1752–1757 by Nicolai Eigtved, who also designed the district, and it was completed by Laurids de Thurah. The building was converted to a museum in the mid-1920s by Ivar Bentsen and Thorkild Henningsen, and naturally, Kaare Klint was responsible for the interiors. For many years the museum's politics of acquisitions and exhibitions was also 'Klintian', which apparently meant that disciples more zealous than the master himself worked to exclude dissent. After the Museum of Modern Art in New York had acquired *FJ45*, the Danish museum waited twenty years to follow suit. By his own account, at a party hosted by Kay Fisker (at which Finn Juhl was present), Erik Lassen proclaimed loudly and with satisfaction that the Danish Museum of Art & Design was now "the only museum in the world that did not exhibit Finn Juhl's furniture".[100] Lassen, who resigned as director in 1982, must have eventually regretted this policy.

Engaged and energised, Juhl threw himself into preparations for the exhibition. He estimated that he spent between 800 and 1000 hours working on it. Naturally, he was nervous. It had been many years since his last commission. Would anyone really be interested in seeing his outdated objects? He wrote to Edgar Kaufmann, describing the exhibition design in detail. He was worried that mounting 22 chairs on podiums would seem pretentious. This was once more his old fear that people would think he could not distinguish between furniture and sculpture. In a sequence of photographs he presented his furniture *in situ*, not least from his house on Kratvænget. *Finn Juhl – a retrospective exhibition of furniture and other works* opened on the 4th of November 1982. It was received warmly in the press.

The retrospective Finn Juhl exhibition at the Danish Museum of Art & Design in autumn 1982. Furniture and posters, stringent, with a limited range of colours and effects. Finn Juhl's concern that setting his furniture on podiums would be seen as stilted or pretentious seems unfounded.

From the exhibition at the Danish Museum of Art & Design, which turned out to be a great success. Finn Juhl had spent hundreds of hours working on the exhibition. This photograph shows a board with images from his own house, flanked by the *FJ45* Chair and an easy chair that was produced for the Cabinetmakers' Guild Exhibition in 1955.

Classic Modern – Nordic in New York Once More

That same autumn, an exhibition of Nordic design opened at the Cooper-Hewitt Museum in New York: *Scandinavian Modern: 1880–1980*. A reviewer in *The New York Times* took the opportunity to retell the story of Scandinavian Modern, the Nordic strand of modernism and functionalism that Finn Juhl had been brought up in. It is this tradition that Juhl from the outset had felt an obligation towards and had been driven by. From the article's opening lines, the figure of Finn Juhl is easily recognisable:

"SCANDINAVIAN was modern for a generation of Americans – indeed for the whole world – in the years following World War II. The Danes established a beachhead on these shores in the late 1940s, at the Fifth Avenue and 53rd Street quarters that Georg Jensen then occupied. Soon the Scandinavian style, the curvaceous walnut and teak chairs and tables, the colorful ceramic tableware and the sinuous and shimmering metal flatware, were warming the homes of the modern minded from coast to coast … Rooms, combining the best of Nordic design, were dominated by a sense of humanism and craftsmanship. Most people felt at home in such interiors. And a surprising number wanted to live with the undulating lines of chair frames, lighting fixtures, silver and glass."

According to the reviewer, the exhibition demonstrated "the appreciation that Nordic designers have always shown for materials and craftsmanship – whether in furniture, metal, ceramics or glass. The emphasis is on naturalism …"

In a thoroughly industrial and commercial society like the United States, 'the natural' is external, something scarcely perceivable in those products that keep the wheels of the economy moving. Mass production is about volume; individual items and their individual consumers are no more than specks in the statistics of a marketing strategy. This is no place for carefully selecting the length of wood best suited for a particular chair. That is why Nordic design always appears more natural for Americans. The *New York Times* reviewer notes this was clear "… in, among other selections, the organic designs of Alvar Aalto and Finn Juhl, the tradition-oriented furniture of Hans Wegner and the witty and innovative chairs of Arne Jacobsen. Finn Juhl's modern classic armchair, designed in 1945, represents the epitome of this sculptural style. The curvaceous teak design with its sweeping arms and rakish rear legs was imitated but never equalled over the next two decades by designers throughout the world, including some in the Soviet Union. The Danish architect's design is as fluid in its ribbon-like shaping as the Art Nouveau style that inspired him, even though it bears no resemblance to the turn-of-the century mode."[101]

Note that *FJ45* is described as both modern and classic. This was a significant point.

In many ways, this conclusion to Finn Juhl's story was more important than the reception of his retrospective exhibition or the fine words on the occasion of his birthday. As the review of *Scandinavian Modern* in *The New York Times* continues, "When Scandinavian design was upstaged by Italian modern in the late 1960s, the furniture lost much of its appeal …"[102] Thus, the golden age of Danish furniture design is written into the familiar story that is, of course, far from over. Today, the awareness of the influence of market forces and shifting fashions on the field of design is probably an important condition for recognising that design products can hold qualities *other* than those defined by markets or the changing fashions, and that in this way, they may reach beyond the time in which they were created. Three years after Juhl's death (in May 1989) Finn Dam Rasmussen, owner of a new boutique specialising in second-hand Danish design, held a Finn Juhl exhibition featuring 30 of Juhl's best works. Rasmussen opened the exhibition with the words, "Finn Juhl's furniture distinguishes itself from the mainstream of Danish design by pursuing the boundary between abstract sculpture and applied art."[103]

Details of the *Chieftain Chair's* 'wishbone' element on a poster for a Finn Juhl exhibition in the lobby of the Danish newspaper *Politiken* in Copenhagen, in spring 1990, the year after Juhl's death in May 1989.

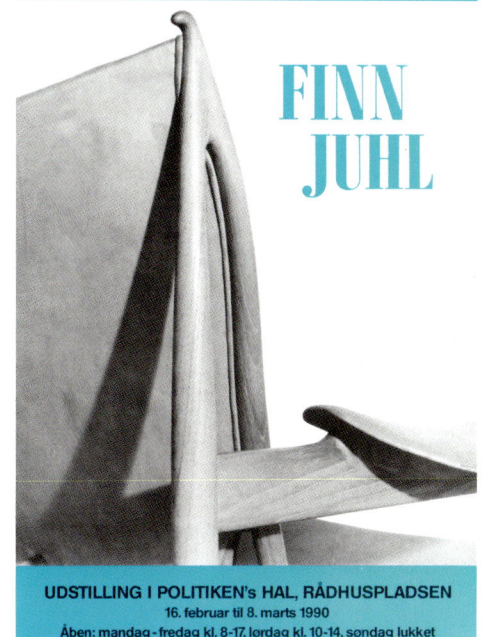

FINN JUHL

UDSTILLING I POLITIKEN's HAL, RÅDHUSPLADSEN
16. februar til 8. marts 1990
Åben: mandag - fredag kl. 8-17, lørdag kl. 10-14, søndag lukket

Heritage

Juhl was probably being coy when he called his chairs 'outdated' as he prepared for his retrospective. It is quite true that he felt he had fallen from fashion throughout the 1960s and 1970s, but then, so did most of his colleagues from the golden age of Danish Modern. Even Arne Jacobsen's products were of varying popularity, Poul Kjærholm's were respected but impossible either to sit in or purchase for ordinary people, while Verner Panton was considered so characteristic of his times that it took a retro wave to bring his works down from the attic. Besides, the rise and fall of fashion was an abhorrent phenomenon that had no bearing on the quality of furniture and design. Juhl probably felt that he had done the best he could, and that the demand for high-quality chairs would return when the time was right. And indeed it did, from the 1990s on. Take a stroll down Bredgade in Copenhagen or check out the furniture auctions online. Old wood commands a high price. In 2002, a well-preserved model of Juhl's *Pelican Chair* in black leather was sold for 425,000 Danish kroner at auction.[104] Even the critic Arne Karlsen, who had led the charge when he and Børge Mogensen confronted what they took to be a slackness in Danish furniture design around 1960, was far more reasonable – and as usual, peerlessly insightful – in his discussion of Finn Juhl in his two-volume *Danish Furniture Design in the 20th Century*:

"It was not easy for the furniture industry to deal with Finn Juhl's furniture constructions. They required major investment in complicated tools and a great deal of finishing by hand … Finn Juhl revised some of the basic types that he had developed for handcrafted production for industrial manufacture, and he designed new models with a simple frame and uncomplicated upholstering. But he himself felt that his industrial furniture was not on a par with his best handcrafted pieces, and the new manufacturing techniques that had been developed after the Second World War did not really appeal to his talents. In 1967 he worked on developing a link chair with a tubular frame and loose seat and back cushions supported by moulded plywood shells. But his heart does not seem to have been in it. The project's shaded drawings do not have the spirit or unreserved joy of his watercolours for the Cabinetmakers' Guild Furniture Competition. The furniture in fact remained on paper.

In 1970, Finn Juhl ended his active career with a retrospective exhibition of his own work at Charlottenborg.

For a few decades, Finn Juhl's furniture was relegated to museums. But this ensured that his ideas survived … When his idiom captivated a new generation at the end of the 1980s, it was easy to recreate the best of his models and put them in production. At the beginning of the 1990s, Finn Juhl's furniture was once again current. A cycle in the history of furniture design has come full circle."[105]

How should we manage our heritage? It is always a controversial question, since some will claim that the core idea has been lost, as nobody can ever really know with certainty what was. Should we even keep traditions alive that have ceased to mean anything to us? Should we save the things once useful which are now superfluous? Art and architecture are especially vexing things to inherit, for they call continually for reinterpretation. What have we actually received? Timelessness has to be forever re-established. Perhaps that is what makes 'classics' so durable.

Our heritage from Finn Juhl is of course, first of all his tangible legacy: the house on Kratvænget and the rights to his furniture. Hanne Wilhelm Hansen, Juhl's life partner since 1961, knew that something needed be done to regain the timelessness of Juhl's work. She withdrew the rights to produce Juhl's furniture from the cabinetmaker Niels Roth Andersen and granted it to House of Finn Juhl, a manufacturer in Ringkøbing. They in turn put the necessary resources into the production of a profitably scaled and internationally oriented, trendy line. Their marketing strategy manages the legacy of this elegant man of the world faithfully. Royalties from House of Finn Juhl's sales contribute to an award that Hanne Wilhelm Hansen founded in Finn Juhl's name. Due to the success of House of Finn Juhl, it is thus possible to award a sum of 300,000 Danish kroner each year to one or more architects, designers, educators or others who contribute to Danish furniture design and the applied arts. Among the previous prize-winners are a talented younger generation of designers, including Louise Campbell, Kasper Salto, Thomas Sigsgaard and Astrid Krogh, as well as the gallery owner Maria Westergren, architect Dorte Mandrup and Copenhagen Technical College, all continuing the collaboration between cabinetmakers and designers.

Almost all of Finn Juhl's buildings and interiors are gone. Only his own home and the few other houses he designed are still standing, and of these only his own is unchanged. Then there is his furniture. Wegner once remarked that "… the chair is perhaps the object closest to us, as human beings." The dictum applies in more than one sense to Juhl's bodily, organic, accommodating models. He designed 22 chairs, and together they are world-famous, from America to Japan.

Why Japan? Finn Juhl visited the country in the early 1960s, where he met with the Japanese architect Kenzo Tange. They had already met in Copenhagen, and Tange had introduced Juhl to Japanese architecture, art and literature. Juhl's Japanese books still sit on the shelves at Kratvænget. Japanese craftsmanship involves a special relationship with wood and the way that it is handled that holds striking parallels with the Danish cabinetmaking tradition. And so it was that in Japan volunteers organised a *Memorial Exhibition* for Finn Juhl as early as 1990. Likewise in 2012, to mark the centenary of Juhl's birth, a perfect replica of Juhl's house was erected outside of Takayama, right down to the Danish power sockets. Juhl's furniture was and still is popular in Japan. The simple expression, which comes from an effort to minimise the use of materials to their physical and logical necessity, became an aesthetic goal in itself and was an important strand in the Japanese influence on European and American architects and designers during the 1950s, including Juhl in his America years.

Perhaps the commonalities go beyond the tactile appreciation of the material. Perhaps Japanese furniture designers recognise Juhl's effort, inspired by the oldest artefacts, to allow the modern to be saturated with something that carries tradition, something so old as to be timeless. In this way, both tradition and modernity become more human, more liveable. Japanese design in particular unites both delicate, careful craftsmanship and respect for nature and the ancient world with innovative technological ambition.

Finn Juhl was an architect. Yet he intuited early that architecture takes place in a broader context, which is social, ethical and aesthetic. That there is more to it than building houses, and that the ability to give form to things, which he was convinced was shared by other, freer art forms, was a driving force, an attitude towards life.

His former students at the School of Interior Design recall Juhl as more a guru than a pedagogue. He let his students work freely and then challenged them through honest critique that, given his unequivocal views, could often spark vehement discussions. In his students' eyes, Juhl was world-famous, smartly dressed and drove a stylish American car. He was well-spoken and knew how to get his way. Articulate and headstrong, he might come across as arrogant, but that was counterweighed by his warmth and his own brand of self-deprecatory humour. As he was knowledgeable, curious and spoke foreign languages, he found it easy to make new friends and acquaintances.

When Juhl was interviewed by *Rum og Form* on the occasion of his 70th birthday, the journalist asked him outright how he perceived himself. Juhl responded with characteristic modesty that although he did not have any special talents, he did at least have a rebellious and independent spirit. He continued that since he had not been taught how to design furniture, he quickly discovered what was expected of a furniture designer during the era of the Klint School – and like a young child who insists only on doing the opposite, he went about things his own way. If there was a price to pay for sticking so stubbornly to his own outlook, he had always been able to brush off people's criticisms: "I am, thank God, not the only one able to say they have lived a happy life – and happiness consists in part in a certain tolerance, which means I've been able to push things aside that I find disagreeable."[106]

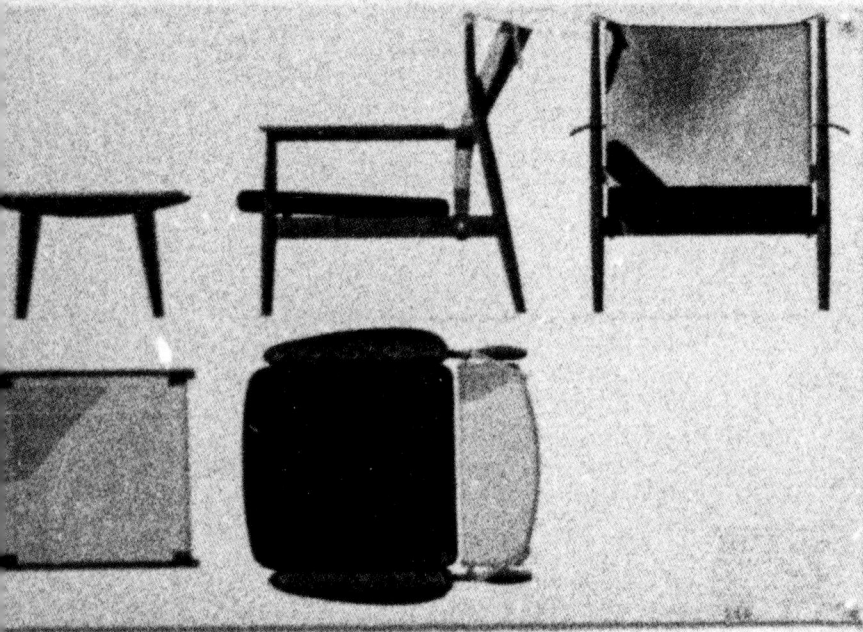

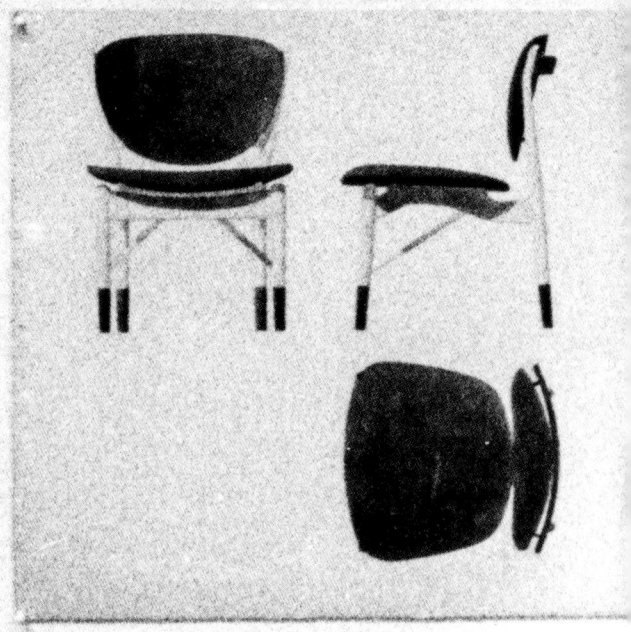

Inventory

Furniture

The list of inventories on pp. 251–265 is based on contemporary Scandinavian architecture and design magazines, Danish and international auction and exhibition catalogues, manufacturers' catalogues, Designmuseum Danmark's archives and other existing literature on Finn Juhl and Danish furniture design (see page 268). As Finn Juhl designed many prototypes and bespoke furniture pieces, which were never put into production – especially during his early years – the list should not be regarded as exhaustive.

1
Chest with legs
for Rothenborg's
house
1930
Unknown manufacturer

2
Early Writing Desk
1936-1937
Niels Vodder

3
Side Chair
1937
Niels Vodder

4
Lounge Chair
1937
Niels Vodder

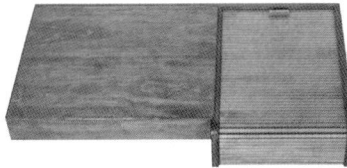

5
Easy Chair
1938
Niels Vodder

6
Side Chair
1938
Niels Vodder

7
Grasshopper Chair
1938
Niels Vodder

8
Wall-Mounted
Bathroom Cabinet
1938
Niels Vodder

9
Unique Cabinet
1938
Niels Vodder

10
Easy Chair
1939
Niels Vodder

11
Easy Chair
1939
Niels Vodder

12
Armchair
1939
Niels Vodder

13
Sofa
1939
Niels Vodder

14
Writing Desk
1939
Niels Vodder

15
Sideboard
1940s
Niels Vodder

16
Pelican Chair
1940
Niels Vodder

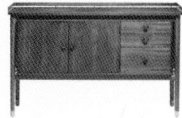

17
Pelican Table
1940
Niels Vodder

18
Low Writing
Desk 40
1940
Niels Vodder

19
Poet Sofa
1941
Niels Vodder

20
Easy Chair
1941
Niels Vodder

21
Side Chair
1941
Niels Vodder

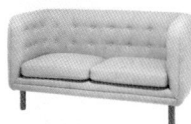

22
Free-Standing
Sideboard
1941
Niels Vodder

23
Unique Sofa
1941
Niels Vodder

24
Shelves
1941
Niels Vodder

25
Unique Wall
Cabinet
1941
Niels Vodder

26
Wall-Mounted
Entrance Drawers
1941
Niels Vodder

27
Sofa
1942
Niels Vodder

28
Easy Chair
1943
Niels Vodder

29
Easy Chair
1943
Niels Vodder

30
Westermann Chair
1943
Niels Vodder

31
Westermann
Cabinet
1943
Niels Vodder

32
Sofa
1943
Niels Vodder

33
Service Table
1943
Niels Vodder

34
Dining Table 44
1944
Niels Vodder

35
FJ44
1944
Niels Vodder

36
Sofa
1944
Niels Vodder

37
Unique Sofa
1945
Niels Vodder

38
Dream Table
1945
Niels Vodder

39
Arm Chair
1945
Niels Vodder

40
Work Desk /
Kaufmann Table
1945
Niels Vodder,
Søren Horn

41
FJ45
1945
Niels Vodder,
Søren Horn and others

42
Sofa 45
1945
Niels Vodder,
Søren Horn

43
Nyhavn Desk 69
1945
Bovirke

44
Stool
1946
Niels Vodder

45
Stool
1946
Niels Voddcr,
Søren Horn

46
Fireplace Chair 46
1946
Bovirke

47
Chair 108
1946
Niels Vodder

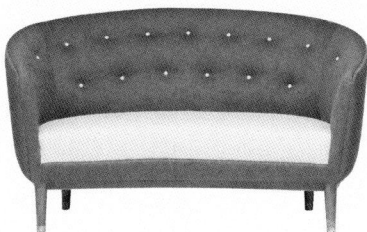

48
Chair 109
1946
Niels Vodder

60
Wall-Mounted Bookcase
1947
Niels Vodder

55
Exhibition Table for Bing & Grøndahl
1947
Lysberg Hansen & Therp

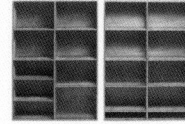

61
Bookcase with legs
1947
Niels Vodder

49
Sofa 46
1946
Carl Brørup

56
Chair 63
1947
Bovirke (Carl Brørup)

50
FJ46
1946 and 1953
Niels Vodder and Bovirke

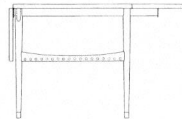

57
Coffee Table
1947
Bovirke (Carl Brørup)

51
Armchair
1947
Niels Vodder

58
Unique Work Table
1947
Unknown manufacturer

62
The Modern Art Chair
1948
Unknown manufacturer

52
Dining Table
1947
Niels Vodder

63
Eye Table
1948
Unknown manufacturer

53
Unique Coffee Table
1947
Niels Vodder

64
Ross Coffee Table
1948
Alf Ross

54
Place Setting Table for Bing & Grøndahl
1947
Jacob Petersen

59
Unique Sofa
1947
Niels Vodder

65
FJ48
1948
Niels Vodder, Niels Roth Andersen

66
Sofa Bench 48
1948
Niels Vodder

71
Organic Coffee
Table with flap
1949
Unknown manufacturer

78
Coffee Table with
shelf and flap
1950s
Bovirke

72
Dining Chair 64
1949
Niels Vodder, Bovirke

67
Easy Chair
1948
Niels Vodder

73
Armchair
1949
Søren Willadsen's
Furniture Manufacturer

68
Judas Table / Silver
Table
1948
Niels Vodder

74
Egyptian Chair
1949
Niels Vodder,
Søren Horn

79
Linen Cupboard
1950s
Søren Willadsen's
Furniture Manufacturer

69
Work Desk
1948
Niels Vodder

75
Chieftain Chair
1949
Niels Vodder

80
Coffee Table
1950s
Bovirke

76
Spoke-Back Sofa
1949
Søren Willadsen's
Furniture Manufacturer

81
Low Sideboard
1950s
Bovirke

70
Floating Cabinet
1949
Søren Willadsen's
Furniture Manufacturer

77
Unique Conference
Table
1950s
Bovirke

82
Sideboard
1950s
Baker Furniture

256

83
Lamp Table
1950s
Baker Furniture

88
Easy Chair
1950
Søren Willadsen's
Furniture Manufacturer

95
Cocktail Table
1951
Baker Furniture

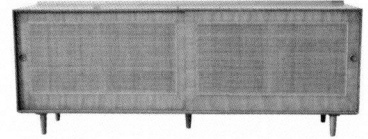

89
Sofa
1950
Søren Willadsen's
Furniture Manufacturer

96
Sideboard
1952
Baker Furniture

84
Coffee Table
1950s
Baker Furniture

90
Coffee Table 50
1950
Niels Vodder

97
Dining Chair
1952
Bovirke

85
Coffee Table
1950
Niels Vodder

91
Baker Sofa
1951
Niels Vodder, Baker
Furniture

98
Chair 96
1952
Bovirke

86
Easy Chair
1950
Niels Vodder

92
Armchair
1951
Baker Furniture

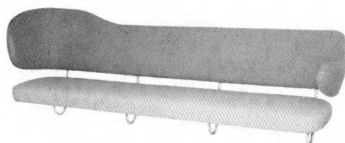

93
The Delegates'
Chair | FJ51
1951
Niels Vodder, Baker
Furniture

87
Sculptural Sofa /
Wall Sofa
1950
Niels Vodder

94
Dining Chair 51
1951
Niels Vodder, Baker
Furniture

99
Easy Chair
1952
Bovirke

100
Table Bench 101
1952
Bovirke

101
Coffee Table with flap
1952
Bovirke

102
Linen Cupboard
1952
Søren Willadsen's
Furniture Manufacturer

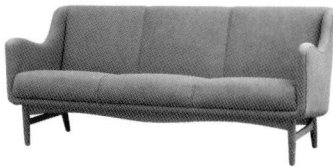

103
Sofa
1952
Søren Willadsen's
Furniture Manufacturer

104
Reading Chair
1953
Bovirke

105
Dining Table
1953
Bovirke

106
Japan Chair
1953
Unknown manufacturer

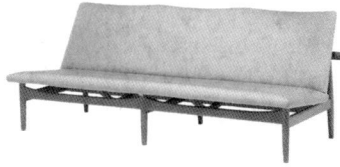

107
Japan Sofa
1953
Unknown manufacturer

108
Easy Chair 53
1953
Niels Vodder

109
Sofa 53
1953
Niels Vodder

110
Chair 86
1953
Søren Willadsen's
Furniture Manufacturer

111
Easy Chair 86
1953
Søren Willadsen
Furniture Manufacturer

112
Easy Chair
1953
Bovirke

113
Sofa 77
1953
Bovirke

114
Dining Table
1953
Søren Willadsen's
Furniture Manufacturer

115
Dining Table
1953
Bovirke

116
Service Cupboard
1953
Bovirke

117
Chieftain Footstool
1953
Unknown manufacturer

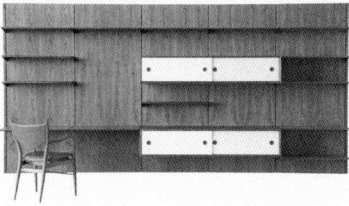

118
Shelf System
1953 and 1956
Bovirke

119
Spade Chair
1954
France & Søn

120
Coffee Table
1954
Søren Willadsen's
Furniture Manufacturer

121
Easy Chair 55
1955
Niels Vodder

122
Armchair
1955
Niels Vodder

123
Stool
1955
Niels Vodder

124
Games Table 55
1955
Niels Vodder

125
Coffee Table 55
1955
Niels Vodder

126
Easy Chair 96
1956
Søren Willadsen's
Furniture Manufacturer

127
Dining Chair
1956
Niels Vodder

128
Lounge Chair
1956
France & Søn

129
Writing Desk
1956
Bovirke

130
Daybed
1956
Bovirke

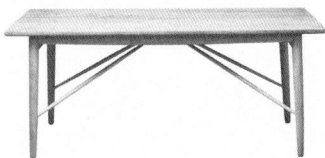

131
Dining Table
1956
Bovirke

132
Lamp Table 635
1956
France & Søn

133
Dining Table 56
1956
Niels Vodder

134
Wall-Mounted
Shelves
1956
Bovirke

135
Chair 116
1957
Bovirke

136
Lounge Chair
1957
Niels Vodder

137
Tivoli Sofa
1957
Hansen & Sørensen

138
Coffee Table 500
1958
France & Søn

139
Easy Chair 136
1958
France & Søn

140
Shelf System
1958
Baker Furniture

141
Sideboard
1958
Baker Furniture

142
Easy Chair 138
1959
France & Søn

143
Sofa 138
1959
France & Søn

144
Stool 140
1959
France & Søn

145
Sideboard
1959
France & Søn

146
Sofa 112
1960s
France & Søn, CADO

147
Easy Chair 112
1960s
France & Søn, CADO

148
Armchair 196
1960s
France & Søn

149
Easy Chair
1960s
France & Søn

150
Coffee Table 612
1960s
France & Søn

151
Coffee Table
1960s
France & Søn

152
Sideboard 527
1960s
Baker Furniture

153
Armchair 144
1960
Bovirke

154
Sofa
1961
L. Pontoppidan

155
Glove Cabinet
1961
L. Pontoppidan

156
Armchair
1961
France & Søn

157
Coffee Table
on wheels
1961
L. Pontoppidan

158
Diplomat Writing
Desk
1961-1962
France & Søn

159
Diplomat Sideboard
1961-1962
France & Søn

160
Technocrat Desk
1961-1962
France & Søn

161
Bwana Chair
1962
France & Søn

162
Bwana Footstool
1962
France & Søn

163
Coffee Table
1962
Unknown manufacturer

164
Double Bed
1962
Unknown manufacturer

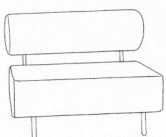

165
Diplomat Chair
1963
France & Søn, CADO

166
Chair 191
1963
France & Søn

167
Armchair 192
1963
France & Søn

168
Chair 64
1964
Unknown manufacturer

169
Tray Table
1965
Niels Vodder

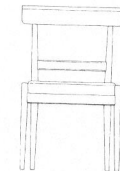

170
Office Chair 210
1965
France & Søn

171
Armchair
1965
L. Pontoppidan

172
Armchair
1966
Unknown manufacturer

173
Chair
1966
Unknown manufacturer

174
Cresco Wall Unit
System
1966
France & Søn

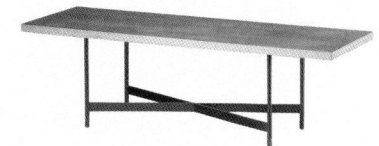

175
Easy Chair
1968
Unknown manufacturer

176
Kidney-Shaped
Coffee Table
Unknown year
Bovirke

177
Round Dining Table
Unknown year
Bovirke

178
Office Chair
Unknown year
Unknown manufacturer

179
Display Cabinet
Unknown year
Unknown manufacturer

180
Coffee Table 57
Unknown year
Niels Vodder

Attributed Furniture

181
Stool
Unknown year
L. Pontoppidan

182
Dining Table
Unknown year
France & Søn

183
Sofa Bench 141
Unknown year
Bovirke

184
Rocking Chair
Unknown year
France & Søn

185
Armchair
Unknown year
Unknown manufacturer

186
Sofa Bench
Unknown year
Niels Vodder

187
Dining Table
Unknown year
France & Søn

Applied Art

1
Wooden Bowls
1951 and 1954
Kay Bojesen

2
Porcelain Service
(Prototype) 1952
Bing & Grøndahl

3
Turning Tray
1957
Torben Ørskov & co.

4
Ice Bucket
1958
Torben Ørskov & co.

5
Trophy for Design Prize
1960
The Kaufmann
International
Design Award

6
Pendant Lamp
1963
Lyfa

7
Table Lamp
1963
Lyfa

8
Wall Lamp
1963
Lyfa

9
Export-Oscar
(Prototype) 1966
Landsforeningen Dansk
Arbejde (National
Association's Danish
Work)

Architecture & Interiors

11
House in Blistrup
1957
Sculptor Erik
Thommesen

12
**Own Design Studio
on Sølvgade**
(Copenhagen)
1957

1
**Own house on
Kratvænget**
1942

6
**Interior-52
Exhibition Room**
(Trondheim)
1952
National Museum of
Decorative Arts and
Design

13
**Interior of DC-8 Jet
Airliners**
1957
Scandinavian Airlines

15
**Interior of Flight
Terminals**
(Barcelona, Geneva,
Manchester, Kolkata,
Gothenburg, Vienna,
Malmö, Johannesburg,
Kuwait City and Munich)
1958
Scandinavian Airlines

17
Interior of Shop
(Westchester, USA)
1959
Georg Jensen Silver

18
**Interior of Flight
Terminals**
(Nice, Paris and West
Berlin)
1960
Scandinavian Airlines

2
**Summerhouse in
Asserbo**
1950
Mrs. Anthon Petersen

7
**Interior of Goods
Office and
Administrator's
House**
1953-1955
Lerchenborg Goods

14
**Interior of Flight
Terminals**
(Alexandria, Karachi,
Baghdad, Athens,
Jakarta, Milan, Beirut,
Cairo, Glasgow, Tehran,
London, Oslo and
Stockholm)
1957
Scandinavian Airlines

16
**Interior of Flight
Terminals**
(Tokyo, Amsterdam,
Bangkok, Budapest,
Prague, Lahore and
Nairobi)
1959
Scandinavian Airlines

3
**Trusteeship Council
Chamber**
1950-1952
United Nations,
New York

8
House in Ordrup
1954
Anders
Hostrup-Pedersen

4
House in Nakskov
1952
Timber Merchant
M. Aubertin

9
**Villabyernes Bio
Cinema in Vangede**
1955
Mogens Fisker

5
Interior of Shop
(New York)
1952
Georg Jensen Silver

10
Interior of Shop
(Toronto)
1956
Georg Jensen Silver

Exhibition Design

19
Summerhouse in
Rågeleje
1962
Anders
Hostrup-Pedersen

23
House in Ørholm
1966-1967
Mrs. A. Roed

20
Interior of Shop
on Amagertorv
(Copenhagen)
1963
Bing & Grøndahl

21
Restaurant, Vester
Farimagsgade
(Copenhagen)
1965
Hotel Richmond

22
Interior of Shop
(Copenhagen)
1966-1967
Wilhelm Hansen's Music
Publishing House

1
Good Design
(Chicago)
1951
Merchandise Mart

2
Design in
Scandinavia
(Traveling exhibition,
USA)
1954-1957

3
Georg Jensen's
Silversmith
Workshop's Jubilee
Exhibition
(Danish Museum of Art
& Design, Copenhagen)
1954
Georg Jensen's
Silversmith

4
Fifty Years of
Danish Silver
(London, Washington,
D.C., and others)
1955-1957
Georg Jensen's
Silversmith

5
Future Home
(Forum, Copenhagen)
1954
Copenhagen
Cabinetmakers' Guild's
Jubilee Exhibition

6
The Arts of
Denmark
(Metropolitan Museum
of Art, New York)
1960-1961
Landsforeningen Dansk
Kunsthaandværk

7
Two Centuries of
Danish Design
(Victoria & Albert
Museum, London)
1968

8
A Century of
Danish Design
(Kelvingrove Museum,
Glasgow & Whitworth
Art Gallery, Manchester)
1968

9
Finn Juhl —
A retrospective
exhibition of
furniture and
other works
(Danish Museum of Art
& Design, Copenhagen)
1982

Notes

1. Finn Juhl interviewed by Ninka. "Møbler og huse er altid tænkt i sammen-hæng", *Politiken*, 7/11/1982.
2. Arne Jacobsen interviewed by Ninka. *Politiken*, 28/10/1971, as quoted in Carsten Thau and Kjeld Vindum: *Arne Jacobsen*. The Danish Architectural Press, 1998, p.27.
3. Characteristically, Arne Jacobsen has recounted how one day at the School of Architecture, his professor in architectural history, Vilhelm Wanscher, took some of his water-colours and said: "I will hang these up in the School of Painting, as that is where they belong."
4. "Fortid, nutid, fremtid. Foredrag holdt af arkitekt Finn Juhl i Landsforeningen d. 14. januar 1949" ['Past, Present, Future. A lecture by the architect Finn Juhl at the National Association 14/01/1949'] *Dansk Kunsthaandværk*, issue 4, 1949, p.57.
5. Nils-Ole Lund: "Den funktionelle tradition" Tobias Faber et al.: *Kay Fisker*. The Danish Architectural Press, 1995, p.182.
6. Finn Juhl interviewed by Ninka. "Møbler og huse er altid tænkt i sammen-hæng", *Politiken*, 7/11/1982. Modernistic approaches and argu-ments can be found throughout Finn Juhl's own articles and newspaper contributions, as where in a book review for example, he praises the book in question for "establishing that furnishing is first and foremost an objective problem".
7. G. Anthony Atkinson: "Technique, Training and Practice in Danish Architecture", *Architectural Review*, Special Issue. London, November 1948.
8. Poul Henningsen: "Stockholms Udstillingen", *Nyt Tidsskrift for Kunstindustri*, May 1930, p.84.
9. Ibid. p.90.
10. Tobias Faber: "Kay Fisker" Tobias Faber et al.: *Kay Fisker*. The Danish Architectural Press, 1995, p.9.

11. In 1949, in his lecture 'Past, Present, Future' Juhl called on his colleagues to rediscover a playful experimen-tation with analytic-rational foundations. He recalled the 'last attempt' of happy youthful days before 'the Fall' and the feeling of 'artistic' freedom, when one didn't quite know what one was doing, in this case "experimental and enjoyable attempts to create new forms in stuffed furniture". Unfortunately this had been "the last attempt *en masse* in furniture design to create something new in a con-temporary idiom. It was not just one figure, it was the whole bunch … The rest of us made things that perhaps tasted more of Mickey Mouse. But we were so wonderfully free from direct precursors and invented for dear life." "Fortid, nutid, fremtid", p.59.
12. Ibid. p.73.
13. Finn Juhl: "Løses Lejlighedens Problem i Massebyggeriet?", *Arkitektens Ugehæfte*, 1946, p.233.
14. Mike Rømer: "Rundt om Finn Juhl – et interview", *Rum og Form*, issue 4, 1981, p.10.
15. "Fortid, nutid, fremtid", p.57.
16. Ibid. p.56.
17. One might not think it of such a warm and cosy design, but *Tired Man* became the most expensive chair in Denmark when in 2014 an example fetched 1,420,000 Danish krone at auction with the auction house Bruun Rasmussen.
18. Arne Karlsen. *Danish Furniture Design in the 20th Century*. Dansk Møbelkunst, 2007, volume 2 p.109.
19. Finn Juhl interviewed by Ninka. "Møbler og huse er altid tænkt i sammen-hæng", *Politiken*, 7/11/1982.
20. See Lisbet Balslev Jørgensen, Jørgen Sestoft and Morten Lund: *Vilhelm Lauritzen, A Modern Architect*, Aristo, 1994, p.246 fn.
21. As quoted in Per H. Hansen: *Finn Juhl and his House*, p. 22.
22. Arne Karlsen. *Danish Furniture Design in the 20th Century*. Dansk Møbelkunst, 2007, volume 1 p.160.
23. Per H. Hansen: *Finn Juhl and his House*. Hatje Cantz, 2014, p.26.
24. "Fortid, nutid, fremtid", p.60.

25. Willy Beck in *Politiken*, 6/7/1971. As quoted in Per H. Hansen: *Da danske møbler blev moderne*. University Press of Southern Denmark and Aschehoug, 2006, p.557. [Trans. *Danish Modern Furniture 1930-2016*.].
26. Ibid., p. 181.
27. Arne Karlsen. *Danish Furniture Design in the 20th Century*. Dansk Møbelkunst, 2007, volume 1 pp.43-45.
28. Kaare Klint: "Undervisningen i Møbeltegning ved Kunstakademiet", *Arkitektens Månedshæfte*, 1930, pp.193-224.
29. Esbjørn Hiort: *Arkitekten Finn Juhl*. The Danish Architectural Press, 1990, p.40. [Trans. *Finn Juhl. Furniture, Architecture, Applied Art – a biography*].
30. See for example Arne Jacobsen's furniture for a study (1927) in Arne Karlsen, volume 1 p.27.
31. Finn Juhl: *Hjemmets indretning*. Thaning and Appel, 1954, pp.17-20.
32. Mike Rømer: "Rundt om Finn Juhl – et interview", *Rum og Form*, issue 4, 1981, pp.6-16.
33. Per H. Hansen: *Da danske møbler blev moderne*, p.73. [Trans. *Danish Modern Furniture 1930-2016*.].
34. Mike Rømer: "Rundt om Finn Juhl – et interview".
35. Arne Karlsen, volume 2 p.185.
36. As quoted in Per H. Hansen: *Finn Juhl og hans hus*, p.38 [Trans. Finn Juhl and his House.].
37. Ibid.
38. Ibid.
39. Mike Rømer: "Rundt om Finn Juhl – et interview".
40. Christian Winther. *The Flight to America*. Trans. Piet Hein. Gyldendal, 1978. [Original: "Flugten til Amerika" 1835.].
41. Per H. Hansen: *Finn Juhl and his House*. Hatje Cantz, 2014, p.49.
42. Edgar Kaufmann Jr.: "Finn Juhl of Copenhagen", *Interiors*, November 1948, pp.96-99.
43. Ibid.
44. Ibid.
45. Olga Gueft: "Finn Juhl – about the quiet life of a Danish architect", *Interiors*, September 1950, p.85.

46. Per H. Hansen: *Finn Juhl and his House*. Hatje Cantz, 2014, p.55.

47. Michael Sheridan: "Foreword", Karsten R.S. Ifversen and Birgit Lyngbye Pedersen: *Finn Juhl at the UN – a living legacy*. Strandberg Publishing, 2013, p.27.

48. According to Esbjørn Hiort: *Arkitekten Finn Juhl*. The Danish Architectural Press, 1990, p.70. [Trans. *Finn Juhl. Furniture, Architecture, Applied Art – a biography*].

49. Ibid.

50. As quoted in Karsten R.S. Ifversen and Birgit Lyngbye Pedersen: *Finn Juhl i FN – et dansk mesterværk i New York*, p.80. [Trans. *Finn Juhl at the UN – a living legacy*].

51. According to Esbjørn Hiort: *Arkitekten Finn Juhl*. The Danish Architectural Press, 1990, p.76. [Trans. *Finn Juhl. Furniture, Architecture, Applied Art – a biography*].

52. As quoted in Karsten R.S. Ifversen and Birgit Lyngbye Pedersen: *Finn Juhl i FN – et dansk mesterværk i New York*, p.88. [Trans. *Finn Juhl at the UN – a living legacy*].

53. Karsten R.S. Ifversen and Birgit Lyngbye Pedersen: *Finn Juhl i FN – et dansk mesterværk i New York*, p.30. [Trans. *Finn Juhl at the UN – a living legacy*].

54. Henry Stern Churchill: "United Nations Headquarters. A Description and Appraisal", *Architectural Record*. July 1952, pp.118-9.

55. Per H. Hansen: *Finn Juhl and his House*. Hatje Cantz, 2014, p.60.

56. Esbjørn Hiort: *Arkitekten Finn Juhl*. The Danish Architectural Press, 1990, p.82. [Trans. *Finn Juhl. Furniture, Architecture, Applied Art – a biography*].

57. Juhl's design studio monthly report, as quoted in Esbjørn Hiort: *Arkitekten Finn Juhl*. The Danish Architectural Press, 1990, p. 83.

58. Ibid., p. 84.

59. Esbjørn Hiort: *Arkitekten Finn Juhl*. The Danish Architectural Press, 1990, p.83 fn. [Trans. *Finn Juhl. Furniture, Architecture, Applied Art – a biography*].

60. Finn Juhl: "Acceptera", *Epoke*, 8/11/1931, p. 10. As quoted in Per H. Hansen: *Finn Juhl and his House*, p.74.

61. Finn Juhl: *Hjemmets indretning*, Thaning & Appel, 1954, p.17.

62. Ibid. pp.17-19.

63. Ibid. p.20.

64. Ibid. p.76.

65. Ibid. p.10 fn.

66. Ibid. p.12 fn.

67. Ibid. p.13.

68. Finn Juhl: *Hjemmets Indretning*. Trans. as quoted in Arne Karlsen: *Danish Furniture Design in the 20th Century*, volume 2 p.120. See also: *Årbog for Nordenfjeldske Kunstindustrimuseum*, 1950, p.20. [Yearbook for the National Museum of Decorative Arts and Design, 1950].

69. Finn Juhl: *Hjemmets indretning*, Thaning & Appel, 1954, p.171.

70. Finn Juhl: *Hjemmets Indretning*. Trans. as quoted in Arne Karlsen: *Danish Furniture Design in the 20th Century*, volume 2 p.117.

71. Tom Wolfe: *From Bauhaus to Our House*. Farrar, Straus & Giroux, 1981, p.4.

72. Per H. Hansen: *Finn Juhl and his House*. Hatje Cantz, 2014, p.85.

73. Finn Juhl: "Danish Furniture Design". *Architects' Year Book*. Paul Elek: London, 1949. p.139.

74. Per H. Hansen: *Finn Juhl and his House*. Hatje Cantz, 2014, p.104.

75. Ibid. p.85.

76. Esbjørn Hiort: *Arkitekten Finn Juhl*. The Danish Architectural Press, 1990, p.42. [Trans. *Finn Juhl. Furniture, Architecture, Applied Art – a biography*].

77. Erik Herløw: "Snedkerlaugets Møbeludstilling 1945", *Arkitektens Ugehæfte*, 1945, pp.173-175.

78. Michael Müller: *Børge Mogensen. Møbler med holdning*. Strandberg Publishing, 2015, p.170. [Trans. *Børge Mogensen. Simplicity and Function*].

79. Børge Mogensen and Arne Karlsen: "Illusion og realitet. Betragtninger over Snedkerlaugets Møbeludstillinger", *Dansk Kunsthåndværk*, 1959, pp.162-177.

80. Børge Mogensen and Arne Karlsen: "Brugskunst på afveje", *Arkitekten*, 1962, issue 1, pp.1-11.

81. Ibid.

82. Svend Erik Møller: "Finn Juhl siger sin mening om arkitekternes egen koksgrå forsigtighed", *Politiken*, 14/01/1962.

83. Svend Erik Møller: "Finn Juhl siger sin mening om arkitekternes egen koksgrå forsigtighed", *Politiken*, 14/1/1962.

84. Finn Juhl: *Årbog for Nordenfjeldske Kunstindustrimuseum*, 1950, p.20.

85. Letter from Finn Juhl to Edgar Kaufmann Jr, 13/9/1982.

86. "Indledning", *Mobilia*, issue 81, 1962.

87. P. von Halling-Kochs debate, ibid.

88. As quoted in Per H. Hansen: *Finn Juhl og hans hus*, p.146. [Trans. *Finn Juhl and his House*].

89. Letter from Niels Vodder to Finn Juhl (05/12/1966). Finn Juhl archive, file 18: Correspondence and Manuscripts. Danish Museum of Art & Design Library (Now Designmuseum Danmark Library). As quoted in Per H. Hansen: *Finn Juhl og hans hus*, p.138.

90. "Modern dansk arkitekt: Vi valde skurgolv!", *Sydsvenska Dagbladet*, 30/04/1948, as quoted in Per H. Hansen: *Finn Juhl og hans hus*. Gyldendal/Ordrupgaard, 2009, p.191.

91. Barbara Plumb: "Dane Decries 'Backward' Furniture", *The New York Times*, 24/10/1963, as quoted in Per H. Hansen: *Finn Juhl og hans hus*, p.174.

92. "Moderne møbelkunst vil forene skønhed og behov", *Politiken*, 13/03/1949, as quoted in Per H. Hansen: *Finn Juhl og hans hus*, pp.189,191.

93. Birgit Lyngbye Pedersen: "Kratvænget 15 – fra hus til museum", Per H. Hansen: *Finn Juhl og hans hus*, p.202.

94. Henrik Sten Møller: "Finn Juhl, 70 år", *Politiken*, 29/01/1982, as quoted in Per H. Hansen: *Finn Juhl og hans hus*, p.156.

95. Mike Rømer: "Rundt om Finn Juhl – et interview", *Rum og Form*, issue. 4, 1981, p.3 fn, as quoted in Per H. Hansen: *Finn Juhl og hans hus*, p.155.

96. Per H. Hansen: *Finn Juhl og hans hus*, p.156.

97. Finn Juhl: "Møblet på møbleringens scene", *Bygge og Bo*, issue 3-4, 1949, p.33.

98. Karsten R.S. Ifversen: "Nordhavn er en ny ghetto for velhavere", *Politiken*, 10/03/2017.

99. Martin Hartung: "Finn Juhl, 70 år", *Berlingske Tidende*, 30/01/1982, as quoted in Per H. Hansen: *Finn Juhl og hans hus*, p.156.

100. Henrik Sten Møller: "En af de store", *Politiken*, 5/11/1982, as quoted in Per H. Hansen: *Finn Juhl og hans hus*, p.154.

101. Rita Reif: "Nordic Design of 50's Gave 'Modern' a New Meaning", *The New York Times*, 16/09/1982.

102. Ibid.

103. Per H. Hansen: *Finn Juhl og hans hus*, p.168 fn.

104. Ibid. p.170.

105. Arne Karlsen. *Danish Furniture Design in the 20th Century*, volume 2. Dansk Møbelkunst, 2007. pp.114-115.

106. Mike Rømer: "Rundt om Finn Juhl – et interview", p.16.

Literature

Andersen, Rigmor: *Kaare Klint møbler.* Royal Danish Academy of Fine Arts, 1979

Andrews, Edward Deming & Faith Andrews: *Shaker Furniture: The Craftsmanship of an American Communal Sect.* Dover Publications, 1964

Asplund, Gunnar et al.: "acceptera". *Modern Swedish Design: Three Founding Texts.* The Museum of Modern Art (New York), 2008

Bundegaard, Christian: "Om arkitekturens oprindelse". *Kritik* 193. Gyldendal, 2009

Dickson, Thomas: *Dansk design.* Gyldendal, 2006

Dirckinck-Holmfeld, Kim: *Guide to Danish Architecture 1960-1995.* The Danish Architectural Press, 2003

Faber, Tobias et al.: *Kay Fisker.* The Danish Architectural Press, 1995

Hansen, Per H.: *Danish Modern Furniture 1930-2016.* University Press of Southern Denmark, *2016*

Hansen, Per H.: *En lys og lykkelig fremtid. Historien om FDB-møbler.* Samvirke, 2014

Hansen, Per H.: *Finn Juhl and his House.* Hatje Cantz, 2014

Harlang, Christoffer, Nils Fagerholt & Ole Palsby: *Poul Kjærholm.* The Danish Architectural Press, 1999

Hiort, Esbjørn: *Finn Juhl. Furniture, Architecture, Applied Art – a biography.* The Danish Architectural Press, 1990

Ifversen, Karsten R.S. & Birgit Lyngbye Pedersen: *Finn Juhl at the UN – a living legacy.* Strandberg Publishing, 2013

Juhl, Finn: *Hjemmets indretning.* Thaning og Appel, 1954

Jørgensen, Lisbet Balslev: *Vilhelm Lauritzen – a modern architect.* Aristo, 1994

Karlsen, Arne: *Danish Furniture Design in the 20th Century.* Volumes I-II. Dansk Møbelkunst, 2007

Müller, Michael: *Børge Mogensen — Simplicity and Function.* Strandberg Publishing, 2016

Olesen, Christian Holmsted: *Wegner – just one good chair.* Hatje Cantz, 2014

Sommer, Anne-Louise: *Kaare Klint.* Aschehoug, 2006

Sommer, Anne-Louise: *Watercolours by Finn Juhl.* Strandberg Publishing, 2015

Thau, Carsten & Kjeld Vindum: *Arne Jacobsen.* The Danish Architectural Press, 1998

Wolfe, Tom: *From Bauhaus to Our House.* Farrar, Straus and Giroux, 1981

Illustrations

The publisher have attempted to identify all the license holders for the illustrations used in the book. If we have missed any, we kindly ask you to contact the publisher, and you will receive the standard fee.

1stdibs.com — 116
Acceptera — 196 bottom
Barbara Hepworth © Bowness — 15
Bent Oue — 120, 122 left
Brahl Fotografi — 78, 80, 114, 115, 148
Bruun Rasmussen Auctioneers of Fine Art — 62
Børge Mogensens Tegnestue — 42
Danish National Art Library — 19 bottom, 32 bottom, Keld Helmer-Petersen 202
Dansk Kunsthåndværk — (1953) 23 bottom, (1949) 29, (1953) 215
Dansk møbelkunst i det 20. århundrede — 32 top right
De Agostini Picture Library / G. Dagli Orti / Bridgeman Images — 44
Design Museum Denmark / Finn Juhl Archive — 12, 14, 15, 16, 22, 23 top, 32 top left, 33, 34, 35, 38-39, 65, 123, 198, 221, 243
Design Museum Danmark / Photo: Pernille Klemp — 21, 64, 73, 77, 86-87, 95, 96, 102, 109, 110, 124-125, 135, 139, 158, 161, 162-163, 167n, 168, 172, 173, 174, 176, 178, 180-181, 182-183, 187n, 188, 189, 190-191, 192-193, 199, 200, 204, 205, 207, 219, 220, 223h, 224-225, 226
Erik Hansen — 206, 216-217, 218
©Ezra Stoller / Esto — 167 top
Form & Space — 232
France & Son – British pioneer of Danish furniture — 213
Hans Ole Madsen — 118, 119, 169, 170-171, 177, 228, 236, 237, 238-239, 241, 242
Hjemmets Indretning 196 top
House of Finn Juhl — 81, 92, 94, 97, 112, 150, 214, 246-247
©Jean Arp / VISDA
Keld Helmer Petersen — 187 top, 201, 203
Klassik — 104, 108
Laura Stamer — 58, 60, 61, 66, 68, 70, 72, 74, 76, 82, 84, 85, 88, 90, 91, 98, 100, 101, 107, 111, 126, 128, 129, 132, 134, 136, 138, 140, 143, 146, 149, 152
Maarbjergs Atelier — 46, 48, 51, (Fotografisk illustration) 52
National Museum of Decorative Art and Design, Trondheim — 208-209
Ole Woldbye — 210
Ordrupgaard — 8, 24, 45, 49, 54, 69, 106, 156, 159, 186, 212, 230, 231, 233, 234, 235
Polfoto / Photo: Holger Damgaard — 17, 18, 25 right
Private Collection Lucien Herve / Bridgeman Images — 19 top
Scanpix — 40-41, Egon Engmann 26, 37, Bjarne Lüthcke 43 right, Sven Gjørling 47, Hakon Nielsen 154, Arne Magnussen 130-131, 223 left, Erik Petersen 240
Svensk Form / Designarkiv.se — 25 left
The Danish National Archives, FDB Arkiv — 43 left
The Royal Danish Library — 20, 30, 47, 50, 103, 142, 211
UN Photo — 166
Wikimedia Commons / Photo: Staib — 28
Aage Strüwing — 53, 144-145, 160, 164-165, 175, 179, 184, 185, 194

Inventory, page 251-265

Furniture:
 1stdibs.com — no. 9, 44, 82, 83, 84, 96, 134, 140, 141, 145, 151, 152; Designmuseum Denmark — no. 56, 57, 69, 92, 125, 157; House of Finn Juhl — no. 40, 47, 48, 50, 62, 63, 64, 91, 95, 118, 137, 138, 155, 168, 169; Klassik, Copenhagen — no. 68; Laura Stamer — no. 7, 35; Noritsugu, Oda — no. 3, 4, 5, 6, 10, 11, 13, 20, 21, 28, 29, 32, 36, 39, 45, 51, 67, 72, 85, 86, 112, 123, 127, 128, 135, 136, 153, 154, 156, 167, 171, 172, 173, 175; Bruun Rasmussen Auctioneers — all others
Applied Art:
 Architectmade — no. 3; Bruun Rasmussen Auctioneers — no. 4; House of Finn Juhl — no. 6, 7, 8, 9; Keld Helmer-Petersen — no. 5; Laura Stamer — no. 1; Aage Strüwing — no. 2
Architecture & Interiors:
 House of Finn Juhl — no. 9, 10, 12; Ordrupgaard — no. 1; The Royal Danish Library — no. 19
Exhibitions:
 House of Finn Juhl — no. 3

Index

Finn Juhl
Life, Work, World

© 2018, 2025 Christian Bundegaard and Strandberg Publishing
Translated from Danish by Max Minden Ribeiro
Editor: Lil Vad-Schou
Picture editor: Birgit Lyngbye Pedersen
Editorial co-ordination: Mille Bjørnstrup
Consultant: Anders Brix
Proofreading: Dorte H. Silver
Research: Caroline Lemvigh-Müller, Christina Damstedt
    and Claudia Rebecca Juul Kassentoft
Index: Josephine Lund Leviné and Rasmus Fynbo Hansen
Design: Rasmus Koch Studio
Cover photo: *FJ45 Chair* (Laura Stamer)
    and Finn Juhl with *FJ45 Chair* (Ordrupgaard)
Illustrations: Bruun Rasmussen Auctioneers of Fine Art,
    Laura Stamer etc. See page 269
Printing: GPS Group/Grafotisak
Litho: Narayana Press, Gylling
Printed in Europe 2025
ISBN 978-87-94418-67-6

Strandberg Publishing
Klareboderne 3
DK-1115 Copenhagen
www.strandbergpublishing.dk
mail@strandbergpublishing.dk

Part of the Gyldendal Group

MIX
Paper | Supporting
responsible forestry
FSC® C118234
FSC
www.fsc.org